# Becoming a Mathematics Teacher

# Mathematics Education Library
## VOLUME 53

*Managing Editor*

A.J. Bishop, *Monash University, Melbourne, Australia*

*Editorial Board*

M.G. Bartolini Bussi, *Modena, Italy*
J.P. Becker, *Illinois, U.S.A.*
M. Borba, *Rio Claro, Brazil*
B. Kaur, *Singapore*
C. Keitel, *Berlin, Germany*
G. Leder, *Melbourne, Australia*
F. Leung, *Hong Kong, China*
D. Pimm, *Edmonton, Canada*
K. Ruthven, *Cambridge, United Kingdom*
A. Sfard, *Haifa, Israel*
Y. Shimizu, *Tennodai, Japan*
O. Skovsmose, *Aalborg, Denmark*

For further volumes:
http://www.springer.com/series/6276

Tony Brown · Olwen McNamara

# Becoming a Mathematics Teacher

## Identity and Identifications

 Springer

Prof. Tony Brown
Manchester Metropolitan University
Institute of Education
799 Wilmslow Road
Didsbury
Manchester
M20 2RR
United Kingdom
a.m.brown@mmu.ac.uk

Olwen McNamara
University of Manchester
School of Education
Oxford Road
M13 9PL Manchester
United Kingdom
olwen.mcnamara@manchester.ac.uk

*Series Editor:*
Alan Bishop
Monash University
Melbourne 3800
Australia
Alan.Bishop@Education.monash.edu.au

ISBN 978-94-007-0553-1          e-ISBN 978-94-007-0554-8
DOI 10.1007/978-94-007-0554-8
Springer Dordrecht Heidelberg London New York

Library of Congress Control Number: 2011920958

Printed on acid-free paper

Springer is part of Springer Science+Business Media (www.springer.com)

# Acknowledgments

This book reports on work taking place over some 15 years, during which time many people have been involved. The research derives from two United Kingdom Economic and Social Research Council studies (R000222409 and R000223073). Particular thanks go to Tehmina Basit, Una Hanley, Liz Jones and Lorna Roberts. We are especially appreciative of the many trainee teachers who offered their time in being interviewed. Finally heartfelt thanks from Tony to Alison, Elliot and Imogen for their love and help throughout. And from Olwen, thanks to John, James and Kate for their support, love and understanding.

# Contents

# About the Authors

**Tony Brown**  is Professor of Mathematics Education at Manchester Metropolitan University. Originally from London, Tony trained in Canterbury and Exeter, before returning to London where he taught mathematics for 3 years at Holland Park School. This was followed by 3 years as a mathematics teacher educator for Volunteer Service Overseas in Dominica in the Caribbean. In 1987 he completed his PhD at Southampton University. His doctoral research focused on language usage in mathematics classrooms, especially where the fluent use of English could not be assumed. After a spell as a mathematics coordinator in a middle school in the Isle of Wight, Tony moved to Manchester Metropolitan University. Tony has headed the doctoral programme in education as well as participating in a range of other courses and became a professor in 2000. Projects have included Economic and Social Research Council funded studies examining teacher education; piloting a distance-teaching programme enabling British volunteers based in Africa to research their own teaching practice within a programme of professional development; a General Medical Council funded project on how senior doctors learn; and leading a team of emergency medicine doctors carrying out professionally focused research. Tony also spent 2 years on leave from Manchester at the University of Waikato where he became the first Professor of Mathematics Education in New Zealand. There he led a project funded by the New Zealand Council for Educational Research on Pasifika teachers working in New Zealand Schools.

Tony has published two other books in Springer's Mathematics Education Library series. *Mathematics Education and Language*, first published in 1997, outlines his interest in mathematics in schools. A revised second edition appeared in 2001. *Mathematics Education and Subjectivity* (forthcoming) explores mathematical learning from the perspective of contemporary social theory. Meanwhile, Tony has also authored *Action Research and Postmodernism* (with Liz Jones), which explores how teachers might carry out practitioner research within higher degrees. *Regulative Discourses in Education: A Lacanian Perspective* (with Dennis Atkinson and Janice England) offered an analysis of teacher practices through psychoanalytic theory. *The Psychology of Mathematics Education*, edited by Tony, introduced psychoanalytic theory as an alternative to more cognitive understandings of psychology. Tony has also written extensively in journals such as *Educational Studies in Mathematics, For the Learning of Mathematics*, and the *British Educational Research Journal*.

**Olwen McNamara** is Professor of Teacher Education and Development at the University of Manchester and has lived and worked in and around Manchester most of her life. Her first degree was in mathematics, which she subsequently taught for over 20 years; latterly combining teaching with bringing up a family and studying for a PhD at Manchester Metropolitan University. After completing her thesis in 1996, she worked at Manchester Metropolitan University as an educational researcher, and also managed a research-based partnership of local schools, local authorities and universities. She moved to the University of Manchester in 2002 where her main management role was initially in teacher education. She is currently Director of Initial Teacher Education and Director of Post Graduate Research at the University.

Olwen's research interests are in the area of teacher professional learning, and she has a special interest in mathematics education, social justice and practitioner research. She has undertaken research projects for funders including the Economic and Social Research Council, the Nuffield Foundation, the Training and Development Agency, The Department for Education, the National College and NASUWT – the teachers' union. She has authored a number of reports for these funders and published widely in international journals. Her previous books include *Becoming An Evidence-Based Practitioner* and *Practitioner Research and Professional Development in Education* (which she wrote with Anne Campbell and Peter Gilroy). She has served on a number of national committees including the British Educational Research Association Council, where she was chair of the conference committee for a number of years, and the Research and Development Committee of the Universities' Council for the Education of Teachers, where she is Vice Chair.

# Chapter 1
# Introduction

Clare is in her final year of training as a teacher. She is aware of the many demands that she will face upon entering her chosen profession. Apart from meeting the academic and professional requirements of her university, she is keen to succeed at the school where she is to be placed in her final teaching practice. Clare enjoys working with young children. She takes pleasure from being popular with them and obtaining the approval of their parents. On her final school placement she will be teaching a broad range of curriculum subjects including mathematics, our particular concern in this book. She has needed to develop a way of teaching this subject that is enjoyable to her pupils whilst adhering adequately to the curriculum. She will need to be sensitive to noticing and minimising pupils' anxieties with mathematics, and perhaps, as we shall show, attend to some of her own. But above all she will need to hold on to some of her own personal aspirations that have brought her this far.

Yet, in reflecting on such demands, Clare is aware that in so many ways she is acting on behalf of others and their own particular priorities. Her discussions with colleagues in schools, tutors at university, and children have become a pastiche of things that she feels other people would want her to say. Clare has become quite alarmed by the absence of her "own voice". But then again, she conjectures, maybe this is now her "own voice", steeped as she now is in the professional way of talking about the job of being a teacher in a school. Her sense of self is fashioned by the expectations of others. Her personal aspirations of what it is to be a teacher have become aligned with the language she feels compelled to speak in order to secure accreditation and then employment, where she will undoubtedly encounter ongoing scrutiny from government inspectors. But then again, even if it were possible to find the real Clare, who would this be? The Clare she thinks she is? The Clare she wants to be? The Clare she was before her training? The Clare who is seen by others? Or the one "others" want her to be? But which others?

How might Clare make sense of all this? Suppose that we imagine Clare lying back on a psychoanalyst's couch where she talks of her life, her motivations, fears and aspirations. And in pinpointing these in words spoken to the analyst, they somehow become more real and tangible for her. As such they emerge as guiding principles for how Clare lives her life thereafter. The words and the way they are put together become part of her. The story that Clare tells of her life shapes her

T. Brown, O. McNamara, *Becoming a Mathematics Teacher*,
Mathematics Education Library 53, DOI 10.1007/978-94-007-0554-8_1,
© Springer Science+Business Media B.V. 2011

1

actual experience by providing a framework against which she understands what she is doing. Nevertheless, these ways of making sense can deceive as well as enlighten. It's a complex world and there is no unique story of how things make sense. Some versions of self may feel more comfortable than others. Clare may choose a version that she feels she can work with or simply stick with the one she knows as familiar. Yet each story of what she has done or of what she is doing provides alternative trajectories into the future.

More generally we build images of how we collectively conduct ourselves and develop particular understandings of normality, and especially of how teachers like Clare should behave. These images provide a backdrop to individuals making sense of their own lives within this wider frame. For Clare, the final stage of her training seemed to go hand in hand with meeting all the obligations entailed in being fully inducted into the profession. She felt she had been speaking with all manner of unfamiliar voices, much as a surrogate ventriloquist's dummy. But, despite this, her personal aspirations still surfaced.

This book is centred on people preparing to teach mathematics to children in the first half of their schooling. But how do we understand mathematics? We do not start out by supposing that there is a "correct" version of what mathematics is or should be. We centre our attention more on the ways in which beginning teachers talk about teaching mathematics to children aged 4–11 in schools currently. That is, we do not commence with our own advance understanding of mathematics and see what people are saying about it. Rather, we start from what people are saying about learning in schools and see how this points to particular ways of understanding what mathematics is in contemporary school practices and more widely. For whatever reason, most countries have decided to teach mathematics in schools and this decision has shaped the activities that we call "mathematics". Ultimately in schools, understandings of mathematics emerge in the interplay between pupils, teachers and the societal structures they inhabit. These understandings derive from a variety of culturally based assumptions as to the nature of mathematics and the associated forms of accountability they produce. And this situated meaning impacts on the evolving practices of trainee and new teachers. For these individuals mathematical understanding is shaped between the new teacher's grasp of the subject and the institutional definitions of it. Trainees and new teachers reconcile their own sense of what mathematics is with how it might be taught, against the demands they face from a variety of sources. Difficulties arise, however, from inconsistencies between alternative understandings of mathematics, the teaching of it, the perspective we assume in describing this teaching, and the issues underpinning the teacher training process. Moreover, teachers of young children generally need to teach a broad range of subjects with teaching mathematics just one of the many duties. Mathematics as a subject in its own right has had a tendency to be drowned out in the bustle of different agencies selling their wares to trainee teachers as they pass through their training.

How do these people begin to think of themselves as teachers? How do would-be teachers experience their own professional learning? How do they change how they are, or even who they are, as they proceed through a teacher education programme into their first teaching post? With many years of experience as pupils in school behind them, student teachers are required to re-orient themselves towards the demands of teaching and they eventually progress into salaried classroom practitioners with a particular brief of teaching children in the primary[1] (or elementary) classroom. The professional landscape guides the aspiring teacher's individual practice against a backdrop of diverse and complex social demands that cannot necessarily be reconciled. The work of schools is targeted at enabling pupils to participate in a rapidly changing world where consensus on educational objectives seems difficult to achieve. Once again the diverse criteria that apply in setting educational priorities can result in teachers being pulled in many directions. Yet the demands of employment often play the trump card. Specifically, teacher identity is set against the regulative policies and highly structured frameworks that have come to define teaching in many countries. In this scenario, teachers have needed to craft their understanding according to the legislative framework in which their practices have become ever more strictly articulated. These in turn structure the learning environment and curriculum encountered by children and the style and content of mathematics.

Those charged with providing training for such individuals need to understand the processes and the impact of this training. An appropriate balance needs to be achieved. On the one hand new teachers need to be nurtured to become autonomous professionals, responsible for developing and delivering the mathematics curriculum in schools. On the other hand, trainers need to engage with policies that prescribe their own practices in training institutions and also the practices of their student teachers in schools.

A social environment of great complexity results in personal liberty vying with social control. The individual teacher juggles between deciding for herself and being told what to decide. She shares space with others in a way that meets common and alternative needs, but collective arrangements entail personal restraint. Yet surely in spite of all this complexity, teachers themselves do have some say, and would want some say, over how they conduct their own lives. They are not infinitely susceptible to social conditions and the guidance of their mentors. Teachers do have a voice of their own through which they express their own aspirations of what it is to be a teacher. How might teachers stick their heads above the parapet to speak more firmly in voices that might be claimed as their own? Yet, the notion of such ownership brings its own problems. The complex nature of teaching and its depiction in the social sphere prevents singular views of one's own participation. Many contemporary analyses dispute the individual's capacity to be aware of his or her own immersion in such collective arrangements. Here a culture of cynicism is observed, where, despite everyone's knowing that they are governed through a matrix of ideological hype, their actions remain largely unaffected.

---

[1] The British term "primary" will be used where the focus relates to the education of children aged 4–11.

Would-be teachers face two simultaneous journeys during the training process: first, the path followed by the teacher pursuing her personal aspirations and second, how the official story portrays the journey as a sequence of criteria to be fulfilled. How do these stories co-exist and in which ways do they intersect? How do they knowingly and unknowingly support each other and resist each other? And how do understandings of mathematics emerge from each?

In the first journey, the survival of mathematics must depend on the individual's wanting it to survive in her story. It would be so easy to downgrade mathematics to "just one of the subjects that I have to teach". For those with uncomfortable memories of mathematics in their own schooling, this might be the preferred option. How then might the pre-service teacher be assisted in advocating mathematics a little more strongly? How might the training process, with its multiple objectives and attendant budgetary and time constraints, impact a little more on the student teacher's inner motivations to work with the subject?

In the second journey the trainee is more like a robot on a production line collecting the components required to assemble the final product. Recent reform in a number of countries has seen governments wrestle with teachers and teacher education providers in deciding the content of the curriculum and the style in which it is delivered. Many policy initiatives have worked to a supposition that prescriptive adjustments to the professional environment will influence the activities that take place. For example, the resulting package in England, to be outlined in Chapter 4, comprised tight guidelines specifying and legislating what must be taught. This included a detailed curriculum prescribing how lessons should be administered, statutory guidance on how pre-service teachers should be trained and supplementary tests of mathematical content before they entered the profession. Few risks were taken. Mathematics as a school subject was largely down to official conceptions dictating its terms of reference.

These two journeys are, in English schools at least, happening at a time when new understandings of professionalism and managerialism are impacting on public conceptions of the teacher's role and external descriptions are being privileged over personal or professional motivations. The personal motivations, characteristic of the first journey, seem increasingly to be expressed in terms of fulfilling the requirements of the second journey. In this book we examine these two journeys, or perhaps alternatively, give an account of and account for "the" journey undertaken by trainee teachers from the two perspectives. But in centring itself in a project concerned with sharpening the definition and objectives of research in mathematics education, the book sides with the teacher in pursuing the development of her own professional voice. The professional landscape is highly populated with people supposing that they are acting in trainee teachers' best interests, whether they be university tutors, teachers encountered during school placements, government inspectors or researchers. This book privileges the task of creating a better understanding of how teachers might be equipped to assert their own voices.

Nevertheless, we do not see ourselves as liberators of oppressed teachers seeking release from restrictive structures. The structures often meet the demands of teachers themselves, providing support in areas where they lack confidence. Official versions of events can easily become the common sense of the day. Yet, we see our research task as being to challenge these boundaries. We investigate the claim that in accepting the 'rulebook', teachers are complicit in limiting their professional judgement. The very fantasy of a quick fix in "raising standards", "redefining professionalism", securing an "evidence base" in research seems to appeal to teachers and their employers alike. Administrators or politicians need to be able to present policies in clear terms no matter how unclear or contradictory the underlying premises might be. Consequently, researchers in mathematics education need to assert a language that resists the onslaught of over-simplistic solutions.

To summarise, the book is primarily concerned with examining how trainee teachers conceptualise their own professional learning from the time they enter training through to the end of their first year of teaching in school.[2] That is, we are centrally concerned with issues of teacher identity. Yet conceptions of teacher identity fix understandings of mathematics and its teaching in schools. The book offers empirical and theoretical perspectives.

Empirically, we draw on two studies funded by United Kingdom research councils and conducted by the authors over a 5-year period. The studies were concerned with the professional learning of trainee teachers focusing on their experience of the training process. Two groups of around 30 trainees were interviewed in detail at different stages of their 4-year training. Many others responded to questionnaires. We hear their voices at various points in the training process to show how these voices adapt to include more of the official language required of them. In due course this language becomes part of them, even in terms of how they see themselves as teachers. Thus we examine how such trainees make the transition into the teaching profession. We further consider the influences which impact on the trainee during this period, such as university tutors, school-based mentors, government policy, curriculum materials. These studies took place at a time of great change, comprising a major programme of curriculum reform in which new policies for the teaching of mathematics took centre stage. Since the book is able to document aspects of this major initiative from beginning to end, we are able in a very limited way to evaluate the capacity of a holistic policy intervention to bring about qualitative adjustments to teaching practices. Many countries have experienced major curriculum reform in recent years. The English initiative, however, penetrated deeply, spanning the regulation of teaching in schools and radical changes to teacher training. It was truly an experiment on a grand scale into how much centralised control could be achieved. We can learn much from this attempt about the limits of centralised control and

---

[2] In the light of recent changes the book rethinks and builds on our earlier book *New teacher identity and regulative government: the discursive formation of primary mathematics teacher education* (Brown & McNamara, 2005). That book had comprised a substantial presentation of two projects funded by the UK Economic and Social Research Council: Brown, McNamara, Jones, and Hanley (1999), Brown, McNamara, Basit, and Roberts (2001). Other material arising from these projects from which our data is drawn include Brown, McNamara, Hanley, and Jones (1999), Hanley and Brown (1999), Jones, Brown, Hanley, and McNamara (2000), McNamara, Roberts, Basit, and Brown (2002), Basit (2003a, b), Brown, Jones, and Bibby (2004), Roberts (2004), Brown (2008e).

how this is processed through the actions of individuals. The studies pointed to this national programme being seen in a positive light by many teachers in primary schools. It provided clear guidance in an area where many such teachers experienced anxieties in relation to the subject. Some pointed to its being a trigger to creativity. Some others saw it as a possible challenge to their own professional autonomy. Longer-term benefits were less clear. The initiative had limited impact on raising pupil outcomes and its wind-down and impending closure were announced in 2009.

Theoretically, we turn to recent work in the field of psychoanalysis, and, in particular, the work of Slavoj Žižek, a Slovenian commentator influenced by the Freudian psychoanalytical work of Jacques Lacan. Žižek has had major impact on contemporary social theory. This theoretical avenue affords excellent views of how individual trainee teachers encounter the social framework in which they operate. Leaning to Foucault, we also consider alternative "technologies of self" that produce teachers in schools. Žižek argues that the seduction of an overarching rational structure guiding practice can provide a substitute for the deeper desires that we wish to satisfy. Such compliance, he argues, can give rise to particular forms of "enjoyment". Teachers, for example, may secretly like the rules they have to follow as they can give them a clear framework to shape their practice, and a quick fix in getting their achievements validated. Similarly, even though people may know that their actions or the stories that support them do not make sense, that may not inhibit their being pursued in the absence of clear alternatives. Žižek portrays a prevalent culture of cynicism, where there is an acceptance that actions by individuals do not make much difference. There are now too many versions of life for one centralised rational structure to have credence. This very complexity can activate the desire for simple solutions or for simple metrics to evaluate the suggested change. Yet the failure of these attempts to explain social processes opens a space for individuals to assert their own agency. Additionally, we look at how this production of discursive apparatus generates reductive conceptions of mathematics. Mathematics is situated amidst a multitude of alternative versions of what people claim it to be. Yet not one of these versions quite pinpoints it. People and places have been affected by the existence of mathematics. We suggest, however, that it is necessarily the discursive constructions that teach us what mathematics is. In the light of this analysis, we conclude by looking at how policy, teacher learning, school mathematics and research might be alternatively conceptualised.

These empirical and theoretical aspects are raised in relation to a number of concerns. First, we present an account of how trainee teachers understand their journey into teaching mathematics in the primary school. Second, we examine the conceptions of mathematics that pervade early schooling and how these conceptions might develop. Third, we discuss how policy, as implemented in major initiatives, impacts on such teachers. Fourth, we consider the role that research in mathematics education might have in accounting for the process of trainees' becoming teachers in school and in stimulating development in this area. Finally, we offer a theoretical frame that accommodates evolving and alternative conceptions of mathematics, how it is taught and the social parameters that guide these conceptions.

We open our theoretical work in Chapter 2 by considering how personal experience encounters social demand in conceiving school mathematics, in understanding how it might be taught and in deciding how teachers might be trained to teach it. Alternative theoretical models from contemporary hermeneutics and psychoanalysis are introduced to provide a framework for discussing mathematics teaching and teacher identity. As a prelude to the data being introduced in Chapter 4, these models provide a framework to consider how trainee teachers construct their identities through the training process and in response to policy frameworks.

Chapter 3 surveys some of the research that is available and relevant to the processes of pre-service teacher education. Whilst emphasising the paucity of research coverage in the British context within major journals, the chapter argues that wider coverage, such as that on offer in the United States, does not deliver the uniformly clear story or confidence one might wish for in building wider curriculum reform.

We then move in Chapter 4 to a case study of recent education reforms in England to contextualise the empirical studies upon which we draw. We document how regulative aspects of policy have shaped conceptions of teaching in schools, teacher education and curriculum reform. After introducing the empirical studies, we discuss the successive phases in the training process with respect to key transition points in the journey from school pupil to primary teacher of mathematics. Many of the trainees we encountered had been nervous about mathematics as pupils. Their anxieties clouded their entry into university. Yet university sessions provided a fun version of mathematics that became an effective blueprint for their future teaching. The impact on practical teaching approaches, however, seemed less obvious. Survival in the classroom and fitting into school occupied their attention. And since they had suffered with mathematics in their own schooling they felt they would be able to sympathise with children who were struggling with mathematics. The trainees' conception of teaching did not develop sufficiently for alternative styles to be effectively implemented in their own teaching. Teaching remained a delivery of mathematics but with an attempt to make it more enjoyable. Different influences impacted in successive phases of the training with uneven reconciliation being achieved of the many conflicting discourses. Mathematics was subsumed within broader conceptions of classroom administration. Yet wider policy changes had re-asserted an identity for mathematics that had become lost within broader primary education practices. These policies had resulted in teachers emphasising procedure rather than mathematical content. New teachers felt confident working within this guidance, which also enabled them to conceal any remaining unease with the subject.

Chapter 5 reflects on the empirical studies as a resource in building a more theoretical account of teacher identity and how this might be accounted for through research processes. We depict how individual trainee teachers see their own emerging sense of identity as a teacher. The multiple demands they face are combined in moving towards a coherent account of professional functioning. The chapter commences with some discussion of how the data represent teacher change and teacher conceptions of their own situations in relation to theoretical models of identity. It provides examples of how trainee and new teachers produce an account of their professional practice against a backdrop of some unresolved issues. It further shows how trainee and new teachers appropriate the language of policy directives within their own vocabularies and how they use this language to encapsulate their own personal experiences. We propose, however, that any supposed resolution of the conflicting demands trainees encounter is illusory and that trainees work at producing images of themselves to conceal continuing difficulties.

Chapter 6 commences by discussing the data against a more theoretical treatment of the social construction of school mathematics. The chapter focuses on how trainee teachers discuss mathematics in the context of their own teaching and shows how school mathematics is a function of broader discursive practices. We shed light on the way in which conceptions of school mathematics are derived through this process. We then offer a more theoretical account of how school mathematics has become *commodified* through social processes. We argue that an administrative language used to articulate teaching practices interrupts a more direct focus on the mathematical content of the children's work. The apparatus associated with this administrative layer shapes classroom mathematics and children's experiences of this. For a teacher setting a mathematical task, there is the activity as performed by the child, the mathematics supposed to underlie it, and also the more unconscious desires being mediated by those forms. Yet it is argued that mathematics will always exceed specific versions of it in educational contexts.

We conclude in Chapter 7, switching from our research voice to our opinions, by arguing for alternative trajectories and implications for practice with respect to our key themes: teacher development, mathematics, policy and research. It is anticipated that the readers of this book would have professional involvement and potential impact in each of those areas.

First, teacher development, we shall argue, is a function of multiple and diverse priorities that are more or less achievable with the given educational resources, most notably the actual supply of teachers. Yet these teachers are answerable to a professional calling that is far from unambiguous. Teachers are required to respond to multiple demands that cannot always be reconciled in the practices of individual teachers. Set policy as they may, school authorities cannot secure absolute control. There are limits to what teachers can distil from the diverse demands they encounter. And they can only define themselves in relation to the constraints they see themselves as having recognised and accepted. For an individual entering training his or her sense of agency is modified and read differently against an emergent understanding of a new environment and of how he or she will be received. This entails a tricky meeting of a newly conceived agency rooted in personal aspirations and an expectation that he or she will be told how to teach. Agency on the part of the trainee mingles with dependency and gets shaped by the form of the external demands encountered. And the assistance on hand is similarly governed by conflicting priorities. For example, as we shall see in Chapter 4, in English schools the input of university-based teacher educators has been substantially reduced in favour of school-based training led by mentors with their own classroom responsibilities. Such changes are governed as much by cost and by ideology as by issues of quality.

Teachers are recognised to the degree to which they comply with external role determinations. There may be a perverse pleasure achieved through performing correctly within a given regulatory frame. Yet the gap between the cover story that the teacher tells and the conflict of priorities can be seen as a potential site for resistance where a more autonomous individual identity could be asserted.

Second, we contemplate how mathematics as a notion emerges from the training process. Mathematical achievement in schools is increasingly read through a register of *commodified* procedures and performativity, in a one size fits all model, spanning diverse nations and communities. Learning outcomes are dependent on the learning theories and assessment instruments being applied. Conceptions of mathematics are heterogeneous, socially derived and motivated by a range of ideological perspectives meaning that we cannot finally decide *what mathematics is*. Yet these social forms have a real effect on classroom practices and their governance. Mathematics gets to be known through, for example, particular results or standard methods. The activities of primary school mathematics have a strong association with the organisational and philosophical discourses of primary education more generally, and the link with a more explicitly mathematical discourse is increasingly marginalised through successive phases of training. School mathematics has been bureaucratised and is held in place by regulation. As teachers and as researchers, we need to learn how these social practices operate if we are to exert any influence.

Third, we consider the policy environment and the role of research. We first consider how policy is conceived and implemented and thus how a teacher's professional domain is shaped. What policies might bring about effective change? Yet the grip of educational policies on practice is generally rather more tenuous. Policy-making is not an exact science and control of educational practices, insofar as it operates, is dispersed across a number of diverse agencies governed by a range of alternative, and often conflicting, agendas with varying degrees of influence. At a structural level, policy makers do not readily identify as a coherent unit in relation to policies governing school mathematics and other stakeholders, such as advisory groups, trainers, mathematicians, research funding agencies, potential employers and universities/colleges work according to a variety of perspectives and priorities. Curriculum pronouncements that do not necessarily achieve harmony emerge from these various groups resulting in possible disconnections between policy setting, implementation by teachers and how such implementations are conceptualised by researchers. Moreover, no one person really knows how much influence he or she exerts in this panoply of political exchange, and no one quite knows who is in charge, or through which routes influence might be achieved. One consequence of this tussle is that teachers do not know who they are ultimately answerable to. Also, there is no one person who has a final word on how we might understand mathematics. We suggest that policy *diktats* cannot assume the behaviourist response their initiators desire. Yet it would be wrong to assume that the complexities defy all analysis. The task of analysis is more complex and cannot be predicated on the assumption that clear solutions will be found. It is not easy to locate simple causal links. This, however, does not stop interested parties claiming them, or others believing them, or, at least, acting as if they believed them.

Finally, how might we move forward in understanding research in mathematics education? The production of educational theory and research is a site of ideological and political struggle. Research intervenes in ideological exchange by providing empirically or theoretically supported arguments, but generally in relation to fairly localised contexts. Yet research discourses and the policy discourses they seek to support rarely meet in a shared language. Policy initiatives cannot be seen as products of individual politicians' imaginations. There is always a gap between conception, declaration and implementation, opened up by the complexity under-lying any supposedly causal relationship. And such policies have had mixed results with a high cost in terms of teachers' being left out of the decision-making process. Teacher working practices are increasingly susceptible to external definition, yet still they participate, and seem to enjoy this participation. We argue that researchers need to resist the apparent narrowing of their domain, centred on current techni-cist or managerial conceptions of mathematics. Mathematics education is a social science and its resources and ambitions need to reflect that. There is a need for a language that does not trap us within restrictive styles of analysis to merely service the current priorities. This is about troubling certainties rather than producing them. There is no endpoint to be reached in a perfect set of guidelines.

# Chapter 2
# Mathematics Teaching and Identity

## 2.1 Introduction

This chapter outlines some of the theoretical ground that will underpin the arguments to be made after the empirical material has been presented in Chapter 4. The alternative frames to be offered enable an analysis of how mathematics and its teaching manifest themselves differently in individual and social perspectives. Distinctions between the individual and the social bring with them a host of difficulties with regard to teacher agency. The image of the lone teacher reflecting on her practice and building her control is challenged. The teacher cannot easily separate her own aspirations from those that are demanded of her by her employer. The very definition of the individual human subject draws on socialised accounts of what it is to be human, or, more specifically, what it is to be a teacher. In short, to a large extent a teacher is *identified* against particular social structures. Individual teachers express their personal aspirations in terms of participation in shared agendas. They understand themselves and are understood by others through that common sense.

The three words that comprise the label *primary mathematics teacher* each have a meaning that is specific to that particular configuration and relate to the circumstances in which the job takes place. As authors, we are addressing members of the mathematics education research community and mathematics educators more generally. Yet the core of our data derives from would-be or practising primary school teachers charged with addressing all aspects of the primary curriculum. Mathematics is just one subject among many for them. Nearly all children in the primary years learn mathematics until the age of eleven from teachers with a generalist brief. Research relating to the teaching of mathematics at primary level needs to be tackled at this more general level. The brief extends beyond the normal territory of mathematics education researchers and the extension requires that mathematics be thought about differently. As we shall show later, primary teachers are not easily persuaded into talking explicitly and exclusively about mathematical content. For them, the distinction of mathematics as a school subject from other areas in the curriculum is too slight for it to have a discourse of its own. Yet clearly they have considerable influence over the conception and practice of primary mathematics, even when that influence is largely restricted to mediating a centralised curriculum. This is very

T. Brown, O. McNamara, *Becoming a Mathematics Teacher*,
Mathematics Education Library 53, DOI 10.1007/978-94-007-0554-8_2,
© Springer Science+Business Media B.V. 2011

different to the situation faced by their colleagues in secondary schools, where most of those teaching mathematics have some sort of specialism in the area.[1] Rather, as we shall see later, many primary teachers experienced difficulties with mathematics in their own schooling. These were not just conceptual difficulties but very often the difficulties involved significant emotional turbulence. We face a disturbing scenario in which many teachers who, as pupils, did not like the subject now teach many primary aged children. This scenario clearly presents a challenge to those responsible for administering the mathematics curriculum at primary level, and for those training the teachers concerned. It is from this perspective that we examine how conceptions of school mathematics come into being. In short the prefix "primary" has a strong influence over how the word mathematics is understood in this location.

Meanwhile, policy moves in recent years have been indicative of a new conception of professional learning. The development of educational organisations has dictated the terms of teachers' personal learning and development. This has resulted in teachers conceiving their professional task in terms of following a set of rules. These rules specify what teachers have to get through for the good of their institution, set against a wider externally defined conception of good practice or standards. This orientation to professional development works against conceptions of teacher professionalism centred on personal authority. Earlier conceptions of developing professional practice had been seen more typically in terms of personal development activated through reflective practitioner models (to be discussed in the next chapter). Recent policy trends have led to suggestions that teachers are participating in their own de-professionalism.[2]

The trainee and new teachers to be encountered in this book, however, have known nothing else. Their emerging professionalism is constructed in this new topography. The very support structures have become the new common sense of what the trainees are learning to do. These structures mask the alternative conceptions of professionalism and mathematics teaching that had been assumed by their predecessors. Against this backdrop, the educational authorities are telling teachers what they need to be. Trainee and new teachers understand the process through which they become teachers in these terms. It is in this sense that the chapter addresses issues of identity among trainee teachers. That is, it considers how teachers begin to understand who they are as they become teachers against this new regime of common sense. What is it that they *identify* with? We suggest that personal understandings are increasingly expressed through the more collectively derived explanatory apparatus that forms the dominant *modus operandi* of the day.

A theoretical account is to be presented here of how individuals understand themselves against the backdrop of the multiple social demands encountered during the training process. Firstly, alternative hermeneutical models are outlined that offer different perspectives on mathematics, its teaching and how teachers are trained. This

---

[1] There are, however, significant problems recruiting teachers with appropriate mathematics qualifications to teach in secondary (or high school) education in England.

[2] Bottery and Wright (1996).

permits a better understanding of how individual and social perspectives on school mathematics might be reconciled through frames that enable them to co-exist. Secondly, we build the ground for a more sophisticated apparatus for discussing identity. Teachers *choose* to tell a particular version of events, and this choice predicates a selective account governed by the teacher's own self-image. An analogy is drawn between these self-disclosures in the interviews carried out and psychoanalytic procedures. Trainees are depicted as mediating self-understandings through the demands of government policy instruments, such as inspections and curriculum initiatives. Yet participation in the institutions of teaching results in the production of languages that serve to conceal difficulties encountered in reconciling these multiple demands with each other.

## 2.2  Hermeneutics to Psychoanalysis

### 2.2.1  Four Models of Hermeneutics

How does language shape the life that it describes and how does life shape language? Individual humans interact with social structures. Specifically teachers interpret social structures and *enact* them in their own "individual" teaching practice. They "speak" understandings of these social structures through their own voices. Social understandings of school mathematics and the teaching of it are reified in the apparatus of schools, policies and associated practices. The individual practices of teachers are recognised and assessed through the filter of more collective understandings of the teachers' professional task. In this way collective social practices shape the practices of individual teachers. But at the same time the summation of individual practices comprises the collective social practices. Primary school mathematics *is* what primary teachers make happen. Policy directives may seek to impact on collective practices but this impact will always be a function of how those collective practices are currently understood and how that understanding might be influenced. Collective practices depend on the interpretation of individuals. In this respect, this book is exploring how a large-scale policy initiative works through the actions of individuals. Such wider concerns have significant impact on conceptualisations of mathematics education research and the routes through which such research might seek to influence practice.

How might we understand this theoretically? A strictly rule-governed apparatus only works if it is in touch with normative practices. Meanwhile normative practices are generally accountable to some agreed regulative framework. Such circularities underpin hermeneutics, the theory of interpretation. Ricoeur (1981) situates the *hermeneutic circle* in the interplay of understanding and explanation. Understanding is continuous in time, forever susceptible to temporal disturbance. Explanations are encapsulated in a form of words fixed in time and discrete. Our understanding of our experience can be translated into an explanation and these resulting explanations can then condition our subsequent understandings. The focus of such analysis is on how people experience the world and make sense of it. There is no necessary supposition of an underlying truth. Hermeneutics can be usefully applied to how we as humans make sense of the flow of our experience. It is often combined with the term "phenomenology", the logic of the world as experienced. In this book we are not so much concerned with the truth of the world as such, as with how teachers make sense of specific curriculum guidance, of the mathematics they teach, of the training processes, of the people they work with, and how they act accordingly. And *in* acting accordingly they assert what those things are.

What difficulties do we face in seeking to encapsulate experience in a set of words? Gallagher (1992) categorises four alternative modes through which such linguistic processing can happen, which each offer a way of understanding how an individual relates to language. In particular they can be seen as modes of understanding how teachers relate to the discursive parameters that shape their practice. But also they are modes of understanding the transfer of mathematical knowledge.

*Conservative hermeneutics* is exemplified in the task of reading a text where the primary objective of the interpretation is to understand the author in the way that the author intended.

> Verbal meaning, being an intentional object, is unchanging, that is, it may be reproduced by different intentional acts and remain self-identical through all these reproductions . . . Since this meaning is both unchanging and interpersonal, it may be reproduced by the mental acts of different persons.[3]

Within schooling, the learner's task is restricted to understanding what the teacher had in mind. The aim of education is to "prepare the individual for common participation in the state, the church, free society, and academia".[4] This traditional view might be associated with delivery metaphors where the ideas in question remain unchanged through this process of communication. This is conservative in the sense that education is seen as reproductive, ensuring that the new generation complies with existing norms. The student teacher aspires to teach in the familiar state-sanctioned fashion, but in turn her pupils will be expected to do what they are told. In this model, mathematics is unchanged through the educative process. It exists independently of subjective attitudes towards it.

Meanwhile, *moderate hermeneutics* does not see tradition, or meaning, as fixed. Rather, tradition is transformed through an educative process. Ideas are not seen as fully constituted objects to behold but in a permanent state of evolution. For example, mathematical ideas are seen as a function of their social environment, or of the teacher–student interaction. The leading exponents of twentieth century hermeneutics were Heidegger, Gadamer and Ricoeur. For these writers certain truths orientate our way of seeing things. A range of interpretations is permitted, some of which may be seen as being closer to the truth. Yet no interpretation is ever final. Such understanding never arrives at its object directly as one's approach is always conditioned by the interpretations explored on the way. Here there is an attempt to capture the continuity of understanding in discrete forms, as explanations. These explanations

---

[3]Hirsch, quoted by Gallagher (1992, p. 211).
[4]Schleiermacher, quoted by Gallagher (1992, p. 213).

then feed into and influence the continuous experience of understanding. Whilst one's own understanding may become "fixed" in an explanation for the time being, such fixity is always contingent. Were I to act as if my explanation were correct, the world might resist my actions in a slightly unexpected way. This surprise gives rise to a new understanding, resulting in a revised explanation, providing a new context for acting and so on. If I imagine myself trying to make sense of the world, I will have various thoughts in my mind. At some point, however, I may wish to share my thoughts in words spoken or written. But, as I say something, I may be more or less disappointed with how my thoughts sound once converted into words. And through my attempts to reconcile what I thought with what I said, my understanding of the world might then be modified. So, when I feel ready to speak again, there may be some shift in the way in which I express myself as, in a sense, a different person is speaking, re-positioned as I am with respect to stories of who I am and of the world in which I reside. And so on, in a manifestation of the hermeneutic circle where understandings and explanations continue to disturb each other perhaps for as long as I live. In this account of the hermeneutic circle one might envisage an individual who is visible to his or her self and able to detect the ways in which explanatory words fail. Adjustments can be made accordingly. The human subject predicated in this understanding is generally Cartesian, centred in current cognition, and self-aware. The reflective task is conceptualised in terms of improvement to where I am now, produced as I have been through historical processes. Models of teacher education centred on reflective practice often follow this transformative model. Here the new teacher crafts a conception of her professional role in relation to the support structures being offered. These models are predicated on the individual's building a sense of her own practice and developing this practice according to her particular priorities. In school these models often translate into progressive teaching where children are encouraged to introduce and pursue their own perspectives.

This version of events, however, lacks some key elements that have emerged in more contemporary theoretical work where the visibility of oneself to oneself is less evident. The very notion of self arises through rather different procedures. One might imagine an individual rather less sure of his or her personal and social boundaries. Individuals craft personal experience through socially generated discourses. These discourses may be new and alien but demand (or appear to demand) that individuals fit around them. The individual's subjectivity is a function of this crafting. I define who I am by identifying reflexively and variously with the multiple stories of life that surround me. And this process cannot have clear outcomes since I cannot fully understand who I am in this situation. A strict separation between the individual and the external world can never be achieved within the discursive terrain of the individual and the social parameters that shape her actions. If, for example, you have populations of people introduced to new trends in curriculum design or research findings, the results will always have an unpredictable dimension. Individuals cannot fully assess how their actions will be assessed against the wider movement by a range of others, working to various agenda. But, More prosaically, we shall later encounter new teachers who are rather insecure with their task of teaching mathematics, both in terms of their own sense of what it is to be a teacher but also with respect to their knowledge of mathematics restricting their pedagogical options. Uncertainties resulting from restrictive knowledge of mathematics and its pedagogical forms can result in a conception of teaching that is more transmission orientated, since such teachers are less willing to deviate from a well-prepared script. In this way, we shall see, curriculum documentation provided a support mechanism for teachers less able to articulate their own professional rationale.

In Gallagher's third paradigm the human subject finds a world distorted by the operation of power. Or, perhaps, certain accounts of the world have settled into place even though they now less successfully support new conditions. *Critical hermeneutics* is targeted at challenging such states of affairs. Its chief contemporary exponent Habermas[5] aims for unconstrained language. Critical hermeneutics presents a conception of human behaviour understood in relation to consensual universal principles. These principles might include particular moral perspectives, the existence of God, or specific forms of common sense, which can be called upon in the event of some supposed divergence from rational behaviour. For example, the content of school mathematics may have been decided by a government wanting measurable results within a particular register rather than according to the promotion of higher order skills that are less easily measured. Curriculums have sometimes moved between problem solving or constructivism and "back to basics" agenda. In either model the depiction of mathematics goes through some sort of distortion. Habermas seeks "Ideal" communication without ideological distortion, a view of mathematics for instance unpolluted by local contextual factors. In such situations the human subject is motivated towards some ideal state of affairs that can be apprehended now and, perhaps, could be realised in the future. Contradictions are confronted and action is designed to remove them. For example, the government's short-term ambitions may be exposed in a television debate that results in an adjustment to policy. Habermas is critical of moderate hermeneutics, arguing that language is inherited and replete with many distortions resulting from particular modes of usage. The subject cannot see the world, or see his or her self, in a straightforward way.

For Habermas, education is charged with resolving inequalities, resisting oppressive power relations and the like. These aspirations suppose a set of guiding principles as to what is better. The work of Habermas has underpinned much work in educational practitioner research.[6] Here the practitioner is encouraged to adopt a critical insider perspective towards detecting how her practice has been misdirected

---

[5]Habermas (1972).

[6]Carr and Kemmis (1986), Zuber-Skerritt (1996). The aspirations seem consistent in many ways with other traditions of critical education as evident in the work of some major writers in the area (e.g. Freire, 1972; Apple, 1982; Aronowitz & Giroux, 1985; McLaren, 1995). Such critical perspectives on education have been pursued specifically within mathematics education research (e.g. Skovsmose, 1994, 2005; Frankenstein, 1997; Ongstad, 2006). See also a special issue of the *International Journal of Philosophy of Mathematics Education*, 2010. Meanwhile, Taylor (1996) and Brown (2001) have explicitly discussed the social theory of Habermas as an approach to understanding how educational objectives in mathematics might be framed.

by distortions in the fabric of the language. For teachers entering the profession, the critical task would be to be attentive to the way in which the language of instruction to which they are subjected draws them in to politically charged modes of making sense of the world. In our main example, we shall argue that the possibility of trainee teachers adopting such critical insider perspectives has been eroded in favour of the authorities prescribing school practices.

Gallagher's fourth category, *radical hermeneutics*, more commonly known as post-structuralism, is identified with writers such as Foucault and Derrida. Foucault, for example, rejects the idea of human activity being governed by universal principles, and specifically rejects Habermas' notion of communication based around these. Foucault denies the centrality or permanence of any regulative framework. This includes any framework that defines what it is to be human. Why, as in cognitive psychology, for example, would a description of a human privilege a cognitive entity defined according to its physicality when that physical presence is peripheral to so many of our life experiences. As mathematics education researchers, for example, much of our output takes the form of writing prepared electronically for audiences who receive the work in very specific written forms. Our physical presence is largely virtual with respect to the audience. Student teachers meanwhile are assessed against detailed frameworks targeted at criteria. The assessment of children in schools is always through very specific filters. Through which analytical or evaluative frames do we understand the "person" doing the "experiencing"? People use language in describing the world around them. By implication they set how they see themselves fitting in. We share ways of describing the world, which perhaps lock us into ways of making sense of the world that favour the values of some people more than others. Having left the world of moderate hermeneutics and its self-reflecting subjects for the more troublesome territory of its critical and radical counterparts, the very notion of the human subject is disturbed. And this move into more socially defined space results in a commensurate shift from mind–body dualities in support of autonomous individuals into a potentially more complex duality of subject and structure. The self, or mind, is not the only centre of coherence. Subjectivity relates to individuals whose psychological existence is distributed and understood, across a multitude of linguistic filters.[7] Human subjects are not so much centred in their biological/cognitive selves but rather in the linguistic/narrative accounts that fix who they are. The human subject herself can offer these accounts or other people may set these accounts. As subjects, individuals *identify* with and partake in alternative ways of making sense of the world and through these *identifications* craft their subjectivity. I am who I am through the ways I narrate and am narrated by telling practices of my community. In Foucault we find a human subject who is a *consequence* to the discursive terrain, an effect of discourse. My very own constitution as subject results from my attempts to describe myself in the discursive material that I find available. Or I find myself being located by others in particular accounts of the world that assign a place to me. Other people assess individuals against partial

---

[7] Brown (2008c).

schema focussing on very specific pieces of those individuals. People are teachers to the degree that they comply with official descriptions of what it is to be a teacher. If those people do not comply with these official descriptions, it may be decided that they are not a teacher and therefore not employable. Similarly, a child's mathematical performance is a function of how it is assessed within the assessment framework. Mathematical ability is not a thing in itself. It can only ever be understood against a particular social register.

Derrida meanwhile provides another example for Gallagher's radical model. Derrida (1994, p. 29) has shown how media conditions understandings of the present. Such media could be newspapers or TV but could also be an assessment scheme or more loosely a particular mode of describing certain sorts of activity. Actuality is *made* and "virtual images, virtual spaces, and therefore virtual outcomes" are no longer distinguishable from actual reality. As he put it: "The 'reality' of 'actuality' – however individual, irreducible, stubborn, painful or tragic it may be – only reaches us through fictional devices". And human subjects are similarly produced through these fictional devices, schemes, discursive styles, curriculum frameworks or models of practice. There is clearly a problem with agency in such formulations if the individual is seen as being a consequence of social structures. The individual cannot hope to comprehend or predict the multitude of filters through which he or she could be understood. This invites a question as to how individuals experience this and how we might again centre attention on the options the individual might take. It is this shift of positioning and perspective that disrupts conceptions of psychology rooted in notions of the mind.

## 2.2.2 Psychoanalysis

Subjectivity in educational contexts is consequential to particular social arrangements that define specific roles for teachers and students alike.[8] For example, Walls (2009, p. 258) conceptualises change from such arrangements in terms of children "as mathematical subjects-in-process" or as "selves in narration". For reasons that will unfold in due course, we are opting for an approach that centres on the individual's conceptions of self, and in particular on how trainees or new teachers experience their immersion in social structures. Yet, as we have seen, these conceptions are troubled by the individual's inability to secure a full picture.[9] But we want to be attentive to the new teachers that we have interviewed. We are placing

---

[8]Excellent books by Valerie Walkerdine (1988), Margaret Walshaw (2007), and Fiona Walls (2009) have each carried out detailed explorations of how we might understand Foucault's theory in the context of mathematics education. These books document educational scenarios and classroom situations from the point of view of how we might read teachers and children's engagements in terms of subjectivity. See also Hardy (2004).

[9]Foucault's work does not provide much insight into the subject's sense of her own situation. This aspect began to be more important later on in his work and has been pursued more by Butler (1997, 2005). Davies (2006) has situated this aspect in educational context. Davies stresses Butler's point that the subject is constituted, not determined, and this constitution is the very precondition for its agency. Oppressive relations can be reworked and resisted by the individual.

a lot of emphasis on the sense they are bringing to the situations that they have encountered. It's all very well being subject to discourse but it is helpful for us to know how people experience that discursive immersion and how they explain their actions with respect to the real pressures they feel. Also, we are not wanting to know the psychology of teachers or of the children they teach so that we can control them. But, perhaps, we do want to know something of what new teachers feel and how they respond so that a dialogue with them (whether that be from an educative or policy perspective) is more likely to succeed.

Radical hermeneutics focuses on how discourse shapes human actions but it says less about how the individual experiences of this discursive immersion. Psychology has taught us how the mind works, yet so often psychology is set on explaining the human as some sort of object responsive to particular conditions. One alternative to both radical hermeneutics and mind-centred psychology is rather the more precarious world of psychoanalysis with its alternative centring in the *subject* and the *unconscious*. In psychoanalysis, the human subject is central in making sense of the situation that she confronts. This approach has the advantage of opening up the ways in which we might explain how individuals partake in the social world and how they are governed by a multitude of possible influences, where the degree of influence from any source is never fully resolvable. We are all governed by collective as well as individual consciousness, where collectivity is expressed in a variety of alternative forms. Sigmund Freud is at the heart of contemporary psychoanalysis.

> Freud dealt with the occurrence of systematically deformed communication in order to define the scope of specifically incomprehensible acts and utterances. He always envisaged the dream as the standard example of such phenomena, the latter including everything from harmless, everyday pseudo-communication and Freudian slips to pathological manifestations of neurosis, psychosis, and psychosomatic disturbance. In his essays on cultural theory, Freud broadened the range of phenomena which could be conceived as being part of systematically distorted communication. He employed the insights gained from clinical phenomena as the key to pseudo-normality, that is to the hidden pathology of collective behaviour and entire social systems (Habermas, 1976, p. 349).

In this way, Freud's work underpinned Habermas's critical quest to detect the faults in society more generally and find ways of repairing these. Hermeneutics is about interpretation and so is psychoanalysis. Freud's psychoanalytic sessions were predicated on "helping the subject to overcome the distortions that are the source of self-misunderstanding".[10] This account of Freud provides a helpful metaphor for the new teacher who is seen as a psychoanalyst's client constructing her life through a depiction of it in words. In some interpretations of Freud's model, such as those followed by the United States ego psychology school, the psychologist sometimes purported to know what to do to achieve this result where therapy was seen in terms of calming the ego to be more conformist. The ego was understood as a biological entity to be strengthened in line with a supposed model of good citizenship. Such an approach to psychology became enshrined in United States social policy.[11]

---

[10]Ricoeur (1981, p. 265).

[11]The British government meanwhile has made it official policy for its subjects to be "happy" since "happiness" is compatible with employability. A number of Cognitive Behaviour Therapy sessions

An alternative interpretation of Freud's work, more in line with radical hermeneutics in some respects, is to be found in the writings of Jacques Lacan. Lacan sees the human subject as being caught in a never ending attempt to capture an understanding of his or her self in relation to the world in which he or she lives. There is no final version of the human subject to be located. The human is constantly shifting with respect to the language that describes who she is. But here the language we use is altogether more complicit in our understandings of who we are. The story we tell makes us, but it is a story that does not stop. In this formulation the human subject is a consequence of the discursive terrain. That is, the human subject is necessarily a product of the ways in which she is described. Here we understand the term "subject" "as a particular or individual view of the world"[12] or "the nature of the agency that says 'I'".[13] Foucault's post-structuralist human subject describes the world and how she fits in using the language that is available. Yet for Lacan there is always something that exceeds Foucault's encapsulation of the subject in discourse. This enables the subject to rise above the limits of the language available. Lacan's human subject is always incomplete and remains so, where the subject identifies herself in a supposed image. In this model, the individual can never be fully self-aware, and never fully explained within the language that is available. The individual has an image of the world and of his or her place within it. Yet Lacan insists that we should always be wary of this image since there is no final certainty through which we might authorise this understanding of self. Here, the individual is forever on a quest to complete the picture she has of herself in relation to the world around her and the others who also inhabit it. Yet language is never quite up to the task of achieving a final version. She responds to the fantasy she has of the wider social network and of how this network might reserve a space for her. The identity thus created evolves through a series of interpretations (and mis-recognitions) through interactions with others.[14] It is this notion of an image that guides us here. Lacan's model provides us with a very powerful tool for understanding how new teachers work towards fitting in with what they see as being required of them. They can only guess but never know since the demands upon them are so diverse that there is no singular correct answer (And as we shall see there are real restrictions on the teachers' becoming autonomous professionals equipped or positioned to make their own decisions). But it is through such "guessing" that models of teaching are produced and that certain representations of mathematics *actually* come into being in the classroom. As a teacher, I may fully subscribe to the national curriculum or I may fully accept the conditions of my employment. But somehow it is not quite "me". There is always something about me that exceeds the way that I am designated by others.

---

have often been provided to "unhappy" people on the grounds that the cost of the therapy is lower to the government than the cost of 6 months of unemployment benefit (e.g. Fitzpatrick, 2009).

[12] Myers (2003, p. 12).

[13] Kay (2003, p. 8).

[14] A much fuller account of Lacan's work considered in the context of mathematics education has been provided by Brown (2008a, forthcoming).

For Lacan there is always a gap between aspirations and outcomes. It is this gap that locates desire, the essential point of impossibility that motivates life. According to Lacan, we are all motivated by desire, but a desire that always mistakes its object.[15] I aspire to a future that would never quite satisfy me if I actually got there. The narratives we offer about who we are never catch up with us, but that need not stop us from trying. And our misses can nevertheless be informative about who we are or where we are. Narratives hold our desires in place even if they do not take us to the place that satisfies them. The stories we tell do not pin down life for inspection but rather stimulate this life for future growth. Yet there is also a risk that we begin to believe the stories we tell, as though they provide the final answer (such as that the school curriculum effectively encapsulates mathematics, that sufficient research evidence would enable more certain action, that if I responded positively to all the demands placed upon me then I would be a good teacher, content with life). There is a cost for the individual as a result of gearing in to the shared outer world. Through expressing oneself through social codes and procedures, personal and social boundaries are reshaped, causing a troubling compulsion to settle these boundaries. Žižek, for example, suggests that individuals may get a perverse pleasure in working to formulae, templates, set pieces, models, regulative frameworks *et al.* He sees such behaviour as a manifestation of what Freud calls "drive" where "we get caught into a closed, self-propelling loop of repeating the same gesture and finding satisfaction in it".[16] As we shall see, some of the new teachers that we interviewed gained some considerable satisfaction from following rules, fitting the image, as it relieved them from making their own decisions in unfamiliar territory where they often lacked confidence. And such attitudes confirmed a certain model for the delivery of mathematics.

### 2.2.3 Hermeneutics, Mathematics and Training to Teach

How then do these alternative attitudes to hermeneutics and the proposed link to psychoanalytical theory enable us to gain further insight in to how we might read our data towards better understanding how mathematics and its teaching are conceptualised by new teachers? The alternative formulations of hermeneutics have different ways of positioning truth and of viewing the authorisation required to secure particular understandings of mathematics. They also have very different perspectives on the efficacy of the social norms that govern its teaching. Let us take, for instance, the possible conflict between the trainee teacher's perspective on the mathematics they are engaged in and the way in which that mathematics is specified in curriculum documentation, the distinction between "what you see" and "what you are

---

[15]Garetsky (2004) argues that it was this ever desiring, never satisfied, being derived from Freud that fed in to early conceptions of people living within twentieth century capitalist economics.
[16]Žižek (2006, p. 63).

meant to see". In conservative hermeneutics, the supposition is that these perspectives become aligned. Yet the other three hermeneutic attitudes entertain distinctly alternative modes of viewing the teacher–student exchange, in which the individual teacher or student is altogether transformed through his or her situation in the social network, as is the knowledge they share. These attitudes span many potential conceptions of mathematics teaching, from transmission to discovery. Another potential conflict is between seeing the teacher's task as enabling children to build their own mathematical thinking and seeing the task as ensuring that pupils attain requisite skills. Yet the possible conflict that will occupy us most will be the one between the trainee's personal aspirations in respect of their professional training and the official demands they face in carrying this out.

Each of these potential conflicts can be seen as dichotomous and may often be experienced as such. Each comprises an individual insider's perspective set in opposition to a more socially constructed overview. In each case, the former is spoken of in qualitative perhaps personal terms, whilst the latter requires a more "objective", or structural style of analysis. Yet each potential conflict can be resolved through adopting a hermeneutic perspective. This will be achieved by highlighting how the first item can be seen in the second and vice versa. Yet such conflict resolution is not about happy endings but more to do with alternative integrations of individual and social. We shall discuss these in turn.

### 2.2.4 Phenomenological Versus Official Versions of Mathematics

Alternative views of mathematics are dependent on where their proponents are positioned in any educative process. As indicated, the "noun" mathematics has multiple usages. It is easy to slip between numerous or conflicting versions. For a tutor charged with the initial or in-service training of teachers, qualitative or ecological concerns are clearly of importance. There is a need to equip one's students with particular mathematical insights, to prioritise a positive attitude to the subject, to value personal understandings and to develop these. Meanwhile, a policy maker promoting effective performance in public examinations or tests to be used in official statistics or international comparisons is likely to be motivated differently. Here, perhaps, formats of learning and assessment delivered as hard data rather than more personal notions of mathematical understanding underpin the currency required to make such quantitative comparisons possible. And so the emphasis is on the pupil's being required to describe particular mathematical ideas in an acceptable language and to filter any personal insights through this language.

Policies developed in the light of international comparisons of mathematical achievement in schools have resulted in changes to the demands made on teachers. The teacher in school is increasingly governed by achievement criteria influenced by these comparisons. Mathematics is more frequently conjured in a form that can be more easily assessed through quantitative measures. And, commensurately with this, after an era in English schools where child-centred approaches had dominated primary education, there was a return to the teacher being positioned primarily at the front of the classroom ensuring that the content-oriented curriculum was adequately covered.

As a consequence, university training programmes have, through both choice and obligation, changed to be more in line with these moves. The university training, to be discussed in this book, had earlier offered a view of mathematics that valued the learner's point of view and emphasised engagement with mathematics at primary level rather than extending the student teacher's own mathematical knowledge by introducing new content areas. Against this backdrop, mathematics, in early training at least, was seen primarily as a learning experience to be enjoyed to counter any earlier unease in the area. This learning was centred on the learner in humanistic terms rather than being defined by mathematics according to external criteria. This mirrored a widespread view among educators at the time as to how the learning might best be seen. Within such a view of school mathematics, there was an emphasis on mathematical processes and application. The quality of student's learning experience was privileged over objectives defined in terms of procedural knowledge. This, however, did not provide a comprehensive picture of the style of mathematics then to be faced by student teachers as they returned to school as teachers in the new policy climate. Here they were to encounter again mathematics not unlike that which they had faced in school as pupils. Consequently, in response to these changes the university diet was extended to focus more on externally defined measures of the trainee's mathematical abilities. Not only did the style of learning change but also the style of regulation was modified as a result. This version of mathematics was predicated on rather different aspects of the mathematics. Ability was understood more in terms of performance of prescribed procedures.

These two aspects of mathematics display a certain amount of incommensurability but nevertheless coalesce under the same heading of "mathematics". Thus we have two sorts of mathematics that tend to get confused:

Mathematics 1: The *phenomenological* view places emphasis on the student exploring mathematics, making connections, seeing structure and pattern and the teacher's task is understood more in terms of facilitating learning from the learner's current perspective rather than didactic teaching. Such an approach, which is often seen as being more "student centred" or "discovery" oriented, emphasises process and the using and applying of mathematics, but a mathematics that is understood fairly broadly. Assessment is often targeted at the student's attempts at articulating their perspective. As an example of a teaching strategy, electronic calculators are seen as an effective aid for developing numerical understanding, since they encourage a focus on conceptual understandings in place of mechanical and tedious pencil-and-paper methods employing poorly understood algorithmic procedures.

Mathematics 2: In the *official* view, mathematical achievement is understood more in terms of performance of prescribed mathematical procedures. This is quantifiable through diagnostic testing, and broader understanding is anchored around test indicators in a statistically defined environment.

Mathematics itself is understood as being describable as a list of mathematical content topics, and thus a transmission approach may be favoured since there is a precise content to be delivered. The teacher's task is to initiate students into these conventional procedures perhaps by demonstrating them and assisting children while they are practised. Proponents of such a view of mathematics are often opposed to calculator use since they perform the very procedures featured on the preferred forms of diagnostic test.

The two sorts of mathematics are governed by different criteria; the phenomenological focuses on the learner's experience, the official on the production of pre-defined and quantifiable mathematical output. There appears to be an irreconcilable conflict between nurturing personal experience and utilising measuring devices. This apparent conflict, we suggest, can be softened through recognising that both perspectives are oriented around the same social phenomena. The individual cannot claim a wholly personal perspective. The space s/he occupies, the mathematics being studied, cannot be observed except through socially derived filters. Personal insights (understandings) are relatively meaningless to others unless they can be hitched to common forms of expression (explanations). Meanwhile criteria-referenced metrics are dysfunctional unless they are derived from careful examination of normative practices. This social derivation of mathematics will be assumed throughout this book. The implications this has for teaching are briefly discussed next.

The potential dichotomy between phenomenological and official versions of mathematics in university training is to some extent mirrored in some supposed alternative teaching orientations in schools. The choice between discovery and transmission appears as an apparent conflict between valuing what children "do see" and measuring what they "should see". For example, Askew, Brown, Rhodes, Johnson, and Wiliam (1997) associate what we are calling Mathematics 1 with discovery, a learner perspective prioritised style of teaching, and Mathematics 2 with transmission favouring a teacher or official perspective. These authors coined the notion of "connectionism" which appears to be a reconciliation of the two perspectives. Here teachers draw links between alternative perspectives as offered by children and discuss how these "connect" with the curriculum topics being addressed. Personal insights or understandings are sought of shared phenomena. This sharing takes place in explanatory forms and develops during lesson time with children and teacher working together. Mathematical meanings are socially constructed at the level of classroom activity through attempts at achieving shared understanding of ideas derived from curriculum topics.[17] This sort of moderate hermeneutic reconciliation suggests possible theoretical frames for combining apparently incommensurable perspectives.

Yet critical or radical perspectives would not necessarily assume the benevolence of the official perspective. Curricula are set in the form that they are for many different reasons, including political expediency, management of large numbers of

---

[17]cf. Cobb (1999).

pupils, working within a budget, supplying appropriate composition of workforce, selectivity of students, not to mention variation down to educationally oriented ideological preferences.[18] Teachers or their trainers may not necessarily be in agreement with official conceptions of how mathematics is presented, identifying the needs and priorities of their students differently. Pupils in schools may themselves choose not to comply with officially sanctioned modes of mathematics education and resist these approaches in many ways, such as with bad behaviour, truancy, dulled senses or mere non-engagement. And some pupils may not report this experience of mathematics in entirely positive terms when they themselves aspire to be teachers.

## 2.2.5 Perceptual Versus Structural Understandings of Trainee's Task

Similarly, the individual trainee's experience of their own training may differ from the way in which that training process is conceptualised by schools, training providers and government agencies. Later, we shall present an account of the phases student teachers pass through in making the transition from learner of mathematics to teacher of mathematics. We shall be pursuing two perspectives on how conceptions of mathematics emerge in students' minds in line with the two journeys that we pinpointed at the beginning of this book. On the one hand, we shall focus on how students report on the affective or perceptual aspects of mathematics and its teaching. This formats the structural space they see themselves inhabiting. On the other hand, we consider how the structure of the training and associated demands shape perceptions of the teaching task. This circularity might be seen as two complementary hermeneutic arcs, from perception to structure and from structure to perception.

As we shall show later, in reflecting on their own experiences of mathematics, the students in our study generally seemed unable to articulate their understanding of mathematics except in affective terms.[19] For those interviewed prior to initial training, mathematics was often conceptualised as a bad school experience. For those later on in the course mathematics was subsumed within the discursive practices of teaching as perceived within the broader primary education space. That is, mathematics was understood primarily through administrative filters such as those to do with classroom organisation. Mathematics did not acquire much of a subject identity in terms of its content. Teaching strategies, meanwhile, were drawn from a more general pool of teaching strategies applied across the various subjects.

More broadly empirical research relating to the teaching of school mathematics has had a tendency to gravitate to one or other of two perspectives. The first of these

---

[18] Jablonka and Gellert (2010).
[19] cf. Grootenboer (2003).

comprises work based around individuals' insider perceptions of their situations discussed in qualitative terms, such as teachers expressing their beliefs in relation to teaching mathematics, or children articulating their learning. The second perspective concerns work focusing on the measurable achievements of such individuals in relation to the structure in which they are working, such as how children perform in formal tests when taught according to a particular method. Research from the insider's perspective is fairly extensive but sometimes rather weakly connected to work focusing on an outsider's analysis of that insider's performance. Research from the second perspective has often excluded the teacher's voice.

Often affective or perceptual concerns have dominated the training discourse while structural accounts dominate the discourse of policy. Resolution of these alternative perspectives might be seen as requiring a softening, or compromising, of each within the life perspective of the individual concerned. This would highlight how the individual's understanding of mathematics is generated through social activity and regulated through socially defined parameters. That is, we can see the two journeys as mutually supportive where the individual knowingly and contentedly makes the social apparatus part of his or her everyday functioning in pursuit of aspirations to be a teacher. But also, the structure is responsive to its new intake and adjusts its practices and demands to accommodate the new generation.

Yet again, critical and radical perspectives would trouble this easy accommodation. Trainees do not have full awareness of the social processes shaping their actions. Nor do they fully appreciate what is concealed in the priorities of these processes. Mathematics, how it is taught and the processes through which teachers are trained are not singular entities. They can be contested. They depend for their existence on the perspectives being taken of them. And there are good reasons as to why different agencies view them differently. In subsequent chapters, we shall pursue this analysis further through the route that we have already identified, namely, the teachers' construction of self and of mathematics, which will be considered in relation to the external demands they encounter. We shall further develop a theoretical treatment of how trainee teachers understand their own training process and the mathematics within that in particular, as an attempted reconciliation of the diverse demands they encounter in a social sphere, defined through explanatory apparatus. At this point, however, we turn to a discussion of how we might frame our understanding of how teacher identity and how this evolves through the training process.

## 2.3  Personal Aspirations Meet External Demands

Interviewer:   So what do you see the purpose of teaching as being?
Nathan:        As being just to educate children and make a difference in their lives
               really. Just to make things – it's just a very small part of their lives
               you know the year in which I teach them, really, but hopefully to
               make a difference really – you know I can see a purpose in it
Interviewer:   What sort of a difference would you want to make?

Nathan:          To give them – I don't know – *confidence* in themselves to *enjoy*
                 school, *enjoy* learning, *enjoy* books and, you know, just have a real
                 … just have an *enthusiasm for life,* you know, not be resigned to
                 thinking things are not worth doing, you know, and yeah preparing
                 them for secondary school so they don't go having a negative attitude
                 towards school.

Identity has become a key term in contemporary social analyses that has productively motivated many recent instances of mathematics education research.[20] In the
chapters that follow we shall be suggesting that identity is produced at the intersection of the trainees' personal aspirations of what it is to be a teacher and the multiple
external demands they encounter *en route* to formal accreditation as a teacher. Or
more strictly, in line with the theorists we shall follow, there are no *identities* as
such. There are just *identifications* with particular ways of making sense of the
world that shape that person's sense of his self and his actions. Fortuitously, for
our analysis, the arrival in school of the trainees to be encountered later in this book
coincided with the introduction of a major curriculum initiative that provided one
timely example of an "external demand" that we could examine in detail. We depict
how trainees mediated this initiative and the multitude of other demands associated
with their training. This mediation will be seen as formative of their evolving professional and personal identities. Interviews provided us with data relating to how
the trainees expressed their personal aspirations in relation to these demands and
how these aspirations were revised during the training period. Our assumption was
that such conceptualisations shaped the actions of the teachers concerned within
their classroom practice. Information was also available on how the trainees perceived the various factors that shaped and regulated their changing professional and
personal environments. We do not apologise for this partial perspective. Where we
address mathematical discourse directly, we are choosing to avoid perspectives in
which we suppose that there is a "better" truth of the students' perspective than the
one encapsulated in their own accounts. These accounts provided the rationale to
students' actions. Their on-going transition towards qualification was understood as
being a function of the narratives they offered in the interviews. We are accepting
that there are limitations to this, however, and will be offering some of our own
interpretations of these accounts. Thus we consider how the trainees create a sense
of their own evolving identities as teachers. The psychoanalytic metaphor invoked
in this frame compares our interviewees with clients in a psychoanalyst's surgery
laying back on a couch and speaking about their lives. Such a metaphor has been
central in the Freudian inspired work of Lacan and Žižek that will feature throughout
this book. For the remainder of this chapter we restrict ourselves to looking at how
trainees proceed with creating a picture of themselves as teachers.

---

[20]See, for example, Walshaw (2008), DeFreitas (2008), Solomon (2009), Black, Mendick, and
Solomon (2009), Krzywacki (2009), and Walls (2010). Walshaw (2010b) documents how student
teacher identity is shaped in school practicum elements of teacher education. Cotton (2010) explicitly addresses issues of identity with a group of teacher education students. Sfard and Prusak (2005)
have also conceptualised identity within mathematics education contexts.

Nathan was a new primary teacher talking about the sorts of motivation that underpinned his early developing practice as a professional teacher.[21] Nathan's comments pointed to a desire to participate in an educational enterprise aimed at making things better for the learners in his class. He hoped that they would "enjoy school" and as a result build an "enthusiasm for life". Such sentiments seem unsurprising for someone entering the profession. The motivation of buying into such a strong mission must be appealing to young adults mapping out a future career. In this perspective the task of the teacher is not just about getting a job and raising standards in accordance with the latest government directive. The motivation is to improve the quality of educational experience more generally and hence the subsequent lives of the pupils. Teaching is about empowering young learners and as such can be seen as a worthy profession. Around such a higher ideal one can harness more personal aspirations, such as feelings of social worth and professional purpose. These aspirations can shape actual engagement.[22] However, in adopting this broader account of how social improvement might be achieved, the role of individual teachers can often take second place to the broader social agenda. Collective arrangements require compromise from the individuals that take part. These arrangements can get to be meshed with the requirements for accreditation as a teacher and the regulations governing everyday teacher practices.

Also, for many trainees interviewed the idyll of teaching encapsulated by Nathan was somewhat punctured by a sometimes unwelcome component of the overall job description, namely, the actual need to teach mathematics in the first place.[23] For many trainees that we interviewed that specific demand seemed to have been the down side in having elected to pursue training as a primary teacher. Beyond the emotional turmoil involved in their own experience of mathematics, it seemed that some had received excellent training for becoming compliant individuals. As one student teacher from our study puts it:

> It was just a case of doing the sums but you didn't realise why you were doing the sums, it was just to do the sums to get as most marks as you could. So I mean I never enjoyed maths. ... It was always a case of, oh if you haven't got above a certain percentage then you need help or you're having problems, so you always felt if you weren't meeting that standard you felt like a failure and I think that really didn't, it really didn't boost my confidence at all.

The student goes on to consider the role of a teacher in this:

> I think the teacher's role played a big part in it as well, because the atmosphere she created. ... It was just a case of if you can't do it, you should be able to do it now. It wasn't very helpful ... She wasn't very approachable. You didn't feel like you could go to her and say I'm having trouble with this and I need some help.

---

[21] This was part of Bibby's study (2001, 2002) also concerned with new teachers. Bibby (2010) introduces a psychoanalytic perspective to examine student disengagements with mathematics in school.

[22] Robertson (1997), Hanley (2007), Nolan (2007).

[23] Brown, Jones, and Bibby (2004).

As we will see later, attitudes such as those expressed here were common in our data. These attitudes resisted a clear passage to the trainee feeling comfortable about teaching where her personal aspirations could be achieved.

But in analysing such data there seemed to be a need to adopt a certain amount of caution. What is concealed in such a story? Story telling can be used as a support device to sustain teacher learning.[24] But surely this interviewee did not have just one teacher, introduced here as "she". The trainee appears to be personifying his entire experience of many teachers in just one teacher. This teacher, it seems, is required to carry the weight of this individual's perceived suffering at school. We may speculate as to which narrative devices individuals employ as they are requested to recount experiences happening maybe some 10–20 years earlier. We had many intriguing accounts thinking back to when the respondents were in their primary years evaluating their teachers' performance. For what reasons do they construct such images of themselves? And what present demands or needs are concealed in these images? How do teachers tell the stories of their lives, to rationalise their current motivations and hoped for futures? The repetition of such a story may be a form of resistance. There is an insertion of a fixed image, which blocks off the possibility of building memories in a more creative way. For Freud, the reworking of memory into a story is not the memory of a linear narrative "as it was". Rather it is a probing that creates something new, a present day building of past. As Kay (2003, p. 159) puts it: "The psychoanalytical view of time is that it does not progress in a linear way but in a kind of backward loop, so that the crucial tense is the future perfect: what 'will have been' … significance is always grasped retrospectively". The motivations that individuals pursue in becoming teachers of mathematics may not be revealed transparently. Where do these motivations come from? And how are they mediated in the teachers' actions? Such educational motives can be read against teachers' identifications with particular ways of being. Our chief example is to do with how individual teachers enact policy in their everyday practice. But they may paint themselves in more heroic terms.

We are viewing the process of becoming a teacher from two perspectives, the phenomenological and the official. A psychoanalytic model is used to inspect how social demands are embraced and how they are or might be resisted or rejected. The trainees re-script their personal storyline to accommodate external demands that disrupt their original aspirations of what it is to be a teacher. Such aspirations and new storylines are, however, illusory phenomena that always conceal desires that will remain unfulfilled. Yet our empirical results, as we shall see, suggest that these new story lines are generally found to be quite palatable. But there are costs associated with individual teachers overly pursuing collective demands specified by government agencies. What options then are open for teachers in asserting more ownership of their professionalism?

Later we shall offer some alternative conceptions of the human subject from contemporary work on social theory. In these notions of subject, individuals speak the

---

[24]For example, O'Connell Rust (1999).

"society" of which they are part; immersed as they are in social discourses. But in
this social construction of self we question which representatives of the "social"
are privileged. And what image does "society" have more generally of individuals performing particular social roles? For a trainee proceeding through his or her
training numerous alternative accounts of what it is to be a teacher will be encountered from people and agencies with varying degrees of influence. Yet, as we shall
show, our empirical study points to these messages being complex such that trainees
were unable to absorb and reconcile all of these. This resulted in a partial realisation
of many often-contradictory perspectives. How might we understand the options
available to trainees? We shall seek to better understand some of these contradictory perspectives and the effects they produce in the trainee's practice. Giddens
(1999, pp. 47–48) has argued that Freud's work is especially relevant in contemporary society where we have increasingly less anchorage in established traditions
guiding human action:

> Self-identity has to be created and recreated on a more active basis than before. This
> explains why therapy and counselling of all kinds have become so popular in Western coun-
> tries. When he initiated modern psychoanalysis, Freud thought that he was establishing a
> scientific treatment for neurosis. What he was in effect doing was constructing a method for
> the renewal of self identity... what happens in psychoanalysis is that the individual revis-
> its his or her past in order to create more autonomy for the future. Much the same is true
> in the self-help groups that have become so common in Western societies. At Alcoholics
> Anonymous meetings, for instance, individuals recount their life histories, and receive sup-
> port from others present in stating their desire to change. They recover from their addiction
> essentially through re-writing the story line of their lives.

In this respect we will be viewing our interview transcripts as being akin to the rev-
elation of psychoanalytic encounters. The interviews provided a forum in which a
reflective layer to the trainees' conceptions of their professional task could be developed. This reflection generated a storyline of their own professional development as
teachers. This provided a framework against which they could make sense of their
evolving professional self.

As we shall show later, Lacan addresses the issue of how an individual confronts
the many conflicting perspectives encountered. He suggests "the ego is ... always
an inauthentic agency, functioning to conceal a disturbing lack of unity".[25] That
is, the human subject is "fragmented" and does not succeed in reconciling all of
the contradictory discourses acting through her. We shall later use this metaphor
in examining how the trainee teacher confronts the multiple demands of the training process. In particular we use such analysis in conceptualising trainee teachers
encountering the major curriculum initiative to be described shortly and the resultant
shift in the trainee's understanding of their own teaching task. We shall argue that the
trainee's growing ability to participate in the discourse of this initiative resulted in a
re-orientation of the trainee's professional self. In this process, mathematics anxiety
that trainees may have experienced as students at school is removed or suppressed.

---

[25]Quoted in, Leader and Groves (1995, p. 24).

# Chapter 3
# How Teachers Learn: A Review of Research

## 3.1 Introduction

The initial education of teachers is the key focus of this book so let us now turn to consider in more detail how the task of student teachers learning to teach mathematics has been researched within teacher education contexts. We commence with an overview of some of the ways in which the process of teacher education is understood and represented within the research literature. We consider how the constituent elements of the process have been defined, and in particular examine some of the mechanisms through which students have been enabled to articulate their own understandings of the process.

Our survey of research literature began with a commission from the British Educational Research Association to create a literature review of British research focusing on both Initial Teacher Education and Continuing Professional Development (Brown & McNamara, 2001). Not believing the paucity of results from our initial electronic search, partially restricted by the technology of the day, we physically went through the hard copies of many major journals to confirm that very little had been published or validated on this theme from a British perspective in the major journals in the few years prior to our search. It seemed that most research of this sort remained confined to the pages of conference proceedings comprising reports focusing primarily on small-scale studies. Large-scale research assessments in the United States were much more extensive, as they are today[1] yet so much of this work has been context specific, and not immediately transferable to other international locations. In recent years the *Journal of Mathematics Teacher Education* and *The International Handbook of Mathematics Teacher Education*[2] have made a difference to the prominence of this field internationally. Yet there remains a tendency in mathematics education research more generally to downplay the mediating role of teacher education and its capacity to supply the teachers able to implement

---

[1] United States Department of Education (2008).

[2] Sullivan and Wood (2008), Tirosh and Wood (2008), Krainer and Wood (2008), Jaworski and Wood (2008).

T. Brown, O. McNamara, *Becoming a Mathematics Teacher*,
Mathematics Education Library 53, DOI 10.1007/978-94-007-0554-8_3,
© Springer Science+Business Media B.V. 2011

any changes that might be proposed within policy initiatives or mathematics education research.[3] And, as we shall see in this chapter, it remains difficult to build an over-arching sense of how teacher education works or might work across populations as opposed to localised situations specific to the researcher. The next chapter will demonstrate some of the difficulties experienced in a major national reform of a mathematics curriculum where so much of the research claimed to underpin the reform was either absent, inadequate, ignored or contested. And it will also show how difficult it is to mobilise a population of teachers to follow a new mode of practice and the professional compromises that can entail.

If it is to be successful, initial training must prepare teachers to become effective operators within what is a highly politicised educational context. In England this is enacted within a "partnership" of school, university and government, which is itself complex and evolving under the influence of many competing forces and agendas. Trainees ingest this oft-times uneasy alliance into their own developing professional sense of being a teacher and, as a consequence, can find themselves being drawn simultaneously in a number of directions according to the diverse motivations[4] and demands of the contributing agencies. As we shall show in Chapter 4, trainees often experience their training and induction into the teaching profession as a complex and disjointed transitional process that embraces multiple and shifting conceptions of teaching and mathematics.

Despite this maelstrom of pressures operating in the training milieu, many descriptions of trainee teachers in the literature and elsewhere, present a somewhat uncomplicated and unilateral account of the complexities of professional training and induction. Some have, for example, furnished an overly rational and socially disembodied model. Others have presented cognitively oriented descriptions which neglect to account for the social dimension. Others still have concentrated on the development of professional skills and competencies: knowledge about subjects, pedagogy, assessment and learning. The wider methodological debate regarding the nature of educational research towards the end of the twentieth century began to be reflected in this mathematics education literature some 20 years ago. McLeod (1992), for example, argued for the integration of affective and cognitive perspectives, and the greater use of a mixture of quantitative and qualitative methods, to counter a weakness he identified in theory building within mathematics education research. Brown, Cooney, and Jones (1990, p. 652) blamed a strong analytic tradition for the fact that even "ethnographic type strategies have tended to be more piecemeal than holistic in their efforts to understand the culture and evaluation of its beliefs". Eisenhart, Behm, and Romagnano (1991, p. 51) found "no systematic body of knowledge about the relationship between good teaching and (mathematics) teacher education" and concluded that anecdotal accounts, not informed by explanatory theoretical frameworks, were largely responsible for such incoherence.

---

[3]This has been discussed by Brown (2008b).
[4]Phelps (2010).

Albeit a number of different theoretical models, sociological, phenomenological and anthropological, have been used over the years to conceptualise the student experience of learning to teach. These include "apprenticeship of observation"[5]; "development of expertise"[6]; "rite of passage"[7]; "performance theory"[8]; "activity theory"[9]; "post-structuralism"[10]; "legitimate peripheral participation"/"community of practice".[11] The influential work of Lave and Wenger (1991), for example, saw the development of expertise and understanding as situational and contextually grounded and learning resulting not "from talk" but "to talk", in a master/apprentice relationship which functioned to confer legitimacy rather than to provide teaching. Yet critics pointed out that learning in a school context "requires understanding of the structure of pedagogy"[12] and needs to take into account "teaching", as well as "learning". Additionally, the whole notion of defining a "community of practice" within a classroom, whether it be in the university or in school, implies a degree of homogeneity of identity and purpose that is not always to be found. In Initial Teacher Education, in particular, the "apprenticeship" model, it has been argued, can construct a false dichotomy between university and school-based elements, and importantly negate the value of reflection and educational theory.[13]

Overall the picture is of a lack of systematic, coherent and cumulative evidence base. A major review of teacher education, commissioned by the US Department of Education, examined more than 300 research reports about teacher preparation and found that only 57 met their criteria for inclusion. They concluded that the "research base concerning teacher preparation is limited. . . The lack of depth of research on teacher preparation poses challenges for a review".[14] A more recent review evaluated 16,000 studies of mathematical learning but again the overwhelming majority did not meet the standards of rigour required. This later review concludes:

> High-quality research must be undertaken to create a sound basis for the mathematics preparation of elementary and middle school teachers within pre-service teacher education, early career support, and ongoing professional development programs. Outcomes of different approaches should be evaluated by using reliable and valid measure of their effects on prospective and current teachers' instructional techniques and, most important, their effects on student achievement (United States Department of Education, 2008, p. 38).

Despite this cautionary note pointing to the continuing inadequacy of this vast research base, the United States is still a good way ahead of the United Kingdom

---

[5]Lortie (1975).
[6]Berliner (1988).
[7]White (1989).
[8]McNamara et al. (2002).
[9]Twiselton (2004), Edwards and Protheroe (2004).
[10]Brown and Jones (2001), DeFreitas and Nolan (2008), Walshaw (2010a).
[11]Lave and Wenger (1991), Maynard (2001).
[12]Adler (1996, p. 9).
[13]Jones, Reid, and Bevins (1997), Smith and Hodson (2010).
[14]Wilson, Floden, and Ferrini-Mundy (2001).

and many other countries in developing a research base on teacher preparation. A number of large-scale initiatives such as the Teacher Pathways Project (2003–2007), a multi-year data-rich analysis of programmes and routes into teaching and their impact on student achievement in the classroom, have been funded. Focusing on the New York City public school system, the study includes detailed programme information on fifteen traditional teacher preparation programmes and two alternative route programmes serving the New York City area. It analyses and identifies the attributes of programmes and pathways into teaching that positively impact on student outcomes. By comparison the United Kingdom research evidence base about teacher preparation is fragmentary. With a few other notable exceptions, much of the existing United Kingdom research evidence relates to single case studies or contexts, and literature is often generic in content and does not identify subject- or phase-specific differences. Some studies have been of seminal importance such as the Leverhulme Primary Project, which tracked students through their training programme and into their first appointments.[15] There was also the "Modes of Teacher Education" study,[16] which was the first systematic attempt to explore the landscape of teacher training. The largest and most systematic of recent United Kingdom studies has been the "Becoming a Teacher Project" (BaT) (2003–2009), which tracked 5,000 trainee teachers for 5 years, charting their experience of training and early professional development and has published a number of extensive reports.[17] Like much of research literature from the United Kingdom this latter study only includes trainee self-report comparative data relating to the "effectiveness" of the routes. Of the studies and commentaries that are mathematics specific in focus, much of the research relates to the mathematics subject knowledge of trainee teachers. In the specific case of the education of primary teachers it is uncommon to find aspects particular to mathematics education covered in isolation from issues relating to more general "professional" issues other than in the area of subject knowledge.[18] In addition, since United Kingdom devolution in 1992 there has been an increasing divergence in policy and practice of the devolved United Kingdom administrations of Northern Ireland, Scotland and Wales in relation to the legislative, strategic and executive functions of education.[19] This has created a complex and fluid landscape.[20]

---

[15] Bennett and Carré (1993).

[16] Barrett, Whitty, Furlong, Galvin, and Barton (1992), Furlong, Barton, Whiting, and Whitty (2000).

[17] Hobson et al. (2005), (2006), Hobson et al. (2007), (2008), Hobson, Malderez, and Tracey (2009), Ashby et al. (2008).

[18] Brown and McNamara (2001).

[19] This book will occasionally refer to the British government, which sets educational policy in England. Other countries within the United Kingdom have relative autonomy over their educational policies.

[20] Raffe, Brannen, Croxford, and Martin (1999).

## 3.2  The Transition from Scholar to Authority

### 3.2.1  Embarking on the Journey

We shall now embark upon a brief journey through the international evidence base, to observe what teacher educators in England might be paying attention to as they seek to understand the transitions that their trainees must make in the long and some-times treacherous journey from learning mathematics as a school pupil to teaching mathematics as a trainee and then new teacher. In our particular framing of the literature we shall present the complex process of learning to teach as developing from a subtle interplay of the parts to the whole. Fundamental to the process, are "ghosts from the past" potentially unhelpful even unpleasant memories of math-ematics, mathematics teaching and sometimes of mathematics teachers. Lack of attention to these "may help to account for why teacher education is often such a weak intervention – why teachers, in spite of courses and workshops, are most likely to teach math just as they were taught".[21] Thus the transition from pupil to teacher, if it is to be successful, must for many involve a considerable degree of "unlearn-ing" and discarding of mathematical baggage, subject misconceptions and attitude problems followed by the (re)learning of some mathematics subject knowledge. We begin then by considering what evidence educators might draw upon in relation to changing conceptions, beliefs and attitudes.

### 3.2.2  Changing Conceptions, Beliefs and Attitudes

The first thing that educators will draw from the literature base is that there is a widespread ambiguity about definitions and significant lack of consistency in the use of the terms "conceptions", "beliefs" and "attitudes".[22] Thompson pro-posed that teachers' conceptions were "conscious or subconscious beliefs, concepts, meaning, rules, mental images, and preferences concerning the discipline of math-ematics".[23] Schoenfeld argued that "beliefs" can encompass "understandings" and "emotions" that "shape the way an individual conceptualises and engages in mathe-matical behaviour".[24] Whereas Ernest proposed a model encompassing "beliefs" – about the nature of mathematics and models of teaching and learning mathematics, together with the principles of education – and "attitudes" – about mathematics and its teaching.[25] Lack of clarity also arises from researchers attempting to delineate

---

[21] Ball (1988 p. 40). See also Ball (1990).

[22] Andrews (2007), Speer (2005), Leder and Forgasz (2002), Furinghetti and Pehkonen (2002).

[23] Thompson (1992, p. 132).

[24] Schoenfeld (1992, p. 358).

[25] Ernest (1989a).

between beliefs and knowledge.[26] Others consider any distinction between beliefs and knowledge to be unhelpful and not sustainable.[27]

The second thing of which educators will be persuaded when reviewing the literature, is that there is compelling evidence that "experiences as a learner of mathematics", "conceptions including knowledge, beliefs, attitudes and emotions about mathematics" and "instructional practices as a teacher of mathematics" are all profoundly interconnected.[28] The corpus of work is relatively recent, one of the first studies having concluded that "the observed consistency between the teachers' professed conceptions of mathematics and the manner in which they typically presented the content strongly suggests that the teachers' views, beliefs and preferences about mathematics do influence their instructional practice"[29] and may impact on their effectiveness as a teacher. More recently a 4-year longitudinal study concluded, "a teacher's experiences from her university studies, actual classroom practice and in-service education interact and influence her beliefs and professional development".[30]

In terms of beliefs about mathematics, there is evidence to indicate that many pre-service teachers have an instrumentalist or absolutist view of the discipline,[31] a finding that we will see in the next chapter is reflected in our data garnered from students upon entering the course. Also widely accepted is the existence of a gap between beliefs and practices.[32] The distinction is conceptualised variously as espoused beliefs or theories against enacted beliefs or "theories-in-action" or "professed" against "attributed" beliefs.[33] We will also see in Chapter 4 that in a significant number of cases once in front of a class, the "child-centred" discovery model of teaching espoused by many trainees at the beginning of the course, reverted to a transmission model when modified by the pragmatics of classroom concerns.

Further, attitudes and beliefs may affect the degree to which curriculum reform is realised.[34] For example, a survey of secondary teachers' conceptions of mathematics suggested that "substantial numbers of serving teachers and many applicants for teacher training, may have perspectives on mathematics which counter the successful fulfilment of (current British government) curricular expectations".[35] Although,

---

[26]Furinghetti and Pehkonen (2002) posit as a solution two types of knowledge: objective and subjective, the former grounded in a notion of "truth".

[27]Leatham (2006), Lester (2002).

[28]Lerman (1990), 2002, Meredith (1993), Stipek, Givvin, Salmon, and MacGyvers (2001), Leder, Pehkonen, and Törner (2002), Sztajn (2003), Szydlik, Szydlik, and Benson (2003), Ambrose (2004), Forgasz and Leder (2008).

[29]Thompson (1984, p. 125).

[30]Potari and Georgiadou-Kabouridis (2009, p. 7).

[31]Ball (1990), Lerman (1990), Ernest (1989a).

[32]Ernest (1989b).

[33]Argyris and Schon (1974), Putnam and Borko (2000), Speer (2005).

[34]Cooney (1988).

[35]Andrews and Hatch (1999, p. 220).

beliefs do to a degree accord with national perspectives/curricular frameworks.[36] Certainly, our study indicates that many trainees' conceptualisations of mathematics were primarily utilitarian and focused upon number, which accorded with the current primary national perspectives/curricular framework.

The literatures on emotions are in many ways more coherent in their messaging than those on beliefs and attitudes. Recent mathematics education literature reveals, "mathematics is often experienced as an intensely emotional subject"[37] and often involves negative experiences for learners and student teachers.[38] Hardy (2009) observes the "faintly noticed essentialising shift" from "What's the problem with mathematics teaching?" to "What's the problem with primary student's mathematics?" (pp. 188–189). In one study conducted, one-third of pre-service teachers reported high levels of anxiety and a further third, medium levels.[39] Again we will see in the next chapter that trainees from our study reported similar levels of mathematics anxiety. Black et al. (2009) bring a coherent theoretical perspective to a range of factors including ability, pedagogy, emotions and relations with mathematics teachers[40] and peers[41] by exploring mathematical identities as framed by relationships that learners form with the mathematics and pedagogic methods/practices. They ask what socio-cultural, discursive and psychoanalytical positions on identity can bring to understanding issues of inclusion and exclusion from mathematics. In the same volume George (2009) argues "The curriculum regulates what mathematics students are exposed to and constrains the mathematical identities they develop" (p. 203) and questions what might happen if the "way of learning they find on offer in school mathematics classrooms does not fit with the nexus of identities in the making they bring with them" (p. 207). Such identity work is often mediated by the use of resources and textbooks.[42]

As to how much teacher educators can substantively influence beliefs and attitudes during initial training courses, opinion is open to question. Some research indicates that frameworks are already fairly firmly fixed before training.[43] A study of pre-service elementary teachers' beliefs, conceptions, practices and pedagogical content knowledge found that their conceptions of mathematics remained constant during a mathematics methods course.[44] A study of mature entrants to teacher education programmes in mathematics also found that their beliefs and conceptions

[36] Andrews (2007), Correa, Perry, Sims, Miller, and Fang (2008).

[37] Bibby (2002, p. 705). See also Bibby (2010).

[38] Boaler, Wiliam, and Brown (2000), Bulmer and Rodd (2005), Drake (2009, p. 162) posits that many people see mathematics as Lacan's "rule-bound symbolic Other" and exhorts educators to take account of student teachers' "emotional relationship with mathematics knowledge as well as their intellectual grasp of it".

[39] Cady and Readen (2007). See also Bekdemir (2010).

[40] Bibby (2009).

[41] Davis and Williams (2009).

[42] Davis (2009), Haggarty and Pepin (2002), Pepin (2009).

[43] Zeichner, Tabachnick, and Densmore (1987).

[44] Foss and Kleinsasser (1996).

were dependent on previous career experiences and were resistant to change.[45]
Further, primary undergraduate students sometimes hold images of teaching formed
from their own school days that are highly influential in moulding their classroom
practice.[46]

The effect of training courses does vary and belief systems are not as resistant to
change as some research suggests.[47] We will hear in Chapter 4 that trainees in our
study began upon entering the course to see mathematics as less absolutist – but that
their new found "ownership" of mathematics was very vulnerable to measures such
as the government's introduction of numeracy skills testing. Many, however, have
acknowledged that the influences of "pre-program beliefs" and "culturally based filters",[48] employed as interpretative frameworks to make sense of classroom contexts,
must be made explicit and challenged if changes in behaviour are to be achieved.[49]
Indeed some courses have had significant impact upon students in shifting beliefs
about mathematics from absolutism towards relativism[50] and supportive contexts
such as coordinated developmental field placements have generated change.[51] One
teaching programme was based upon a critical epistemology in which trainees'
models of knowledge and beliefs about teaching and learning were explicitly challenged and a language developed for describing, understanding and developing
practices and positions.[52] They created, as an analytical tool, a two-dimensional
matrix which charted trainees' practices (with respect to subject knowledge; beliefs
and values; pedagogical positions and power relations) against their moral/social
positioning as "compliant"; "reflective" and "interrogative". One of the most enduring theoretical conceptualisations of changing belief systems, however, is Lacey's
(1977) typology of student teachers' behaviours that included "strategic redefini-
tion", "strategic compliance" and "internalised adjustment". "Strategic compliance"
denoted behaviour changes that had been brought about under pressure whilst underlying beliefs remained unchanged, whereas "internalised adjustment" indicated that
changes had occurred in both behaviour and beliefs. The most important tool in
the teacher educators' armoury in recent times to advance professional learning and
promote change in beliefs and attitudes has been reflection.

---

[45] Harel (1994).

[46] Calderhead and Robson (1991). Su (1992) meanwhile, in a study of 29 training establishments,
found the teaching experience and the class teachers of greatest influence and the course curriculum
less so and Cheng (1990) found humanistic views of teaching and learning developed in college
sessions were tempered by realism after teaching practice experiences.

[47] Bramald, Hardman, and Leat (1995).

[48] Hollingsworth (1988).

[49] Ahmed (1987), Bird, Anderson, Sullivan, and Swidler (1993).

[50] Carré and Ernest (1993), Carter, Carré, and Bennett (1993).

[51] Swars, Smith, Smith, and Hart (2009).

[52] Miller and Baker (2001).

### 3.2.3 Developing Reflective Skills

Another transformation, which our trainee teacher are required to undertake is that of becoming "reflective" about their professional learning, pupils' learning and their teaching skills. This seems especially pertinent to the present study insofar as this approach provides a forum in which trainees can develop their philosophy of education and their personal accounts of "what it means to be a teacher". The "reflective practitioner" is a model that teacher educators in England have traditionally endorsed. A survey of training providers in 1991 found that over 80% of courses claimed to espouse a particular philosophy or model of professionalism and in over 70% of these cases (across primary, secondary, undergraduate and postgraduate courses) the model was that of the "reflective practitioner".[53] In the late 1980s and early 1990s such faith was shown in the notion that "a reflective teacher is an effective teacher", that reflective ability was employed as a criterion for selection into some training courses.[54] Poor reflectors meanwhile were found more likely to drop out or fail – arguably, perhaps, due to the fact that the courses were designed centrally around an approach with which they were not comfortable.

Generally traced to the work of Dewey (1933) modern frameworks of reflection involve some element of systematic enquiry into one's own practice. "Discourses of reflection" in the literature include content free "reflective teaching", "reflection on/in action", and "reflection as critical inquiry".[55] Reflective processes themselves are often represented in 3 level hierarchies,[56] loosely derived from Habermas (1973); or protocols such as "reaction, repair, review, research, retheorizing and reformulating".[57]

Strategies, which are claimed in the literature to foster reflection in pre-service teachers, include action research,[58] case studies,[59] ethnography,[60] micro teaching,[61] theorising on others' practice,[62] dialogic reflection[63] and structured curriculum tasks.[64] A number of educators feel that reflective work provides a forum in which students can reconstruct their own identity as they become inducted into

---

[53] Barrett et al. (1992).

[54] Leat (1995).

[55] Adler (1991), Cruickshank (1987), Schön (1983, 1987), Zeichner and Liston (1987).

[56] Van Manen (1977), Carr and Kemmis (1986), McIntyre (1993).

[57] Griffiths and Tann (1992).

[58] Carr and Kemmis (1986), Liston and Zeichner (1990).

[59] Ross (1989).

[60] Beyer (1984), Zeichner (1987).

[61] Sparks-Langer and Colton (1991).

[62] McIntyre (1993).

[63] Hatton and Smith (1995) claim dialogic reflection occurred in one third of the essays they read based on their "critical friend interview" technique.

[64] Smith (1991).

professional discourses.[65] Good reflectors have been shown to be warm, spontaneous, adaptable, creative, self-confident and in control.[66] And reflection on beliefs
allows mathematics teachers to connect thoughts and actions and resist tendencies to
separate mathematical and pedagogical beliefs.[67] Stinson and Powell (2010, p. 202)
employ reflection through the perspective of post-modern theory within mathematics teacher education contexts as "an opportunity to challenge and 'trouble' both
traditional mathematics teaching and the reform efforts".

Despite its considerable popularity with teacher educators, there have been
numerous critiques of the use of "reflective practitioner" techniques in initial teacher
preparation. Some claim that the skills required for reflection are very different from
those required in teaching and that the process of reflection could easily become an
end in itself.[68] Many studies indicate that the standard of most trainees' reflective
writing remains seriously under-developed, mostly at a descriptive level. It has been
suggested that there is scant evidence in the literature to suggest that "reflection
on practice in initial training is an opportunity to connect any sort of pedagogical
theory with practice".[69] A study of 150 newly inducted teachers found that only
5% mentioned reflective practice as an important mechanism of support.[70] Rather,
trainees found it a distraction from the serious business of learning to teach and
another "hurdle" to get over.[71] Still others argued that theorising classroom practice was difficult for trainees and more productive for experienced practitioners.[72]
More recent international studies, considering reflection in relation to mathematics
teaching suggest that it works better if the student teachers are less troubled by the
mathematics itself.[73] Outright health warnings about the use of reflection in initial
teacher education include the potential damage caused by its capacity to expose
personal deficiencies, pose threats to classroom teachers and produce anxiety, low
self-esteem and disempowering self-doubt by emphasising the disparity between
actual and intended classroom practice.[74]

There are grounds for suggesting that reflective practice as a model became less
dominant in England at the turn of the century, in response to the pressures of
an increasingly regulated curriculum, which we will hear about in Chapter 4. The
"reflective practitioner" was to a degree a casualty of this intensification of initial
teacher education, "while many teacher educators aspired to maintain the ideal of
the reflective practitioner by working in collaborative partnerships with those in

---

[65]Tann (1993), Hanley and Brown (1996), (1999), Jones et al. (2000).

[66]Gipe, Richards, Levitov, and Speaker (1991), LaBoskey (1993).

[67]Wilson and Cooney (2002).

[68]McNamara (1990), Valli (1993).

[69]Edwards (1995, p. 600).

[70]Tickle (1994).

[71]Bolin (1990).

[72]McIntyre (1993), McNally, Cope, Inglis, and Stronach (1994).

[73]Britt, Irwin, and Ritchie (2001), Tzur (2001), Roth McDuffie (2004).

[74]McNamara (1990) McLaughlin, (1994), Leat (1995).

schools, in reality that was increasingly difficult".[75] In England this depleted a key forum in which trainees could articulate their aspirations. But 2007 saw the introduction of Masters level postgraduate training pathways, which have put reflection back on the agenda, and 2009 saw the piloting of a school-based Masters in Teaching and Learning for all new teachers. If adopted, the latter will undoubtedly secure the position of criticality in initial teacher preparation in England.[76] In schools reflective practice, where it thrives, is nurtured by an army of school-based mentors and coaches.

## 3.2.4 Supporting Learning Through Mentoring and Coaching

Formal mentoring activities in English schools have, until relatively recently, largely been focused on trainee and new teachers. Mentoring featured largely in the literature in the 1990s as a vehicle to encourage reflective practice[77] but a review of mentoring literature (1992–2003) revealed a dearth of evidence on how school-based practices supported trainee teachers' professional learning. The burgeoning body of research that did emerge about mentoring in the 1990s was often single case studies and largely centred on the affective dimension of mentors' perceptions, views, beliefs and experiences.[78] The use of "learning conversations" or "reflective dialogues",[79] however, can be observed through literatures in narrative studies[80]; critical incidents[81]; and empowerment discourses.[82]

A review of primary mentoring concluded that professional, interpersonal and communication skills were important and that guidelines for selection and training of mentors were necessary.[83] Other research concluded that mentors did not take sufficient account of adult learning needs and did not understand the principles underpinning mentoring.[84] A study of the school-based learning of 125 student teachers concluded that mentoring focused on curriculum delivery and was heavily situated in a way that limited their understanding of learners.[85] Primary school-based mentors tended to emphasise classroom management and professional issues

---

[75]Furlong et al. (2000 p. 143).

[76]McNamara (2008).

[77]Watkins (1992), Hagger, Burn, and McIntyre (1993), Jaworski and Watson (1994), Tauer (1998), Jones (2002).

[78]Moyles and Stuart (2003).

[79]Zeichner and Liston (1987).

[80]Connelly and Clandinin (1990), Beattie (1995), Weber (1993), England and Brown (2001), Brown (2001).

[81]Tripp (1993), Brown and England (2004).

[82]Elbaz (1990).

[83]Moyles, Suschitzky, and Chapman (1998).

[84]Jones and Straker (2006).

[85]Edwards and Protheroe (2003).

and did not provide quality subject-specific feedback to support trainees in applying subject knowledge effectively.[86] A study (2004–2005) into the nature of effective coaching and mentoring concluded that despite widespread and significant confusion over the definition of terms and the relative importance of process skills, as opposed to specialist content knowledge, the use of coaching and mentoring was growing significantly.[87] This growth is undoubtedly fuelled in England by the expectation in the professional standards that teachers will become involved in mentoring and coaching.[88]

The reciprocal benefits of the mentoring process are widely cited in the literature.[89] Indeed, overall, reflective practice was generally held to be a more productive exercise for mentors than mentees. However, also noted is the need for school leaders and managers to have greater awareness of its potential; more effectively integrate it into school structures and processes; and employ it as a mechanism for school improvement.[90] Twenty-five years ago school inspection evidence[91] identified links between initial training and teacher professional development as powerful. Two decades later, however, an analysis of all 13,202 primary school inspection reports (1999–2005) found that fewer than 6% made any reference to initial training of teachers and these were limited in the main to statements of involvement.[92] Although all evaluative comments made were supportive, only one example was found of a report explicitly linking mentoring to professional learning.

Thus the potential professional learning gains for primary schools are a positive, albeit unintended, consequence of the initial training process. Teacher education offers the opportunity to give expression to teachers' voices espousing the practitioners' perspectives and generating practical theory. Some consider the ascendancy of this practical theory to have been part of a post-modern development in which wider societal and cultural pressures have engineered the demise of the traditional meta-disciplines of education: sociology, psychology and philosophy.[93] Others believe that education as a practical discipline requires practical theory and the erstwhile meta-narratives have been perceived to fail in the task of determining and validating a practical basis for action.[94] A manifestation of this new cultural dynamic in teacher education generally has been the privileging of practice over theory, which has lauded "performativity" and resulted in classroom competence

---

[86] Brown and McNamara (2005), Ofsted (2007a).

[87] Curee (2005).

[88] Professional Standards for Teachers, Training and Development Agency (2007).

[89] McIntyre (1993), McNally et al. (1994), Goodson and Sikes (2001), Kiltz, Danzig, and Szecsy (2004), Lopez-Real and Kwan (2005), McNally (2006) argued that rather than learning through the formal mentoring process, mentee learning experiences were largely informal and affective.

[90] Price and Willett (2006), Hurd, Jones, McNamara, and Craig (2007), Mentor and Whitehead (1995).

[91] Perry (1985).

[92] Hurd et al. (2007).

[93] Wilkin (1993).

[94] Elliott (1987).

being positioned as the benchmark of accomplishment. We will hear about support for teachers' "practical" understandings over educators' "theoretical" or "idealised" knowledge when we learn more about the teacher training reform agenda in Chapter 4. Here a key driver has been to ensure that teacher preparation is more centrally school based. Yet, as we will hear in the next section, the British government has demonstrated a continued lack of confidence in its school workforce, most especially in respect of teacher subject knowledge.

### 3.2.5  Improving Subject Knowledge

The now endemic and deeply rooted international audit culture[95] will ensure that educational standards, and particularly mathematical performance, stay on the agenda of most governments in the developed world for the foreseeable future. The response of successive British governments to the ostensibly poor performance of English pupils has been to blame the mathematics subject knowledge of its teacher workforce. Indeed, as we shall see in the next chapter, the government at one point itemised in detail the mathematics content knowledge it required primary trainee teachers to demonstrate. Thus, improving their knowledge of the subject discipline of mathematics is another transformation that our trainee must undertake on her/his journey to becoming a qualified teacher. It is perhaps not surprising then that, as we shall see in the next chapter, so many of the trainees in our study were anxious about their mathematics subject knowledge and lacked confidence in their ability. Lack of confidence in mathematics ability is not, however, an ill that can be entirely blamed upon recent governments' focuses on international league tables. Twenty years ago, at the time the first National Curriculum for mathematics was introduced in England, a survey of 400 primary teachers found that they lacked confidence in mathematics subject knowledge. Another strand of the same study tested primary pre-service teachers at the beginning and end of their 1-year post graduate course and found that their subject knowledge across a range of subjects was limited and that there was no significant improvement of content and substantive knowledge of mathematics during the year.[96]

However, even in East Asia, which has been recognised in the international league tables for its high performance in school mathematics, confidence is not high. Eighty-four percent of pre-service primary teachers in China and 80% in South Korea rated themselves with either "limited" or "low" knowledge, understanding and readiness to teach the national mathematical syllabus. The authors contrasted this with the high self-confidence reported by pre-service teachers in the United States.[97] Confidence, however, does not always translate into competence.

---

[95]For example, *Trends in International Mathematics and Science Study* and *Programme for International Student Assessment*.

[96]Wragg, Bennett, and Carré (1989), Carter et al. (1993).

[97]Mullins, Martin, Gonzalez, and Chrostowski (2004), Li, Ma, and Pang (2008), Li and Smith (2007).

A comparative study of Chinese and of elementary teachers in the United States found the Chinese teachers to have a "profound understanding of fundamental mathematics" compared to teachers in the United States who demonstrated a lack of conceptual understanding.[98] Further, despite the reported lack of confidence of Chinese and South Korean pre-service teachers, around 95% of them answered correctly a question on division of fractions to suggest that "prospective elementary teachers in East Asia have a strong preparation in mathematics content knowledge".[99]

But exactly what type and level of content knowledge is required for pre-service primary teachers is far from clear because the relationship between mathematics subject knowledge and effectiveness in teaching mathematics is still vigorously debated. On the one hand, there is a convincing corpus of research evidence which links lack of sufficient subject knowledge to lack of effectiveness in teaching. Insufficient subject knowledge has been linked to less effective classroom performance and in some cases over reliance on commercial schemes.[100] Novice teachers have been observed to lack versatility in this pivotal competence[101] and trainees have been observed to display the same misconceptions as children.[102]

Conversely, "more" teacher subject knowledge does not necessarily mean "better" teaching. Some research has challenged the assumption that the more subject knowledge teachers had (as measured by quantity of instruction received) the more "effective" they were.[103] Indeed, they questioned whether some aspects of higher-level mathematics training might actually be counterproductive in preparation for teaching. Byrne (1983) suggested that one reason why these earlier studies failed to establish a relationship between teacher subject matter knowledge and student achievement is that both notions had been inadequately conceptualised and measured – the first, typically, by multiple-choice tests and quantity of tuition received, the second by standardised tests. A research review  in the United States dating from the 1970s, however, found no statistical significance in the relation between teacher subject knowledge and effective teaching (as measured by "student achievement").[104] A lack of conclusive evidence linking subject study and teaching quality was again apparent in a review of research from the United States, albeit, of the 57 studies included, only seven related to subject matter preparation and, of those, only four concerned mathematics/science and only one was elementary/middle school focused.[105] "Undermining the view that ideal preparation is a subject matter major,

---

[98]Ma (1999).

[99]Li et al. (2008, pp. 58–59).

[100]Wragg et al. (1989), Bennett and Turner-Bisset (1993), Simon and Brown (1996), Ofsted (1994), Rowland, Martyn, Barber, and Heal (2000, 2001), Rowland and Barber (2002), Millett and Johnson (1996).

[101]Alexander, Rose, and Woodhead (1992), Shulman (1987).

[102]Bennett and Turner-Bisset (1993), Ball (1990).

[103]Begle (1979), Ball (1990).

[104]Grossman, Wilson, and Shulman (1989), Wilson, Shulman, and Richert (1987).

[105]Wilson et al. (2001).

three studies had complex and inconsistent results": one study[106] found a positive relationship between teachers' degrees in mathematics and their students' test scores, one was equivocal and one found no effect. Further, one study,[107] of secondary mathematics students' outcomes, found that teachers' subject matter study was positively related to student achievement, but that there appeared to be a "threshold" effect beyond which additional study offered no increased benefit in terms of student outcomes, while having a mathematics major had no effect. Several studies, however, reported subject-specific methods courses useful.

Adding further weight to conclusions of the United States research review mentioned above, an English survey of 90 teachers also found that "more" was not necessarily "better" when correlating teachers' mathematical knowledge, measured in terms of formal qualifications, against average pupil test gains over one academic year.[108] There was a slight, but not statistically significant, negative correlation between level of mathematical qualification and "effective" teaching: indicating that mathematical qualifications are not a reliable indicator of the mathematical knowledge required for teaching. In contrast, the study found that those teachers who had knowledge and awareness of conceptual connections within the primary mathematics curriculum were effective in terms of pupil test gains. Indeed, the amount of extended continuing professional development in mathematics education undertaken by the teachers was found to be a better predictor of "effectiveness" than formal qualifications.[109] A comparative study of Chinese and United States teachers, cited above, also concluded that the Chinese teachers' profound understanding of mathematics might have resulted in part from the continuing professional development opportunities in which they studied teaching materials intensively together with other teachers, and the fact that they were specialist mathematics teachers.[110] Whilst vigorous debate about subject knowledge was ongoing, a parallel debate was gathering momentum, triggered by the 1985 American Educational Research Association Presidential address of Lee Shulman (1986, 1987), in which he proposed a framework of seven categories of teachers' professional knowledge.

### 3.2.6 Transforming Subject Knowledge into Pedagogic Content Knowledge

In the complex "learning to teach" equation, the transformation "learner" to "teacher" is mirrored in the transformation of "content/subject matter knowledge" into "pedagogic content knowledge". The notion that the development of pedagogic content knowledge was the most important and difficult element of learning to be

---

[106]Goldhaber and Brewer (2000).

[107]Monk (1994).

[108]Askew et al. (1997, p. 65).

[109]Askew et al. (1997, pp. 74–79).

[110]Ma (1999).

an effective teacher became popular in the late 1980s. Shulman (1986), its main proponent, argued that too much emphasis had been placed on pedagogical processes and not enough on "the missing paradigm" – "subject content knowledge". The latter he defined as including pedagogic content knowledge, curricular knowledge and content/subject matter knowledge (both "substantive" facts and concepts and "syntactic" mechanisms and processes).[111] The development of pedagogic content knowledge was conjectured to involve the repackaging of mathematics and necessitate facility with the representations, illustrations, examples, explanations and analogies that make mathematical ideas comprehensible to others.

Shulman also distinguished between two kinds of understanding: knowing "that" (rules and procedures), and knowing "why" (conceptual and principled knowledge). "The teacher need not only understand that something is so; the teacher must further understand why it is so".[112] Askew (2008, p. 19) conjectures "that procedural knowledge of mathematics is not the problem. . . . [the difficulty] is not that teachers were unable to reach the correct answers, but they were not able to generalise from their answers". This was also a conclusion drawn in the United States review: "prospective teachers may have mastered basic skills, but they lack the deeper conceptual understanding. . . in mathematics both prospective elementary and high school teachers had relatively sound procedural, or rule-dominated knowledge of basic mathematics, especially in arithmetic but had difficulty when pushed to explain why an algorithm or procedure works".[113]

Critics of Shulman's model of teacher knowledge believed that it was decontextualised, not sufficiently dynamic to allow for a non-absolutist view of mathematics and assumed a simple didactic and transmission view of teaching.[114] Schulman's research was undertaken with secondary teachers and which may explain the "cautiousness that Shulman and his colleagues expressed over generalising the range of their work to primary school teachers".[115] Others question whether the distinction between subject and pedagogic knowledge can and should be made since all subject matter is itself a form of representation.[116] Others stress that pedagogic content knowledge is situational and experientially grounded in classroom experience.[117] Also, the assumption that teachers have full access to subject matter knowledge has been questioned; it has been argued that for both experienced and novice teachers much subject matter knowledge remains as "learner-knowledge"

---

[111] Shulman (1986), cf. Schwab (1978).

[112] Shulman (1986, p. 9). A powerful argument was also provided for this position by Skemp (1976) in his seminal paper on "instrumental" and "relational" knowledge in mathematics.

[113] Wilson et al. (2001, p. 9).

[114] Stones (1992), Meredith (1995), Meredith (1993), McNamara (1991).

[115] Askew (2008, p. 15).

[116] McNamara (1991), McEwan and Bull (1991).

[117] Carter (1990), Lave and Wenger (1991), McNamara (1991).

and is not transformed into "teacher-knowledge".[118] A case study of "Frances" describes conditions under which this transformation did and did not take place.[119]

The capacity to transform personal understanding was posited to depend on what teachers brought to the classroom and, as has been noted, many experienced teachers used their own mathematical experiences as a pupil in the classroom as a foundation for making decisions. Also trainees' pedagogic content knowledge is not thought to be robustly connected to their training but to prior learning, knowledge, experience, values and epistemological beliefs.[120] Its acquisition was as a result of "thinking about subject matter and learning in relation to teaching tasks". A review of the situational nature of teachers' decisions and rationalisations about classroom tasks found that "gaps in subject knowledge undermine the common rationalisation of the teacher's authority in the classroom".[121] Others have claimed that teachers' choice and use of resources such as school textbooks influence students' situational understandings and perceptions of mathematics and learner identities.[122] Gutstein (2008) argues that Shulman's categories might be supplemented by *culturally relevant pedagogy* to acknowledge the struggle encountered by students from minority groups disadvantaged by mainstream cultural assumptions built into pedagogical forms.

Rowland and colleagues undertook a significant corpus of research into trainees' classroom performance and its relation to subject matter knowledge and pedagogic content knowledge. They theorised a "knowledge quartet" that encompassed four dimensions: foundation (knowledge, beliefs and understanding of mathematics and its teaching acquired through study), transformation (knowledge-in-action demonstrated in planning and teaching mathematics including particularly choice and use of examples – Shulman's pedagogic content knowledge), connection (depth, breadth and coherence of relationships demonstrated) and contingency (responsiveness-in-action to events and ideas). The conceptual framework showed a significant association between the assessment of trainees' teaching competence and the score on their mathematics knowledge audit, undertaken 4 months into a 1-year postgraduate training course.[123] These results are broadly in line with the findings reported in the section above, although notably this research audited current mathematics subject matter knowledge, compared to the study undertaken by Askew et al. which used mathematics qualifications as a proxy measure for subject knowledge.

A comprehensive review of the development of pedagogic content knowledge over the last two decades (Graeber & Tirosh, 2008, p. 124) notes that other researchers have extended and modified Shulman's domains. "The more recent

[118]Prestage and Perks (1999).

[119]"Frances", in Rowland et al. (2000).

[120]Meredith (1993, p. 336).

[121]Simon and Brown (1996, p. 7).

[122]Pepin and Haggarty (2007), Davis (2009), Pepin (2009).

[123]Goulding et al. (2002), Rowland, Huckstep, and Thwaites (2005), Rowland and Turner (2007), Rowland, Turner, Thwaites, and Huckstep (2009), Rowland (2008).

frameworks[124] identify aspects of content teaching and curriculum within [peda-
gogic content knowledge]". Graeber and Tirosh pose a number of questions arising
from their review: "(1) the role of beliefs and values in the development of a
teachers' [pedagogic content knowledge], (2) whether different teaching/learning
paradigms require different components of [pedagogic content knowledge], and
(3) what are improved methods for assessing [pedagogic content knowledge]".
They conclude that Shulman's achievement has been to "inform and legitimise the
content of teacher education programmes thereby establishing teaching as a profession with a well-defined knowledge base, along with medicine and law" (p. 125).
However, caution that, "Evidence that such knowledge is unique to teachers and
more evidence that [pedagogic content knowledge] is positively related to student
achievement in mathematics will aid in the field's acceptance of [pedagogic content
knowledge] as a less elusive and a more useful construct" (p. 128).

## 3.3  Conclusion

We apologise for the exhausting and yet incomplete review of the research and literature base relating to learning to teach. Readers may be forgiven for not spotting
the direction of travel of the findings of the various research themes, but we lack
confidence that a more extensive review would have cleared things up. Large-scale
multi-site research programmes are rare and small-scale single case study research
will never offer coverage of all situations in all contexts. This chapter is of course
also based on a questionable premise that teachers and teacher educators in schools
and universities are, or could be, guided by "what is *known* from the research literature". Which epistemological framework would this suppose? Who knows and how
does their knowledge impact on their actions? The chapter is perhaps even more
deluded as regards how we understand the shaping of actions. How is the research
mediated? How does it shape the work of researchers, teacher educators, teachers
and children? How much can people be aware of research? And if they are aware of
it, to what extent are they at liberty to follow its suggestions or implications? This
question is beyond the brief of this study, although we do address this issue more
directly in the final chapter. Certainly, the research impacts on the present authors'
sense of their own obligations as to how they present their work although other
concerns seep out of the edges. It shapes our own reading of events to some extent
but it would be more difficult to pinpoint how research has impacted on the shape of
the environments in which our research subjects see themselves operating. Research
predicated on improving practice will frequently come into contact with policy that
thinks it already knows how this can be achieved.

---

[124]An, Kulm, and Wu (2004), Ball and Bass (2003).

# Chapter 4
# Becoming a Teacher: An English Case Study

## 4.1 Introduction

The key objective of this book is to present a theoretically oriented account of the processes through which primary teachers develop their understanding of the task of teaching mathematics. The theoretical framework was created as we faced the task of building a picture of the training process in England, where the regulative apparatus of the central government impacts greatly on teacher practices and on conceptions of mathematics. At one level these are colloquial concerns. Nevertheless, we are seeking to address an international audience as we feel that certain issues might activate a broader interest. Key among these is the formation of primary teacher identity and the social derivation of school mathematics in a country where the government has legislated how "mathematics" is taught and understood. Consequently, we find ourselves asking the more general question of how conceptions of school mathematics might be shaped through regulative apparatus. Mathematics education researchers will always be obliged to understand their concerns against the specific demands of particular local or national contexts. For example, suggestions as to how teaching practices might be improved need to be integrated into the specific curriculum definitions of mathematics and of how the teacher is expected to facilitate those definitions. The situation in England became quite distinctive in the 1990s, in the degree to which its government pursued an agenda of surveillance and control to unprecedented levels of prescription. As such, England became an interesting research site. What can others learn by observing how one government chose to micro-manage so many aspects of education? In a recent party political debate it was claimed that English school principals had received an average of 4,000 pages per year of governmental instructions.[1] One question that we found ourselves addressing in relation to school mathematics was, "who has the final word on what mathematics is in schools?" In England, as we shall see, the answer seems clear.

---

[1] Lawson (2010).

Each of the next two sections outlines a key aspect of the English situation, the teacher training procedures and the curriculum structures. These outlines show that the policy apparatus was highly intrusive, greatly restricting teachers' capacity to make professional judgements. The scope for research is also greatly hampered by an authority assuming that it already knows so many of the answers. The policy changes were predicated on controversial claims about research that provoked some concern.[2] Is the task of research about supporting a particular model of education or is it to challenge the limits of that model? These first two sections provide a contextual backdrop for the third section, which presents a detailed account of our empirical studies.

## 4.2  The Initial Teacher Education Reform Agenda

### 4.2.1  Setting the Scene

An "overwhelmingly favourable response" to proposals in the policy document *Teachers: meeting the challenge of change* we were told[3] persuaded the British Government to introduce skills testing for trainee teachers in the English system. The aspiration was to "raise the skills levels of the teaching profession. . . . and the professional standing and the profile of teachers and teaching"; and to empower teachers to become change agents "instrumental in raising standards of teaching and learning in our schools and in contributing to the changes needed to extend opportunity for young people and the wider community".[4] The Numeracy Skills Test introduced in 2000 was the first of three tests[5] to be introduced under the aegis of the government.[6] Such testing was but one of a long list of curriculum and assessment prescriptions introduced to regulate initial teacher education.

Thursday 1st June 2000 was to be the National Premiere of this particular performance and as the day drew near detailed local planning was evident in numerous venues around the country. . .

---

[2]This is discussed in the final chapter.

[3]Department for Education and Employment (1998a, p. 3).

[4]Morris (1999, p. 3).

[5]English and Information and Communication Technology were to follow in 2001.

[6]Teacher Training Agency.

The following scene is set at the Institute of Education, Manchester Metropolitan University – Didsbury Campus (one of the largest "Initial Teacher Training" providers in the United Kingdom)...

*The cast*: 830 trainee teachers.

*The audience*: (absent but "overwhelmingly" supportive) the English public who "never forget a good teacher".[7]

*The stage*: 34 rooms across the Campus. The largest held 120, the smallest 16. There were special rooms set aside for dyslexic students, non-native English speakers and latecomers.

*The script*: included oral/mental and written components and was devised by the government and naturally remained undisclosed to the cast until the performance; but was known to focus upon their "wider context of their professional role as a teacher".

*The rehearsals*: practice scripts were available in abundance and managed centrally through "web-based resources", although hard copies and help lines were also available.

*The directors*: worked solidly for days prior to the performance enlisting back stage support, planning, producing room lists, counting out scripts (lack of sufficient spares available made contingency arrangements exceedingly tricky); preparing individualised instruction packs for the stage managers/runners; and (to reduce commotion and disruption) stopping builders from building, gardeners from cutting lawns, and beer lorries from delivering.

*The stage-managers*: 40 invigilators and 20 runners (provided with mobile phones due to the size of the campus) were drawn from amongst the academic and administrative staff.

*The stagehands*: a House Services team worked tirelessly for days setting out the requisite amount of chairs and tables in the 34 rooms and ensuring security and access.

*The props*: audio equipment was provided for each room to deliver the mental/oral test, pre-recorded on audiotape. Above and beyond what was already available, this alone cost £1000. Backup calculators, pens, rulers, paper cups and water were also supplied in great numbers.

---

[7] Teacher Training Agency (1999).

*The pre-performance briefing*: planned, according to the director, with "military precision" this took place in Lecture Theatre A at 10.15am.

*The performance*: almost faultless – the stage managers reported only one audiocassette to be mal-functional. Only 2 of the 830 cast were late and a further one reported with a slight malaise at the beginning of the performance (most probably a case of stage fright). Less impressive, however, was that one in ten of the cast forgot their registration number and/or their photographic identification (a problem in the offing!)

*The post-performance debriefing*: took place again in Lecture Theatre A where slightly less "military precision" was apparent due to the unexpected presence of about 80 of the cast under guard until such time as they could be reunited with their scripts and registration number and/or be identified by an official. Scripts were cross-checked against attendance; missing scripts checked against the absentee list; unused scripts, as instructed, returned forthwith.

*The reviews*: The director proclaimed, "the whole thing was an amazing production". The cast whose views were canvassed after the event proved to be somewhat less enthusiastic. Approximately half found the oral test easy or at least fairly easy; less than 10% rated it hard. Most felt the written test passable when it came to level of difficulty, although a few complained it was "wordy, a lot of looking at tables"; about 10% rated it quite hard. The time allowed for both written and oral tests was an issue for many. Opinion was equally divided as to whether there was, or was not, sufficient time for the oral test. When it came to the written test, however, nearly twice as many students felt the timing too tight as were comfortable with it. When measured against the other four or five performance indicators employed on their course to assess their standard, however, the tests got a massive "thumbs down" – 90% of students rated them "least important/valuable".

"The cultural content of a tradition is organised and transmitted on particular occasions through specific media"[8] and this event was clearly no exception: The Numeracy Skills Test was enacted as a very public theatrical event. Resourced with a kitbag of "ideological state apparatus"[9]: information, advice, instruction and support were made directly available through web site, information line (by telephone, fax and email) and publications. Specifically, each trainee received a substantive pack from the government containing information, numeracy support and sample questions. Individual rehearsals were managed by means of hi-tech "cultural media". Trainees rehearsed on practice tests available as "web-based resources".

---

[8]Singer (1959, p. xii).
[9]Althusser (1971).

They were (re)assured by the government that amidst all of this "state of the art" centrally controlled telematics, their tutors in the training institutions would be kept in touch with developments.[10] Although it has to be said, feeling "in touch" was most definitely not a sentiment articulated by many training providers at the time!

The numeracy test was intended to police the boundaries of the teaching profession in order to assure the public that "every one qualifying to teach had a good grounding in the use of numeracy in the wider context of their professional role as a teacher".[11] The "major social concern" that prompted this particular contemporary spectacle was focused on the quality of mathematics subject knowledge and understanding of teachers. The "growth of the spectacle genre in the modern world is to be understood as a public form of thinking out, of telling stories about certain growing ambiguities and ambivalences".[12] Energised by government rhetoric the "social concern" developed in reaction to the low rating of England in comparative international studies of pupil outcome data and was sustained by a burgeoning national audit culture of league tables and targets.

The Numeracy Skills Test was but one of a multitude of *audit* tools employed by the government to define the skills and the personal characteristics of teachers and generate "consistent and reliable" assessment practices across the initial training sector. Yet it could be argued that this aim was far from achieved, as it appeared to privilege formal testing above the existing self-audit mechanisms at some cost to trainees' autonomy and emergent notions of professionalism. Another long-term unintended consequence might be the shifting of trainees' conceptions of mathematics to become more "hard-edged" and absolutist, when training had previously been reported, as discussed in the last chapter, to be successful in softening such beliefs.[13] Studies conducted at the time of the first numeracy test also reported that trainees felt extreme anxiety and a "deep sense of grievance" about the introduction of the test, as we have discussed elsewhere.[14] This added greatly to the already negative associations and anxiety about mathematics experienced by many trainee teachers and countered the success that training courses at the time were reported to be having in remediating such feelings.[15] Deeply concerning also, at a time when inclusion, and in particular the recruitment and retention of ethnic minority teachers, was high on the government agenda, evidence indicated that certain minority groups were disadvantaged.[16] More generally, however, the testing provides an example of

---

[10]Morris (1999).

[11]Teacher Training Agency (2000a, p. 2).

[12]MacAloon (1984, p. 247) quoted by Stronach (1999, p. 183). Such an event would be defined by MacAloon as "metagenre"; "an increasingly hybrid form of contemporary ritual involving the dramatic enactment of major social concerns, publicly shared and articulated" (Stronach, 1999, p. 183).

[13]Carré and Ernest (1993), Carter et al. (1993).

[14]McNamara et al. (2002).

[15]Brown et al. (1999), Green and Ollerton (1999).

[16]Hextall, Mahony, and Menter (2001), Teacher Training Agency (2000b).

an external demand made of trainees as they struggled to articulate their personal philosophy of education and aspirations for themselves as teachers.

This chapter will now present a, necessarily selective, account of the policy environment within which our empirical studies were carried out, a complex task, given the surfeit of policy apparatus of recent years. We shall focus upon the "official" training process itself and offer a detailed case study of the English government's management of it. We consider in detail four key aspects of recent reforms as they impinge upon training courses: centralisation of control, regulation of the curriculum, inspection of training and the development of partnership.

## 4.2.2  Centralisation: Government Control of Initial Teacher Education

The last quarter of a century has been a period of sustained and increasingly radical reform to the structure, content and regulation of teacher preparation in England. Some ascribe the move of initial teacher education from relative obscurity to strategic significance to an assumption on the part of the successive governments that initial training was an effective mechanism for steering change in the school curriculum and transforming teacher professionalism.[17] The centralising tendencies and the accountability culture which grew apace during the two decades of the Conservative governments (the 1980s and 1990s) were intensified, both in terms of the degree of micromanagement of the sector and the scope and pace of the reform agenda, in the late 1990s when the Labour government took office.

The drive towards centralisation and political control of teacher education had first been signalled in 1984 with the establishment of the Council for Accreditation of Teacher Education that sought to create a more practical and school-based training. Importantly, it sought to regulate more rigorously the assessment and delivery of courses and introduce alternative school-based routes. In the mid 1990s the Council was superseded by the Teacher Training Agency, which was considerably more powerful and wide-ranging in its powers. These included: funding; quality control/assurance; accreditation of training routes; teacher recruitment; and induction. The move from "Council" to "Agency" also signalled a change in the ideology and governance of training and, in particular, a profoundly symbolic shift in the designation of the process from "education" to "training".

The government's Teacher Training Agency, undoubtedly the key driver of change in England, was motivated by a need to increase supply but also by a desire to broaden the type of training offered, and limit the dominance of universities and colleges that at the time provided most of the training. The first national survey of teacher education provision in 1991 showed that 99% of the 45,000 trainee teachers in the United Kingdom were registered on programmes offered through universities

---

[17] Furlong (2001), (2005).

and colleges.[18] Indeed, even in the subsequent decade, despite the best efforts of the government, the overall percentage of trainees following such training routes had still not reduced significantly.[19] The Teacher Training Agency's approach was two-fold. Firstly, to extend the variety of traditional courses on offer and introduce modular and flexible routes, and secondly, to attempt to increase the disappointing uptake of "alternative" routes into teaching through more centrally school-based programmes and employment-based routes. It achieved success in the former; but although there was a very significant increase in the number of secondary teachers training through employment-based routes by the mid 2000s, this pattern was not replicated in the primary sector. Still around 85% of primary teachers are still trained in universities and colleges: 50% on 1-year postgraduate courses and 35% on 3- or 4-year undergraduate courses.[20] It is to one of these that we will later in the chapter turn our attention; our particular emphasis will be upon the 4-year undergraduate Bachelor of Education degree (B.Ed), from which our study cohort was recruited.

## 4.2.3  Regulation: Intensification of the Curriculum

The first change experienced in the 1980s was a gradual but significant increase in the intensification of the curriculum in terms of mandatory requirements for school-based training. By the early 1990s the number of school-based days prescribed on some courses was up to two-thirds of the course length. A comparative review of European teacher education at the time, noted that England was on its own in attempting to erode both its length, and the university based academic rigour, of training.[21] The new proposals were considered "conservative", "time constrained" and lacking the flexibility and intellectual and professional foundation necessary to prepare teachers for the future.[22] Carré and Ernest (1993) expressed concern that an increasingly school-based training would cause the already limited improvement in mathematics knowledge of primary postgraduate students to decline further.

In addition to the time spent in non-practice-based activities decreasing considerably, the detail and prescription of knowledge and skills required of trainees was increasing with the introduction of a "competences" based model of training. The combined effects resulted in considerably greater pressure on the delivery of traditionally university-based components and increased financial pressure overall, due to the apportioning of funding between universities and schools in respect of the latter's greatly increased role. Increasing the level of intensification of courses rendered them overfull and previously key aspects of curricular and professional

---

[18]Barrett et al. (1992).
[19]Furlong et al. (2000).
[20]McNamara (2008).
[21]Holyoake (1993).
[22]Bines (1994), Dart and Drake (1993).

development were squeezed out. Course leaders in a 1996-survey reported curriculum planning was becoming an "increasingly technical affair" and one in which "more and more issues had to be packed into less and less time".[23]

The most radical and comprehensive change was yet to come. The National Curriculum for Initial Teacher Training[24] was introduced in 1998 after a "consultation" which left some commentators "concerned about the state of democracy in England".[25] The curriculum prescribed requirements for courses including length, arrangements for partnerships with schools, selection of trainees and quality assurance processes. It also set down in previously unimaginable detail over 100 standards that trainees had to demonstrate to be awarded qualified teacher status. They related to: knowledge and understanding; planning, teaching and classroom management; monitoring, assessment, recording, reporting and accountability; and other professional requirements. In addition there were further standards relating to the auditing of specified subject knowledge.

The increased pressure generated by the new curriculum and assessment requirements did not escape trainees who perceived the training as overly prescriptive and felt the need for space to reflect and develop their understanding of what it meant to be an effective teacher.[26] A crucial area of immediate reflection might have been how the space could be created, amongst all the other competing demands. And what policies, practices and pedagogies were sanctioned as legitimate objects for reflection, given the competing discourses of "audit" and "standards".

In 2002 this curriculum framework was superseded by the slim-line *Qualifying to Teach*,[27] which contained just 40 standards: the new Labour Government having now explicitly abandoned attempts to prescribe pedagogy and to detail subject knowledge. The profession received this version more positively,[28] not least because of its explicit focus on professional values and practice. The third revision of the curriculum in 2007 was a subtle refinement of the previous version, foregrounding new school curriculum reforms (of which more later) and reducing still further (to 33) the number of standards. Notwithstanding an enduring focus on the core curriculum, learning to be a primary teacher continues to gather an ever-increasing curricular and pedagogic knowledge base and skill set.[29] The aspiring primary teacher is now also required to broaden her key focus on the academic curriculum to encompass contribution to society, safety, health and economic wellbeing, as well as developing an understanding of an extended range of professional contexts, from working with others in the classroom to working in multi-professional teams, providing access to

---

[23]Furlong et al. (2000, p. 103).

[24]Department for Education and Employment (1998b), Circular 4/98.

[25]Mahony and Hextall (2000, p. 323).

[26]Lunn and Bishop (2003).

[27]Teacher Training Agency (2002).

[28]Simco and Wilson (2002).

[29]The latest addition being modern foreign languages.

integrated and specialist services including childcare, parenting and family support, community facilities/learning and, finally, to promoting community cohesion.[30]

A further significance of the 2007 initial training curriculum was that it sat within a coherent developmental framework of National Professional Standards for the whole teacher workforce, which covered initial training up to excellent and advanced skills teachers. Such a framework had been mooted 10 years earlier but was now made possible because in 2005, a decade after its inception, the Teacher Training Agency was re-launched as the Training and Development Agency (*for Schools*) with an extended remit to cover the training and development of the whole school workforce. Initial teacher education was, it seemed, set to take a back seat as the Training and Development Agency faced the challenge of its vastly extended remit. Furlong (2005, p. 132), reflecting on the new positioning of initial training, posited that: "the end of the era is to be regretted".

## 4.3  Inspection: The Standards and Quality Assurance Agenda

A second major change experienced by universities involved in training teachers was with regard to quality assurance mechanisms. The inspection of the quality of training provision, previously managed by an "informed connoisseurship" model was replaced in the mid 1990s by the new "technicist" model.[31] The first "new style" inspection of all primary teacher training was undertaken in 1995–1996; and although there was little to indicate undue weakness, a further round of inspection of all primary training was undertaken in 1996–1998 with a focus on the teaching of reading/numeracy. These first inspections were a considerable cultural shock to the community, and judgements were fiercely contested. A system of grading (very good to non-compliant) was used to measure standards, low grades incurred real penalties in terms of reduced allocation of training places, and even worse non-compliance incurred penalties on all institutional training programmes rather than just the non-compliant course. The new inspection regime heralded an era of surveillance and control that professed greater transparency of criteria,[32] and had the potential to lead to greater inter-inspector reliability of assessment, and greater consistency of judgements across contexts. Lack of confidence was, however, expressed in the piloting, evaluation and rigour of the evidence-base for the (around 160) criteria statements and the validity and reliability of the process.[33] Indeed, in a survey of providers of teacher training, nearly 80% expressed a lack of

---

[30]McNamara, Brundrett, and Webb (2008).

[31]Campbell and Husbands (2000).

[32]Framework for Assessment of Quality and Standards.

[33]Gilroy and Wilcox (1997), Sinkinson and Jones (2001).

confidence in the validity and reliability of the process.[34] When a third round of primary training inspections was announced in 1998, again with a focus on English and mathematics, such was the perceived burden of the high-stakes inspection process that the government's own parliamentary education subcommittee, in an attempt to reign in the excesses of the inspections, recommended the immediate introduction of a minimum 4-year cycle with differentiated light-touch provision.[35] The latter, with a focus on management and quality assurance, was introduced in 2002,[36] although it was not felt by providers to be markedly less onerous.[37] As a result of, or some might say despite, the oppressive inspection regime, in 2006–2007 just under half of primary training inspected in universities and colleges was deemed to be "outstanding" in management and quality assurance.[38]

By contrast to the inspection of traditional university and college training courses, the rapidly expanding employment-based routes into teaching were, until 2009–2010, subject only to "survey" inspections, which did not carry the same punitive consequences. The 2003–2006 survey of employment-based routes concluded that the management of training had improved considerably over the period but that there was still room for further improvement. Primary training was judged to be consistently better than secondary training, but was found in the majority of cases not to offer good enough subject training.[39] Although inspection grades have systematically and transparently been used for a decade to inform the allocation of training places in universities and colleges, ideological drivers can be deduced from the fact that there has been a persistent tolerance of repeatedly less than favourable inspection reports on alternative employment-based training routes which, rather than being cut, have been allowed to grow despite their reported deficiencies.[40]

The combined weight of inspection of universities and assessment of trainee standards cited above indicates a significant increase in quality measures. However, very few providers thought that the overall quality of their courses had improved,[41] and generally felt the whole assessment portfolio was a "bureaucratic nightmare". As noted earlier, rather than appraise the quality of the breadth of training provision, inspection was strategically planned to drive change by focusing the primary sector on particular educational enterprises and nationally defined goals.[42] Further, an

---

[34]Graham and Nabb (1999).

[35]House of Commons (1999).

[36]Ofsted (2002).

[37]Universities' Council for the Education of Teachers (2007).

[38]Ofsted (2007a).

[39]Half of the lessons observed during 2005/06 displayed strengths but 17% still had significant weaknesses (Ofsted, 2007b).

[40]Smith and Hodson (2010) describe students' limited conceptions of theory on such routes.

[41]Mahony and Hextall (2000).

[42]The round of inspections in 1998–2002, for example, was planned to coincide with the introduction of the National Strategies (numeracy and literacy) and focused, unsurprisingly, on English and mathematics; a survey inspection in September 2007 focused on early reading and phonics,

annual monitoring exercise was introduced in 2008–2009 in which all teacher training organisations were required to submit to the Training and Development Agency a report on the self-evaluation of each programme they delivered, identifying its strengths and weaknesses with a particular focus on improvement planning. A relative cost-benefit analysis of this enterprise has yet to be conducted, as has its overall impact on improvement in the quality of training.

Thus we note an improvement in standards in relation to external criteria, but at what cost is yet unclear, as are the key drivers. We have also argued that rather than generating "consistent and reliable" assessment practices, inconsistent messaging is conveyed in terms of the way in which different types of knowledge and assessment regimes are prioritised and training routes differently privileged.

## 4.3.1  Partnership: The Rhetoric and Reality of School-Based Training

Many university and colleges voluntarily made considerable strides in the 1980s and 1990s towards developing formal training links with schools.[43] As "school-based training" evolved into "partnership"; however, a review of contemporary literature characterised it as a "problematic concept"[44] and a "slippery and imprecise word".[45] Bratman (1992) theorised partnership as a shared cooperative activity that has three key factors: mutual responsiveness, commitment to joint activity and commitment to mutual support. Partnership was soon, thanks to the Teacher Training Agency, defined very differently and far more precisely.

Once partnership with schools was mandated in legislation within teacher education[46] many teacher educators challenged what they saw as the government's simplistic depiction of the trainee developing practical skills in schools and subject knowledge in the university.[47] It seemed changes had reinforced "hierarchical relations" and the "demarcation of practice in schools from educational theory".[48] The substantive content of training courses had changed little as a result of the

---

following the publication of a review of the teaching of reading (Rose, 2006). More recently, an annual on-line survey of newly qualified teachers has been used strategically to support inspection evidence on the quality of training and police the introduction of new policy initiatives.

[43] This has been encouraged by the Council for Accreditation of Teachers and much earlier endorsements of school-based training (McNair, 1944). The Oxford Internship Scheme (Benton, 1990) is one such model.

[44] Brown, McNally, and Stronach (1993).

[45] Crozier, Menter, and Pollard (1990).

[46] Department for Education Circular 14/93 (1993)

[47] Edwards (1995).

[48] Dunne, Lock, and Soares (1996), Taylor (2000, p. 55) speculated that "specification of who does what, is less important than the existence of shared values based as far as possible on a common knowledge base".

introduction of the new arrangements.[49] They identified a continuum in partnership models that extended from the university-led to the entirely school-led provision; they argued that neither extreme was truly partnership. They characterised ideal typical models of initial teacher education partnerships as either "complementary" or "collaborative". The former were a "pragmatic response to limited resources" in which the partners had separate roles and responsibilities; in the latter partners were deemed to have different, but equally legitimate, bodies of knowledge. Furlong *et al.* reported that in reality the most common model of partnership throughout the 1990s was still largely university-led, with contributions from school-based colleagues. The introduction of entirely school-centred training and employment-based routes in the mid 1990s, however, undermined the notion of partnership even further, as in the case of these routes collaboration with a university was not a requirement. This was notwithstanding evidence in the literature that primary schools in particular harboured little desire to establish more entirely school-centred primary initial teacher education programmes.[50]

The increase in the regulation and inspection of partnership arrangements in the late 1990s took its toll on the system and when combined with a rapid increase in training numbers, as a result of an impending teacher supply crisis in 2000, disaster seemed inevitable. A major national intervention was devised to address the emergent predicament. The high profile, and extensively resourced initiative,[51] saw partnership, now in its third era, commodified and marketed to schools. The aim was to increase the capacity of the system to provide school placements, enhance the quality of school-based training, and to improve collaboration between partners and other stakeholders in the teacher training, enterprise.[52] Abandoned when the immediate danger was thought to have been adverted, it was far from clear how much had systematically been learnt about the ideological, political and philosophical mechanisms of partnership; and how much it had simply been reduced to a technical-rationalist task.

Despite substantial international interest[53] England and Wales still remain the only countries where "partnership has become institutionalised at a national level as a core principle of provision".[54] A review of partnership comparing England to other parts of the United Kingdom, suggested that the "detachment of some forms of entry away from the university sector perhaps reflects the relatively low standing of teaching within the English culture".[55] A key strength of the university partners it has been argued, "is theorising the epistemological and pedagogical underpinnings

---

[49]Furlong et al. (2000).

[50]Williams and Soares (2002).

[51]National Partnership Project, Teacher Development Agency (2001–2005).

[52]Furlong, Campbell, Howson, Lewis, and McNamara (2006, p. 41).

[53]Brisard, Menter, and Smith (2005).

[54]Furlong et al. (2006, p. 33).

[55]Brisard et al. (2005, p. 50).

of training", so in their absence "(the) complexity and contestability of professional knowledge is no longer seen to be at the heart of what partnership is about;
professional knowledge becomes simplified... it is essentially about contemporary
practice in school".[56]

## 4.4   The School Context: The Rise and Fall of the Strategies

To further contextualise the portrayal of the trainee teacher that will unfold in this
chapter, we shall outline a very brief account of the educational scene in England.
In any such account of the current educational milieu, the government appears as a
more prominent player than at any time in previous history. In general, the fundamental and most significant reason, putting aside for the moment any secondary
agendas, has been the drive to improve educational standards. Since the beginning of the 1990s, educational standards have become a high profile national issue.
Mathematics became a particular focus of attention as indications emerged of the
ostensibly poor mathematical performance of English pupils viewed in a comparative international context.[57] Data was read as a reflection upon the standard of
mathematics teaching and teachers, an interpretation disputed by some.[58] "Official"
accounts commonly attributed the relatively poor performance of English youth to
prevailing "progressive" primary pedagogies of the 1970s and early 1980s in which
the teacher's role was depicted as that of facilitator administering and supervising
pupils working through individualised learning programmes. Too much emphasis
was retrospectively deemed to have been placed on individualised and differentiated work and too little on whole class teaching.[59] A different historic reading, taken
at the time, attributed the emergence of individualised schemes in the 1970s to the
severe shortage of appropriately qualified mathematics teachers. The introduction of
"teacher-proof" programmes was seen as a pragmatic response, and potentially an
effective solution, to the lack of mathematical expertise of, in particular, the primary
school workforce.[60]

An immediate consequence of the prominence given to the educational standards agenda has been over a decade of recurrent statutory change to curriculum
and assessment regulations and the implementation of unprecedented large-scale
reform programmes. The first major reform began at the end of the 1980s with the
introduction of the National Curriculum, a catalogue of prescribed subject content
to be taught to children between the ages of 5 and 16. There was a perception, at the
time of its introduction, that the Curriculum would compel teachers to change not
only subject content but certain classroom management and teaching strategies as

---

[56]Furlong et al. (2006, p. 41).
[57]E.g. Harris, Keys, and Fernandes (1997).
[58]Brown (1999).
[59]Reynolds and Farrell (1996).
[60]Banks (1971).

well; including that of increasing the amount of time spent on whole class teaching. A few years after the Curriculum was "bedded in", the consensus appeared to be that there had been actually only "modest changes" in primary classroom practice as a result of its introduction: most teachers had simply "bolted on" new content and assessment procedures to their existing practice.[61]

An ambitious programme of National Tests[62] was established to assess the attainment of pupils at the ages of 7, 11 and 14.[63] Individual school performance results for pupils leaving primary education at aged 11 were published annually. Many teachers read these "league tables", which were initially unmediated by any reference to local conditions or "value-added" measures, as inequitable representations of performance, particularly of those schools servicing areas of severe socio-economically deprivation. The test results and league tables were later to fuel the government's (and to a degree the public's) thirst for the monitoring of performance and accountability. A profoundly significant consequence of the National Testing programme was that it afforded the opportunity to introduce target setting. Education was to become the model for a paradigm shift that introduced an audit culture of league tables and targets, already an international phenomenon,[64] to a number of other British public services, such as medicine and the policing.

For the new Labour Government, elected in 1997, this was a panacea. "Education, education, education" was its priority. Dissatisfied by the lack of change in teacher practices over the previous decade, and lack of improvement in pupil performance brought about by the National Curriculum, it embarked upon the most radical programme of reform the education system had ever seen. The literacy and numeracy projects, which had been introduced by the previous government as 5-year pilots, were abandoned after only 2 years and launched across England as the flagships of the reform agenda: National Literacy Strategy (in 1998) and the National Numeracy Strategy (in 1999).[65] The resultant combination of curriculum and pedagogic prescription, testing, target setting and inspection in the primary phase was unprecedented in the United Kingdom and likened by Margaret Brown (1999, pp. 14–15) to that of a Maoist regime. An annotated bibliography of evidence that supposedly underpinned the Numeracy Strategy was compiled based on a "careful study of the world's knowledge bases about mathematics education and mathematics teaching" (DfEE, 1999b, p. 2). Interestingly, the bibliography stretches the notion of evidence to include "more polemical and think pieces" (DfEE, 1999b, p. 2) as well as research-based evidence, the assumption being that teachers are grounding their "effective behaviours" in evidence that is a "fusion in practice" of

---

[61] Galton (1995).

[62] Initially known as SATs (Standard Assessment Tasks).

[63] Pupils aged 16, the statutory school leaving age, continued to be assessed through the traditional external examination system.

[64] Power (1994).

[65] Department for Education and Employment (1999a). The National Literacy Strategy had been introduced the year before.

the knowledge bases and literature (Reynolds 1998). Notwithstanding that the status, and the selectivity, of the said evidence remains controversial (Brown, Askew, Baker, Denvir & Millett, 1998) as does its ideological grounding (Noss, 1997).

Alongside the curriculum reform was the most extensive programme of continuing professional development ever attempted in the country. The whole package estimated to have cost £400 million.[66] It involved a "national plan and infrastructure... detailed teaching programmes... 300 consultants ... and part-funding of hundreds of leading mathematics teachers".[67] The stakes were intensified further by targets set for the national performance of primary children at age 11.[68] These national targets were translated into targets for each Local Education Authority, from thence to individual schools and, as is now increasingly common, individual children. Although the Strategies, unlike the National Curriculum, were not statutory, most elements of them appeared in virtually all primary classrooms; such was the pressure to achieve targets and the degree of apprehension regarding school inspection. Albeit, the evaluation team found it "difficult to draw conclusions about the effect of the Strategies on pupil learning" given the "considerable disparity across teachers in subject knowledge, pedagogic skill and the understanding of the Strategies" but warned of a "culture of dependence".[69] The National Numeracy Strategy was introduced a year later than the Literacy Strategy and – if yet another change was welcome in schools, which it was not – was considerably more popular. A feel good factor was noted generally and teachers were reported to be very positive; interestingly, this was true "across all age/experience/expertise/teaching year groups".[70]

Having now developed a sense of the rationale for and initial effects of the Numeracy Strategy, let us now briefly explore its substance. Fully compatible with the mathematics National Curriculum, it was designed to improve pupil performance in mathematics by enhancing schools' management of numeracy (for example, understanding of progression, systematic planning, target setting, monitoring and evaluation) and the pedagogic practice of teachers (for example, effective classroom management, appropriately high expectations and direct instruction). School mathematics coordinators at the time became pivotal in embedding the Strategy, sustaining teacher collegiality and auditing accountability.[71] The Strategy framework, organised in curricular areas of number, algebra, shape and space and data handling, contained yearly teaching programmes of key lesson objectives and medium and long-term planning grids, which included time slots for assessment and exemplar materials for each year group. In addition to what was seen by some as

---

[66] Mansell and Ward (2003).

[67] Earl et al. (2003).

[68] Seventy-five percent of children were to achieve "level 4 or above" in the National Tests for mathematics by the summer of 2002 and 80% for English.

[69] Earl et al. (2003, pp. 3–8).

[70] McNamara and Corbin (2001).

[71] Corbin, McNamara, and Williams (2003).

a further narrowing of the mathematics curriculum content through its rebranding as numeracy[72] the Strategy advocated particular teaching structures and methods. These comprised a dedicated daily mathematics lesson, consisting of interactive oral work with an emphasis on mental calculation, direct teaching, group work with controlled differentiation and a plenary session for reflection. The use of clear learning objectives, a focus on vocabulary and numerous resources such as empty number lines, place value cards, and 100 squares were central to the pedagogic approach.

Despite a high profile failure to meet the 2002 national targets for mathematical performance at the end of primary schooling, the Strategies survived – and apparently grew from strength to strength. However, stung by criticisms of a narrowing of the curriculum there was a move in 2004 to signal the importance of a broader-based primary curriculum.[73] In 2006 the renewed Primary National Strategy for literacy and numeracy[74] was published offering a greater focus upon the use of "assessment for learning" and incorporating fully the Every Child Matters principles and outcomes which had since 2004[75] driven the education agenda in England. There was a growing sense, however, that two decades of reform had delivered little change to the system in terms of curriculum development or pupil performance. Two major and very high profile reviews of primary education were commissioned: the first independently funded[76] and the second a government-funded curriculum review.[77]

The reports came to significantly different conclusions about the curriculum but both called for more autonomy for the profession in terms of curriculum development. Added to this, significant improvements in mathematics performance at the end of primary education continued to be elusive, eventually stalling uncomfortably. In July 2009, in the midst of the brouhaha of the publication of the primary reviews, the demise of the strategies was quietly announced. The recommendations of the official review of the curriculum were adopted for implementation in 2011 but in the event, despite changes having been made in anticipation in many primary schools, it was dropped from the legislative programme just weeks before the fall of the government in May 2010.

A much more extensive account could clearly be given of the rise and fall of the Strategies, and reforms to primary schooling in England more generally, but our aim in this section is principally to provide a backdrop against which to read the narrative more central to the focus of the book. That is, the impact of regulative government and its espoused ideology on education policy and practice; the function and nature

---

[72]Brown et al. (1998).

[73]Department for Education and Skills (2004).

[74]Department for Education and Skills (2006).

[75]In response to a high profile child protection case the Children Act 2004 (updated in the Children's Plan, 2007) provided the legal underpinning for Every Child Matters, a multi-agency approach to protect the well-being of children and young people from birth to age 19 and give them the support they need to: be healthy; stay safe; enjoy and achieve; make a positive contribution; and achieve economic well-being.

[76]The Cambridge Primary Review www.primaryreview.org.uk (Alexander, 2009)

[77]Rose (2009), http://www.dcsf.gov.uk/primarycurriculumreview/

of evidence in terms of warranting said policy making and informing practice; the framework within which school mathematics and its pedagogy is articulated and played out and, last but not least, against which our primary trainees and new teachers begin to understand and identify with as they are inducted into the profession. To which story we now return.

## 4.5   The Empirical Study

### 4.5.1   Introduction

We apologise to international readers who may by now be quite exhausted by the interminable listing of the English policy apparatus. As authors, we feel quite breathless detailing this overwhelming corpus of prescription and legislation. As we struggle to regain our own sense of agency and reality in writing this book, we can only emphasise that the account is concise. It is also time-dependent in that some changes have arisen since the data that we are about to present was collected. A fuller account would have been extraordinarily tedious and left insufficient space for other discussion. In this chapter so far, we have looked at the political, ideological and pragmatic pressures in England that have over the last 20 years imposed particular patterns on the experience of becoming a teacher. A picture of disparate, and at times overtly conflicting, discourses and agendas is apparent but the direction of travel overall clearly identifies it as a "training" rather than an "educational" process. Such outcomes are characteristically a potential hazard of government-led models and are indicative of a fragmentation of, and lack of clarity about, the principles, practices and philosophies underpinning initial training. Our main point is that for the trainee teachers we interviewed, this apparatus could not be ignored. The spectre of government policies formed the parameters of their professional reality. Such competing demands on trainee teachers can "create a role conflict in which they fail to achieve a sense of belonging and confirmation of teacher status",[78] and training is predicated on supposing these seemingly divergent demands can be reconciled.

In the remainder of this chapter we shall begin to discuss how trainees meet this challenge. In order to do this we shall draw upon empirical studies gathered from trainees on a 4-year undergraduate training course[79] at the Institute of Education, Manchester Metropolitan University in England. As noted earlier, this mode of training provides training for about 40% of primary teachers in England and trainees traditionally enter undergraduate courses at aged 18. Primary teachers in England are generalists, it will be remembered, and so trainees study all the National Curriculum "core subjects" (English, mathematics and science) and, to a lesser extent, the "non-core subjects" (history, geography, art, music, religious education, information and communication technology, physical education, design

---

[78]McNally et al. (1994, p. 229).
[79]Primary Bachelor of Education Degree (BEd).

and technology, while most recently modern foreign languages has been added to the primary curriculum). Each trainee, at the time of the study, was also required to choose one subject as a "specialist" subject to study at a greater depth. It will be remembered that trainees characteristically spend time on placement in local partner schools; in the first year 2 years this amounts to a light teaching load encompassing very short periods/part weeks and in the last 2 years the teaching practices are blocks of more prolonged periods.

The empirical studies upon which the theoretical frameworks presented in this book are based took place in two phases.[80] A total of 200 hours of interview data was collected from two sets of about thirty students, one set for each phase. The first phase focused upon examining the cognitive and affective elements of the understandings of mathematics and becoming a teacher that primary trainees brought with them onto the course and the nature of the transition that these conceptions underwent. The intention was to develop an empirically informed theoretical account of how school mathematics and its teaching were constructed by the "non-mathematics specialist" primary trainees. Complete data sets were collected from 20 trainees, five from each of the 4 years of training. The data gathered explored how the trainee teacher as learner negotiated a position within the complex school/university partnership and considered how the course could better enable them to critically engage in the transitional processes that embodied their professional induction and its positioning within the broader contexts of National Curriculum and school mathematics policy. The second phase addressed transition and was based on a cohort of 10 primary trainee teachers who were tracked through from their 4th and final year of training into their first teaching post where they embarked upon their professional induction as a new teacher. During this phase, our embryonic teachers were substantially (in their final year of training) or wholly (in the case of the induction year) based in school. Accordingly, reflection was centred on the social practices that prescribe primary school mathematics and its teaching and the impact that initial training and government policy initiatives had on primary mathematics and the construction of the identities of beginning teachers. The study relating to this second phase was concerned with the question of how conceptions of mathematics and government reform agendas relating to the teaching of mathematics, became manifest in university and school practices. It also considered how they contributed to the new teachers' socialisation into the profession and to their evolving perceptions of their professional self. In these respects, the study was undertaken at a key transitional moment not only for primary mathematics, with the introduction of the National Numeracy Strategy, but also for teacher education, with regulation moving to its most extreme and the inspection regime at its most febrile.

The emphasis adopted throughout both phases of the study was on exploring the phenomenological experience of the trainee and new teacher. It also examined

---

[80]The studies were funded by the UK Economic and Social Research Council: "Primary student teacher understanding of mathematics and its teaching" (1999) and "The transition from student to teacher of mathematics" (2001). See footnote 2 in Chapter 1 for more details.

the interpretative and generative hermeneutic process through which they organised their experiential world. In the remainder of this chapter then, we see our task to be to present the narrative accounts of how mathematics was understood as a discursive field, and how beginning teachers negotiated their position as they attempted to function at the intersection of the many discursive domains. We undertake this analysis using trainees' or new teachers' accounts of their experiences of being and becoming teachers. Methodologically, the data collection process throughout the study as a whole took the form of a collaborative inquiry in which the researcher facilitated the generation of narrative accounts of individuals' evolving knowledge of mathematics together with their developing understanding of self-as-teacher in the context of their past, present and future lives.

The truth of what we say ourselves as researchers in analysing this data might perhaps be seen as comprising moments of suspended doubt[81] in pursuing our broader project. As indicated in Chapter 2, we saw this approach displaying many features of a psychoanalytic process and, as such, strategies for assessing "truth" were seen as potentially being applicable. As suggested, we needed to be cautious in accepting everything that our interviewees said at face value. Teachers' assertions of identity are shaped by what they feel they need to be. MacLure (1993) sees identity as an argument that needs to be made rather than someone's identity being something that needs to be discovered. Convery (1999) similarly suggests a need to attend to where the identity claims are pointing. Specifically, we sought to examine the narrative functioning of the various utterances as part of a more holistic account against which interviewees understood their emerging conceptions of practice. We do not, however, wish to over claim our investment in any developmental staging. In this we are guided by Ricoeur (1984) who sees the passing of time as a function of the narratives we tell about it. Time is shaped by these narratives, and the texture of time and associated concepts like progress, improvement and development can have their character or existence changed by a mere shift of narrative paradigm.

We weave that narrative with warp and weft. The former is constituted from the duel themes of this book: the social construction of "primary school mathematics" and of "new teachers". We explore how, in the dynamic relationship between university and school partnership, the beginning teachers narrate their developing understanding of primary mathematics and its teaching and how they articulate the gradual socialisation and formal induction of self into teacherhood. The latter tells the story of their navigating a journey from school pupil to new teacher; shaped by narrative accounts of their progress. We frame this journey in three key transitions. The first, from school pupil to university student during which new trainees discard a considerable amount of "baggage": negative attitudes towards mathematics, its teaching and teachers. We report the trainees' conceptions of mathematics and how they perceived the course supporting them in relocating mathematics and repositioning themselves with respect to mathematics. In the second phase, students move

---

[81] Schütz (1962).

to young professionals in the middle years of training. As noted earlier, the course involves a certain amount of "front-loading" of university sessions, particularly subject application, and "back-loading" of school placements. It is during these middle years that trainees begin to divide their time more equally between school and university partners and begin to experience the clash of cultures more acutely. The third and final transition is the, at times perilous, move from the final year of training to becoming a full time classroom teacher. This transition necessitates the assuming of diverse identities and the playing of many different roles: learner, pedagogue, assessor, university representative, school employee, carer.[82] Negotiating this final shift in their metamorphosis to professional requires the trainee to navigate the plethora of government and local regulations to be found at the border crossing. They are required to demonstrate, to their tutor's satisfaction, that they have definitive grasp of the numerous standards; concluded their subject audits; qualified on final teaching practice; passed the three skills tests; and completed their Career Entry and Development Profile; together with local end-of-course assessment requirements. For trainees, the euphoria of successfully prevailing to achieve qualified teacher status is inevitably short-lived as the now new teacher is (re)positioned again as novice. In yet another addition to the plethora of barriers that our trainees are required to surmount *en route* to their ultimate ambition of being a classroom teacher, all new teachers since 1999 have been required to complete an induction period of 1-year duration. The statutory induction arrangements provide new teachers with a bridge from initial training to establishing themselves in their chosen profession. The government-funded induction package entitles them to a reduced timetable, mentoring, professional development support, and an assessment of performance against a set of induction standards.

### 4.5.2  Becoming a Primary Teacher: The Construction of School Mathematics

Many of the stories the trainees had to tell about their mathematical experiences were rooted not so much in a cognitive account of the mathematics but in an affective account of the experience. "It was horrific" (Yr. 2). "Hate hate hate" (Yr. 1). When feelings about mathematics were explored intense emotions were often exposed. The trainees' experiences of mathematics at school had been overwhelmingly negative; overall approximately 80% of the study cohort disliked mathematics or found it a struggle. In quite a number of accounts a retrospective "it was alright until. . ." dimension was apparent; moments when things first started going wrong were often remembered as "algebra", "fractions" or "secondary school". A major hurdle in the first transition, from school pupil to university student, was facing the "mathematical demons". The majority of study participants were relatively recent school leavers, it

---

[82]Morgan (1997).

has to be remembered, so the experiences they reported from their secondary school days at least were still very vivid.

The one trainee in year 1 who claimed to enjoy mathematics linked the pleasure to extrinsic reward: "I like mucking about with figures; I got enjoyment when I got it right" (Yr. 1). But even she felt compelled not to voice such positive feelings when she met her peers in the first mathematics session: "I had my first maths core lecture yesterday, they were all going 'its horrible, it's boring' – I wanted to say 'it's not that bad'" (Yr. 1). Another trainee, who declared, "I'm not frightened by maths" (Yr. 2), both denied and acknowledged its potential to intimidate.

Into yet another retrospective account a "victory narrative" can be read: "It scares me. I just hated it. My greatest achievement was doing maths" (Yr. 1). If victory there was, however, it was for one trainee not attributable to herself: "I just worked really hard at the end and I was really surprised to get a [grade] B, I was predicted a [grade] C... it was probably a fluke" (Yr. 3). Most trainees, however, in recalling encounters with mathematics remembered just the struggle: "even though I got a decent grade at GCSE [16+ mathematics examination] I found it very, very hard... I thought I can't do these in the exam, so I just sat at home and worked and worked" (Yr. 2).

Often present in the trainees' narratives was the spectre of "the beast of a teacher [who] used to scare us all" (Yr. 1). One positively traumatic account of ritualised humiliation enacted in the classroom was related:

> We had to stand up if you didn't get it against the clock and if you didn't get it in 30 seconds you had to stand on a chair and if you didn't get it again you had to stand on the table and if you didn't get it again you had a slap across the legs and made you late home for tea... It's stayed with me all of these years even now. I don't think I will ever forget it (Yr. 4).

Where attributes of mathematics teachers were valorised it was for characteristics such as "approachability", "patience" and "humour". They were identified as teachers who "really knew us" and used to "explain things time and time again": "He was funny and he made maths fun and he was kind and took time with us" (Yr. 1).

A significant number of stories about mathematical experiences were nuanced with reflexive accounts of how doing mathematics made them feel about themselves. In regard to this, feelings of "failure" were common: "I just remember not liking it, being weak, and being a bit of a failure at maths" (Yr. 2). Often trainees' accounts of the construction of "self" by mathematics were read against the construction of "others". Such "others" were always brighter and faster: "I have to work and work and work at it – there's other people who naturally it would just click for" (Yr. 3); "I never enjoyed maths... you're struggling and the girl next to you is whizzing away" (Yr. 3). It seems clear from such accounts that the trainees are revealing some anxiety in relation to their immediate task of training to teach mathematics; this might be seen as a processing of the past to allow the trainee to move on.

A commonly held perception of trainees upon entering the course that did, however, militate against them moving forward was a belief that mathematical ability was innate, as illustrated in the comments below:

> I think you have to have a very mathematical, practical brain. I'm a very arty person. ... If you sat there and learnt and learnt and learnt I still don't think you could change the way you are. I don't think you can suddenly become a mathematical sort of person (Yr. 1).

> Some people are good at maths and they just know how to do it (Yr. 3).

> Some people can't get their heads round it (Yr. 2).

Trainees' perceptions of their own success at mathematics often, but not always, correlated positively with these experiences. Overt measures of esteem from peers and tutors did not, however, always translate into self-confidence even in the 4th year of the course: "Everyone around me was saying I was good at maths but I actually wasn't and I think I knew that really" (Yr. 4). Such shifts in trainees' perceptions about mathematics and their ability to be successful provided a catalyst for change and offered the potential for empowerment.

Alongside feelings of intimidation and failure, a sense of bafflement about the purpose of school mathematics was also present in many accounts. The relation to their everyday life of much of the mathematics they studied as a school pupil was far from clear. As one trainee observed: "It's just lots of numbers that didn't make sense. ... You didn't know what you were doing you just knew if you got it right" (Yr. 3). This reinforced notions that the trainees saw mathematics being externally defined such that they, as individuals, could affix no meaning to it. No clearer was the reasoning behind some of the complex algorithms that they were required to execute in order to arrive at the much-valued solutions to their mathematical problem. One trainee recalled, "It was just, oh, here's some quadratic equation or Pythagoras Theorem and you just have to learn it and just do the sums and there wasn't any connection" (Yr. 4).

The teaching model most commonly recalled by trainees from their school days, and subsequently drawn upon, was that of transmission, getting the idea across:

> I think you have to go back to the basics to get it across to people (Yr. 1).

> When you're a teacher you have to be able to explain it for somebody else to understand it (Yr. 1).

> I think you have got to be very clear in your explanations (Yr. 2).

Upon embarking on the course, however, a gradual but significant transformation occurred for many trainees, in that, although memories of school mathematics remained as "ghosts from the past", their potency gradually faded in response to the softer image of mathematics they were proffered in the university course. Second year trainees were no longer reluctant to admit that mathematics wasn't "that bad", indeed a number became very positively disposed towards it: "Since I came to (university) I just so much enjoy maths. I thought that's cool I can do that" (Yr. 2). Trainees in the 3rd and 4th years of the course were markedly less negative overall and the transformation was often quite vividly recalled even years later as can be seen from the reminisces below of four fourth year trainees about their first encounters with mathematics at college:

> I actually thought: hey, this is maths I'm coming out and I've actually learnt something and I feel quite upbeat about it (Yr. 4).

> It was just an amazing feeling to think well it is accessible to me and I can do it (Yr. 4).

> We saw maths on the timetable none of us was particularly happy, we all felt quite threatened by it, but we were made to feel at ease (Yr. 4).

> College sessions made me feel good about myself, it made me feel able to do these maths... loads of people, mature trainees as well, dreaded the maths lesson (Yr. 4).

Analysing the triggers of the change process trainees observed:

> In lessons at college we would sit down and we would all put forward different ways of working it out that enlightened us all (Yr. 4).

> We were given fun activities to do (Yr. 4).

> We've un-picked a lot of things on this course and it's made me think that maths isn't just scary numbers (Yr. 2).

> It's totally different to anything I've ever experienced at school... they say that's great, you're doing fine you have nothing to worry about you're all right with maths (Yr. 4).

A feature common to much of the school mathematics reported above was an implicit privileging of the "answer" over the mathematical processes involved, given that "right answers" were often the only tangible product of, and rationale for, engaging in school mathematics. One particular way in which university sessions did seek to redefine mathematics was to increase the importance vested in mathematical processes. It is perhaps not surprising that trainees, who had been schooled into the privileging of answers over mathematical processes, commonly inverted the binary to read as "getting the right answer doesn't matter":

> It was enjoyable because there wasn't the impact that you had to get everything dead right (Yr. 3).

> It doesn't matter if you don't get the answer as long as you can understand the process and eventually you will come to the answer (Yr. 3).

> Maths should not necessarily be about getting things right it's about the way you work out maths (Yr. 4).

Whilst most trainees reacted positively to this new idea, one reflected sadly upon missing "the ticks on the page" and the "that's good, well done!" (Yr. 2).

There were other ways in which trainees' conceptualisations and representations of mathematics changed over time. Conceptions of mathematics began to change too. Right at the beginning of the first year, their conceptions of mathematics started, and sometimes finished, with "number". They described it variously as: "Working with figures", "Solving problems", "Numbers and how they work?", "Numbers, fractions, equations, algebra". The accounts were often contextualised in a version of "everyday life" which ranged from "bus fares" through "cooking" and "shopping" to "finance". Trainees captured this view succinctly:

I think it's about everyday life really, you've got to do loads of adding up, especially at university with finances (Yr. 4).

used all the time... well I do 'cause I work in a pub so I've got to add up the numbers and know the answers (Yr. 4).

making sense of the world around you in a different way that's pretty concrete that you can measure and apply it to different contexts (Yr. 4).

By the later phases of data collection, the National Numeracy Strategy was embedded, and featured centrally in preparation for teaching. Language and processes particular to its way of seeing and generating school mathematics in the classroom began to filter into trainees' articulations. So there was a slight but observable increase in the sophistication of responses and this was largely as a result of the frequency of National Curriculum language such as "shape and space" beginning to permeate accounts along with processes such as "exploring" and "investigating". So accounts began to take on flavours such as:

Making sense of everything around you – number, space and shape (Yr. 4).

Well, it's to use logic and progression (Yr. 4).

Maths to be about logical thinking, making decisions. I think it's something that you apply all through your life (Yr. 4).

After the first two years of training, it will be remembered, the students spent less time in university learning mathematics and more time in schools teaching it. In this transition a fresh determination to achieve mastery and control of mathematics was evident through a shift to a "can-do" mind-set:

I go away and do two hours work to try and build up my skills and weave them round it... I've got a different state of mind about maths now than I did before... it was all quite complicated, very intense, difficult, hard (Yr. 2).

My past is in my brain so I try to forget about my past, about the bad experiences, and I'm trying to start again with maths in the way in which the lecturers have put it across to me (Yr. 2).

There was even a physical relocation of mathematics in the minds of many trainees, a shifting from what we have described as a Mathematics 2 to Mathematics 1. Mathematics was no longer seen to be embedded in the pages of a book but was a social practice. Trainees' previous experiences of mathematics had been associated most commonly with a "transmission" or a "facilitation" view of teaching where the teacher either stood at the front of the class "telling" whilst the pupils listened passively and then worked through pages of exercises in a text book, or, alternatively, sat at her/his desk facilitating pupils in pursuing individualised work programmes. One trainee observed, "Before maths was on the board and now it's actually working with blocks and things like that and as a prospective teacher I do find that more interesting and enjoyable" (Yr. 2). Another reflected, "I see it as practical now because they are not just sat down working through pages and pages" (Yr. 4).

The transition to more school-based middle years of training did have its challenges; however, for example, the theory/practice dichotomy surfaced on the horizon. "Subject application", as the trainees referred to it, was to a degree a casualty of the structural arrangements of the course at the time, which, as noted earlier, front-loaded subject study at the university. This meant that students completed most of the mathematics sessions in university before they embarked upon the three major school experience placements (in years 3 and 4). A number of trainees felt let down by what they perceived as a lack of support at the time when it was most needed, although the 4th year trainee below was beginning to understand the theory/practice double-bind:

> For the last two years I've not had any maths input at all (Yr. 3).

> I've been let down this year because we've only had maths from September to January and then it finished. . . I'm here to learn I'm here to be a teacher and if I'm not good at maths I need help and they are just dropping it (Yr. 2).

> It would have been useful to look at different types of assessment in core studies. . . but last year I wouldn't have understood as much about assessment (Yr. 4).

Another concern about the structure of the course in the middle years of training was the effect that fragmented school practices could have on the scheduling of mathematics lessons that trainees taught. One trainee recalled a practice in which because of the timetabling she taught the topic "time" at a rate of just one lesson a week:

> I do find it frustrating to come into a classroom and do 'o' clock' one day and then have a whole week in between and then the next week 'it's half past' but I can't do half past straight away [because they have forgotten o' clock from the week before] (Yr. 4).

By far the most prevalent theme relating to the transition from learner of mathematics to student teacher of mathematics, however, was the interface between school and university cultures and norms. A number of dilemmas were apparent between the ideal world of college and the only too real world of the classroom, in which external demands impacted on more personal understandings of how mathematics might be. The most prevalent and explicit centred upon pedagogy and the disparate nature of the favoured methodology for teaching. In university, "college maths", as the trainees often referred to it, was characterised and experienced as *practical, discovery-oriented* and *child-centred*. In school, mathematics was practised as *scheme-focused, transmission-oriented* and *teacher-centred*. Trainees on the whole adopted a "when in Rome do as the Romans" approach to resolving the conflict. One trainee was concerned about the physical and mental demands of teaching "college maths"; for another more experienced trainee it was its appropriateness to context:

> I don't think I could teach the same way as I was teaching today for one thing it's too intensive (Yr. 1).

> [College] is very much a child-centred approach. . . and it's OK in theory but once you get into a classroom and you have got 30 children. . . . It's hard saying that you are not going to teach them a method. . . if I tell them to explore they may not get a basic grounding (Yr. 3).

A second tension lay in the content of "college maths". One trainee had formed the impression that it lacked credibility in school and another trainee reflected upon the apparent mismatch:

> College maths is helpful but the teachers sometimes think it looks like playing in some way or it's not proper maths (Yr. 3).

> College seems to like us to do a lot of practical activities looking at the National Curriculum and thinking up something whereas school, obviously they work from a scheme so it's practical with worksheets... but it's different to college (Yr. 2).

Under the circumstances trainees faced with the pressures of actually having to teach mathematics, not surprisingly, often felt ill-equipped to face the ordeal. The seemingly alternative accounts of mathematics provided by school and university were seen as being mismatched, with the immediacy of school demands revealing apparent shortcomings in the university input. In particular, they sought more direct preparation on a topic or of a pedagogic skill:

> Sometimes you think, if they are not going to tell you how are you going to learn? (Yr. 2)

> Nobody will say to you how do you measure this table, I only learnt that by being in school (Yr. 2).

We've not done anything on time to teach the children very little subject application (Yr. 4).

> They don't tell you right, this is what you should be doing and this is how you should be teaching it (Yr. 3).

Language was a hurdle in many local schools where high percentages of the pupils had English as an additional language. Differentiation, and sometimes lack of it, was also a matter of particular concern as the trainees below observe:

> It scares me a little bit actually to think that I've got to plan for all these different ranges of ability. Differentiation has never really been mentioned at all in maths. We have never actually said you have this range of abilities and you are going to have to do a completely different activity with them (Yr. 1).

> The teacher doesn't tend to differentiate, they're all on the same Heinemann book. And what she does do is there's another book the Peake book, and she uses that like an extension (Yr. 2).

One first-year trainee with remarkable prescience, however, was already beginning to suspect that her fantasy of being given simple recipes would never be fulfilled:

> I sometimes feel that we don't do as much on the topics we cover at primary school... but I don't know whether that's to come or whether that's for us to work out from what we have been taught (Yr. 1).

### 4.5.3  Becoming a Primary Teacher: Mathematical Identities

Very soon after embarking upon their studies a marked shift was evident in the trainees' developing sense of selves as prospective teachers of mathematics. We have discussed the redemption of school mathematics: the transformation that occurred in trainees' disposition towards it and the reconciliation they enacted; its reconstruction as no longer "scary" and its relocation in lived activity rather than the pages of a book. As they (re)positioned themselves in these new discourses about who they now were and how they related to school mathematics and their own school mathematics teachers they storied themselves as teachers with children of their own. In the process their emergent and evolving identities as teachers of mathematics slowly began to take shape. The identity work was clearly articulated by one trainee who observed:

> It doesn't scare me as much as it did last time because I am seeing it from a different perspective as the teacher. I have the control to make this lesson as good or as bad as it can be (Yr. 1).

But the trainees, who were often taught to teach by being positioned as a pupil, were not slow to remark upon the paradox inherent in the methodology college adopted to engineer this identity shift:

> Sometimes they will treat us like children put us in the child's place teaching us and giving feedback... but that is completely different because we are adults and they are children I really don't think on their level I thought that was the whole point of being here (Yr. 2).

> In all our maths lessons we are always the pupils. You don't do a lot in college about being the teacher. The only time we are the teacher is when we are presenting our ideas from the front (Yr. 2).

There was nevertheless some indication that they began to reposition themselves, for example, to consider the learner and where s/he was coming from:

> I started by putting the easy questions because if you start with the harder ones they will just give up straight away. I started through till the subtraction at the end so that I knew that the higher group would be able to get on to that quicker than the others (Yr. 3).

> Trying to understand where the children are coming from and where they got their ideas to start with (Yr. 3).

> If you're trying to teach somebody else and you can't tell them the best way, you've got to help them find it for themselves and then build on that, so you've got a responsibility to guide and help, not work it out for yourself and dictate how it's done (Yr. 4).

> (This lesson) allowed me to see what type of level they were up to, independent of the scheme, if they are just working with themselves with numbers, and it also allowed me to see how they developed in their thinking, how they were working things out here (Yr. 4).

If a meta-narrative can be identified in the trainees' accounts of the changes they underwent in their transition from learners to teachers, it is that their experience as pupils informed, most often in a negative sense, their model for teaching. A commonly occurring theme was a belief in the value of empathy in the mathematics teachers' armoury: "I think I can sympathise more with them because I found it so difficult" (Yr. 1). As we illustrate below such observations often later feed into trainees' accounts of their own professionalism. Many trainees expressed concern to correct the perceived failures of their own mathematics teachers:

> I've realised that I can use my experiences to make sure that I don't teach maths in that way (Yr. 3).

> I feel I would have gained more by physical hands-on experience... which is what I try to do with the children (Yr. 4).

> None could approach this teacher at all. She wasn't people friendly... I think you have got to be approachable for a start (Yr. 4).

> I couldn't make the connections... They have to be able to feel there's a connection between what they are doing and later life, how maths can be used in other subjects (Yr. 3).

When reminiscences about trainees' experiences as learners of mathematics at the beginning of their first interview were compared to later responses regarding their beliefs and attitudes towards the teaching of mathematics, it appeared that the former had a pronounced effect upon their espoused teacher identity:

> Five pupils in our group were really good at maths and the teaching was mainly geared at these people... [and later] my main concern is putting the work at the right level for the children (Yr. 2).

> I didn't enjoy it... [and later] I wouldn't want them to not enjoy a lesson... kids won't learn if it's not fun (Yr. 1).

> She would just sit at her projector and write it all down. We would just sit there it was pretty boring... [and later] I won't just sit behind my desk and say 'this is the question, give me an answer, work it out' (Yr. 1).

> I can never understand why it was done in that way and what it was for.... When I teach maths I have to make sure, number one, that I understand completely what I am doing in order to put it over to the children to get them to understand why they are doing it first and then what they are doing (Yr. 3).

> No discussion, it's not related to anything, you just thought what's the point in this?... You need to be able to put maths into a way that is relevant to children, so that they are involved in it (Yr. 2).

Whilst associations could be tracked from trainees' experiences of learning mathematics as pupils to their nascent espoused theories of teaching, it appeared that in the middle years of training when undergoing the transition from being more university-based to more school-based, although the aspirations may have remained unchanged, in practice, in a significant number of cases, the ideal model was modified by the pragmatics of classroom concerns. That is, once in front of a class, the preferred "child-centred" discovery model of teaching, espoused by many trainees upon embarking on the course, reverted to a modified version of the transmission model, so often reviled by them as a consequence of their own experiences as a pupil at school.

The interview data indicated, however, that for most trainees on school placement the development of their sense of self and understanding of their role as a teacher of mathematics became completely subsumed by wider and immediate pedagogic concerns. In particular, classroom management was the highest priority for all trainees:

> I found it hard to keep the children on task throughout the lesson they were very excitable due to Mrs H not being here. I've had problems with classroom management whenever Mrs H isn't teaching. . . they just don't want to listen to me (Yr. 2).

Whilst on school placement, class teachers and school supervision tutors provided trainees with support and guidance in their understanding of their roles as mathematics teachers. However, there was little in our findings to indicate that discussion with either course tutors or class teachers helped to shift trainees' all consuming preoccupation with pedagogic issues to focus more on being and becoming a teacher of mathematics:

> My tutor didn't really contribute to maths things, everything was just general (Yr. 4).

> I've never had any specific maths feedback during school experience she was more bothered about how I fit the classroom and how I respond to children (Yr. 4).

> As for my tutor I don't think he's seen me teach a maths lesson and if he had I'm sure he wouldn't talk about it explicitly (Yr. 4).

> She is interested in things like differentiation and integrated days. I am not sure I want to get into what integrated days are but that's her agenda (Yr. 4).

> It was quite good the maths he did watch – but then he wanted to talk more on discussional skills (Yr. 3).

> I got a little bit of explicit guidance on teaching a theme. . . [but] it was more organisational (Yr. 4).

One trainee reported feeling reassured by the fact that her school experience tutor also struggled with mathematics:

> My school supervisor didn't like maths when he was in school he shared maths with another teacher. . . he never taught any maths. In a funny way it gave me confidence. . . because he was sharing his insecurities with me that made me feel better. . . He more gave me advice on management and organisation of class, how to motivate children. . . he never actually specified anything in maths (Yr. 3).

Class teachers were, however, valued for the opportunities they provided to observe the teaching of mathematics lessons, if not the potential the observation afforded for the subsequent articulation and discussion of practice: "I find that I've learnt mainly from going into the classroom from observing other teachers who were practising maths" (Yr. 4).

In the absence of other discursive framing of mathematics teaching, the National Numeracy Strategy filled the vacuum in its specification of mathematics pedagogy and its framing of the cultural norms in which mathematics was performed and assessed. Although considered by some to present a reductive account of mathematics teaching (Brown et al., 1998; Noss, 1998), given the trainees' conceptualisation of this as primarily utilitarian and focused upon number, it is perhaps not surprising that they reported little dissonance with much of its ideology:

> Everyone's comfortable with the National Numeracy Strategy... I've certainly found the file the government produced very useful but I've never really used the school policy (Yr. 4).

> You have to do what they tell you to do... you have to be doing this at exactly this time for this amount of minutes but... I've been trained to do it that way, perhaps I would teach it that way anyway (NQT).

Although some were clearly less enthusiastic about the structures it presented for them to work within:

> I don't think we've got a lot of say now in the maths because of this highly structured numeracy hour (Yr. 4).

> the numeracy hour, it's so prescriptive as to what you have to do, when you have to do it and how long you do it for, so it shapes the whole numeracy hour of every day of every week of the school year (NQT).

> I thought OK, for the next three weeks, I would do as she asks but I know that it's not right (Yr. 4).

It was evident that the pedagogy, which framed the Strategy, formed a useful vehicle through which trainees and new teachers could discuss their practices, assess their effectiveness in the performance of their role and articulate their sense of self-as-mathematics teacher. Through it, they were both socialised into primary school mathematics and inducted into the local cultural norms and practices of their schools. The Strategy's discursive patterning thinly veiled their references to key aspects of mathematics classroom practice: "It's sort of ingrained into my head". The description of the mathematics lesson below illustrates how the pedagogic language of the Strategy is used to conceptualise and articulate aspects of mathematics teaching and learning.

> Well the mental starter I demonstrated to begin with and then the children came up and it was interactive – they actually had to move the numbers in pairs. The main part of the lesson started off with questioning, introducing the ideas of the data, demonstrating a frequency chart and then each child had a white board and they had to write their favourite subject on the white board. Then I collected the information so this was all whole class with them on the carpet – collected the information put it onto a class frequency chart ... so I demonstrated really – then the children went into the four groups and did it themselves with me working between the groups and stopping them now and again just to clarify any corrections arising or problems. And then it was the whole class plenary when the children present – the children themselves then presented their findings to the rest of the groups (Yr. 4).

One particularly notable feature of trainees' and new teachers' accounts of their classroom practice was the overt reliance on representational media to the extent that they appeared to completely overlook the underlying mathematics. As two new teachers revealed:

> I've made everything we've got; place value dominoes, number bingo... number bands, number cards, number bond loops (NQT).

> I think it's impossible to teach place value without those arrow cards, they're superb because ... the children can understand it so much easier when you can say – Look it is a ten 'cause the nought is hiding under the unit and you can explode it and they know that that's ... the

unit is sitting on top of the nought and it really helps them understand the nought's the place
holder. . . I decided to use them and just to make the activity more independent. . . it means
they're manipulating the numbers and they're then choosing the numbers they're using and
reading them (NQT).

Another trainee highlighted the importance of kinaesthetic engagement in classroom
mathematics:

You can't have a washing line where I am so I use the children to be number lines. . . . It's
important, that physical act of involvement in the whole class situation. . . we have little egg
men on a little board – in a groove (NQT).

The representational models were not only difficult to manage but at times got in the
way and practical considerations such as the availability of space were important:

We first started off doing tens and units and we did a number line we did it on the floor
actually because it was quite a long number line (Yr. 1).

They had cubes and they had to find combinations of 10 with the cubes but it was far too
easy because they were just working them out in their heads they didn't need the cubes and
they didn't want to use them so they were more of a hindrance really (Yr. 3).

The transition from student teacher to teacher was a considerable ordeal for our
trainees who had the misfortune of undertaking training at the height of the changes
wrought by the new curriculum and inspection regime. They were often left feeling
somewhat aggrieved as regulations regarding assessment were continually revised:

Audits[83] came in our second year, we only had two years to do them. . . having originally
been told the audits were instead of doing a test . . . then the numeracy tests come along
(Yr. 4).

The audits achieved a higher level of gravitas in years when government inspections took place, which at the time were every other year. Inspections in which the
university, placement school and trainees' own practices as teachers were measured
against the whole gamut of externally defined standards were a matter of great concern to all. Tutors, trainees and placement schools and class teachers alike were
vulnerable and had to be extra vigilant:

They would really say that the audits would have to be up to date for (the inspections) and
they (inspectors) are going to come in and . . . might be asking questions (Yr. 4).

It feels as if [tutors] are checking up on you all the time, they're not leaving it to your own
professionalism to be able to cope or not cope. . . but the university have to cover their own
backs don't they, with (the inspectors) coming (Yr. 4).

Particular venom was directed at the most recent ordeal, the Numeracy Skills
Test, as outlined at the beginning of the chapter. As a rite of passage, the test
proved highly effective: trainees experienced fear, powerlessness and humiliation:
"Nervous, stressed, sick" (Yr. 4); "I was vomiting before it" (Yr. 4).

Most read it first and foremost in terms of its (re) positioning of other previously
existing symbols of passage. A few trainees regarded it as a legitimisation of their

[83] Students were required to keep audits as part of the self-assessment mechanisms.

mathematical subject knowledge and thereby their transition into professional teaching: "A good idea to say who can do maths to a standard" (Yr. 4). Most frequently, however, trainees considered that the test denigrated their other mathematics credentials such as formal end of school examinations qualifications, self-audit and internal examinations. A few trainees regarded it as a necessary, and potentially effective, gatekeeper:

> I think they're a good idea because without sort of being bitchy or derogatory I do think there are a lot of people on our course who ... shall we say even in a year 6 class wouldn't have the mathematical knowledge to teach them (Yr. 4).

Many trainees, however, were deeply cynical about the whole enterprise. One Machiavellian reading portrayed the test as designed to incite public anxiety about standards whilst rhetorically demonstrating government concern and simultaneously presenting an opportunity for them to act effectively to resolve the crisis, thereby increasing public esteem:

> Ooh, you know, we're really panicking, we're going to have a general election in a couple of years time and people are worried about the state of our schools... We'd better throw some maths tests in... I'm very cynical... they'll stand up there and they'll say 'Ooh our schools are rubbish'... and then they worry because everyone thinks that schools are rubbish and it's because they've told them that... it's stupid, so yeah, these tests are just for popularity at the moment I think, definitely. I think it's very crafty to put them in now, very vote-winning (Yr. 4).

Once having undergone their third and final transition, that is securing a job, our study cohort now in their first appointment as new teachers, reported markedly different experiences of regulatory governance. This suggested that at local education authority/individual school level there was a loosening of the very tight governmental grip experienced by university and college teacher training institutions. One notable disparity related to the varied experience of the local implementation of the statutory induction arrangements. As noted above, in 1999, a probationary period of 1 year was (re)introduced in England and during this period, new teachers were entitled to a 10% reduction in contact teaching hours, mentoring support from a member of the school staff, access to a professional development programme, assessments each term involving target setting and monitoring by an external tutor.

The new teachers from our study were employed in seven different local education authorities and the extent to which the latter became actively involved in supporting the induction process varied. Provision in five was considered to be good or better by new teachers such as the one who reported her local authority to have:

> Very, very good induction courses and it also goes towards your Masters' Degree if you want to take advantage, they seem particularly keen because I've been talking to friends from X and Y and they hardly get any input from their Local Education Authorities.

For another new teacher the story was very different:

> I've had one afternoon non-contact time so far (8 weeks into the year), I've been to an induction meeting, I've applied for courses and I've been told that they are full so I've not been allocated a single course...they know full well how many NQTs there are so why they don't allocate enough places is beyond me.

Not only were the quality, coverage and availability of professional development programmes varied but so was the extent to which trainees received their entitlement to the 10% funded timetable release. Practices at individual schools clearly varied:

> Can't fault it at all and when I go to these meetings all the other NQTs are sitting there and the only time they get off is for courses and I'm like – oh I get every Wednesday afternoon off and they're like 'WHAT!'

One experience particularly valued by new teachers who encountered it was observing other teachers, sometimes in other schools. New teachers would request visits to support particular professional needs identified in their induction targets: "I'm going to another school to see a music lesson 'cause that was one of my targets you know we are really working together as a team to achieve my targets".

Mentoring arrangements, where they worked well, were excellent: "Because there are four new teachers in my school, we have a group meeting every week and then we have personal meetings so just myself and the mentor every other week". Where the arrangements didn't work well mentoring amounted to "informal contact with my tutor if I want to speak to her, no set time you know, five minutes a week". In another school in the same Local Authority induction was overtaken by other more pressing matters, like getting ready for an inspection, "The Head and I we've had one meeting about my career entry profile and she just said – everything's fine". This new teacher was, however, getting steady support from the teacher in the classroom next door who taught the same age group. Physical and curricular proximity was not, however, always seen as crucial when it came to choice of mentor. Indeed in one large school roles and systems seemed not to be at all transparent to the new teacher involved:

> I've been observed by the Local Education Authority [and] my Deputy Head as well, he's my induction tutor so that's very good... whereas my mentor is another member of staff. I don't know why she is my mentor really... with it being a big school and the mentor's in the other side of the school I don't see her... I don't really know... what I'm actually supposed to do with them to be honest... I don't know if I'm meant to talk to them if I've got a problem... I tend to talk to the year leader.

In terms of identity work, perhaps not surprisingly, the transition to new teachers upon commencing their first appointment represented the most marked shift. Commonly it was represented as a newly found agency in which "ownership" was a key factor. In their accounts the normalising tendencies that were so apparent in the university training were felt less strongly now as they could "be themselves", "do their own thing" and responsibility could be gratifying too:

> It's my own classroom, I put up the displays completely.

> The high points were in September, the initial feeling of, I've made it, I've got my own class, and it's all the excitement that goes with it.

> It feels good to have the responsibility of having 30 children.

There was, however, a flip-side to this initial euphoria: at times the "responsibility" for teaching and learning was awesome, particularly for the new teacher in the local authority where children's future schooling was dependent upon an external examination at the age of eleven:

> When you are stood in front of 33 faces all gazing up at you it's the strangest thing you've got just a duty to the children and that massive sense of responsibility.

> I'm also feeling the kind of pressure of this time next year, when the children will do the 11-plus [exam].

> I think now I feel totally responsible whereas before I was given guidelines on what I would be teaching. It feels heavy that it's all down to you. You feel really that the responsibility is on your shoulders.

The "autonomy", alluded to above, was a third key issue that new teachers tussled with, and one new teacher believed: "Right from the start it's all my ideas"; others were more guarded, and certainly autonomy did not always extend to the curriculum. At least two new teachers were able to reconcile external demands with personal aspirations:

> The actual set up of the lesson is restricted to sort of government requirements and school requirements and Local Education Authority requirements and (inspection) requirements and everyone else but you can still fit your own style in that.

> You have more autonomy... you can be more spontaneous, you can react to the needs of the children better because you're working within your own framework, even though you've got to follow the demands of the... literacy hour and the numeracy hour, you can say – right that's not worked, we'll stop that, we'll do something else.

Even when focused upon their teaching and curriculum responsibilities "managing behaviour" still took precedence:

> The classroom management overrides everything that you're doing in the day.

> I've had children swearing at me when you've told them off they'd say – I don't f** like you, I f** hate this school and one child picked his coat up and walked out of school. That's happened a couple of times with one specific child – it's a shame 'cause they've got problems at home.

> The Head teacher actually said 'if you need to stop a lesson to practise being quiet for example, then do it now get them sorted out in the first month it doesn't matter if one or two lessons go astray'.

Another key issue was the strain of "maintaining energy" for an extensive period and pacing activity levels was often noted: "It's not for 7 weeks it's for a year... you need to spread yourself thinner when you are full time". The cumulative effect of week upon week of such responsibility had not been anticipated: "I've felt a high level of enthusiasm throughout my first year. In the first couple of weeks you have everything so well planned you seem to have time to waste... then all of a sudden..." This issue was of course accentuated by excessive teacher workloads, reported by the workforce as a whole, which could be gruelling:

> I'm working from 7.30 to 6 o' clock at night and then leave the school and get home and still have things to do for the next day... It's not the job. It's the fact that it leaves me no room to do anything else that I want to do.

Above and beyond the actual teaching and learning, there were a "multiplicity of tasks" and responsibilities, that trainees had largely been protected from on school placement, that all took their toll: "It's not the actual teaching that's a problem... there's just so many other things, other responsibilities"; "It's juggling 300 different things at once". The sheer number of matters to attend to was for many new teachers "nerve-wracking" and led them to develop a set of initial coping strategies which they implemented as "short-term" solutions in response to the immediate demands of a situation.

In particular, new teachers were less prepared for the far-reaching array of responsibilities that went with their duty of care inside and outside the classroom not only developing and maintaining relationships with colleagues and children, but managing parents and families:

> I didn't like it all because the way that that man looked at me in the eyes... it felt a bit strange you know angry as well and annoyed because I thought... but it's part of handling parents isn't it?

> I told the child protection officer in the school that I was concerned about one of the children in my class.

Or, indeed coping with the continuing waves of emotional demands and traumas that inevitably punctured daily life inside the classroom. Critical incidents are more on a social level:

> In two terms I've had 3 births and 3 deaths in the class. I had a child who lost a father before Christmas and then the mother gave birth just after Christmas... then just after Christmas one of my little girls her sister in year 1 had a brain tumour and died within 4 weeks of diagnosis. I visited the child in hospital and was invited to go to the house on the day of the funeral to say farewell... and the same weekend a boy in my class his Dad died of meningitis... I felt traumatised but I've managed to cope.

## 4.6  Conclusion

> We are forever telling stories about ourselves. In telling these stories to others, we may ... be said to perform straightforward narrative actions. In saying that we also tell them to ourselves, however, we are enclosing one story within another ... On this view, the self is a telling ...Additionally we are forever telling stories about others ... we narrate others just as we narrate ourselves ... consequently, telling "others" about "ourselves" is doubly narrative. Often stories we tell about ourselves are life historical or autobiographical; we locate them in the past. For example, we might say, 'Until I was fifteen, I was proud of my father' or 'I had a totally miserable childhood.' These histories are present tellings. The same may be said of the histories we attribute to others. We change many aspects of these histories of self and others as we change, for better or worse, the implied or stated questions to which they are answers. Personal development may be characterised as change in the questions it is urgent or essential to answer. As a project in personal development, personal analysis changes the leading questions that one addresses to the tale of one's life and the lives of important others (Schafer, quoted by Felman, 1987, pp. 99–100).

There are clearly difficulties involved in the methodology we adopted, not least being our attempt to understand how concerns were mediated by the presentation of supposed formative experiences. To find ways of pinpointing how students viewed mathematics on their entry to the course, which was for most a transition from being a learner of mathematics as a pupil to studying mathematics as a prospective teacher. Clearly there was some anxiety relating to this but it is more difficult to establish how the reportage of a 20 year old, anxious about teaching mathematics now, recounts the experiences that she believed triggered this anxiety. Unconscious forces are at work and will suppress a fuller picture. Although it may frustrate those among our readership seeking a longitudinal analysis, we feel unable to placate their need for a more progressive story. Yes, a lot of our students were saying that mathematics caused them concern. But our quest is not to provide the truth of this. Rather, our concern is to draw attention to the frameworks through which the trainees look at things and what that says about their approach to such problems. We are dealing with psychic, not material, reality here. However, we need to emphasise once again that they were responding to an interview, not real life as it were, and we are once again conscious of the potential disjuncture between lived time and its narratives.

School mathematics is a function of its social construction and of the discourses and structures that permeate that formation. In this study, socialisation into teaching was examined in terms of trainees' and new teachers' perceptual understanding of the task they faced against a structural account of what they were required to achieve. For the purposes of our analytical frame, we considered the process of socialisation into teaching as being closely aligned to the attempt to resolve these alternative accounts. The illusion that they could arrive at a resolution appeared to be a crucial component in the trainee's and new teacher's essential belief in self as part of a social project. It was through this that their identity and sense of community was defined. We address this in greater detail in the next two chapters. Suffice it to say now that trainees' and new teachers' conceptions of mathematics and being a professional were shaped by their engagement in the social project and their perception of how they lived up to the expectations of the National Numeracy Strategy, inspections etc.

In this present study, we argue that the instruments of curriculum reform such as the Strategy have also become part of mathematics itself – exemplified admirably in the long description of the mathematics lesson given by the trainee above. In virtually all the schools in which the trainees and new teachers taught, the Strategy, as a regulatory regime, had to a large degree taken over the function of the school mathematics policy. It was, however, locally mediated, by particular contextual factors such as the need for a supplementary scheme to assist individuals such as speakers of English as an additional language. This new regime also had a pronounced effect upon the alignment of mathematics with other National Curriculum subjects: defining a hierarchy that extended from numeracy/literacy in pole position, through the other "core" subject (science) and finally to non-core subjects (such as history and geography). There are also ample grounds to suggest that the social quest to improve mathematics teaching in schools has become embodied within the Strategy and the supposed improvement trajectory it offers and the purpose it confers on teachers' participation in the social project.

The shaping of mathematics, now strongly governed by the Strategy, was commonly perceived by the study cohort to be "a helpful framework for developing their professional expertise in an area in which they have often experienced some anxiety".[84] Nonetheless, for some it did augur a loss of professional agency on the part of schools and teachers Responses to the situation that the Strategy presented differed; some appeared naturally acquiescent and for some, reconciliation obviously came at some price. The former, perhaps, was reminiscent of Lacey's (1977) "internalised adjustment" and the latter "strategic compliance" (see Chapter 3), yet the compliance thus activated could be read as supporting the common good, namely the belief in the Strategy as a social project to be taught such that all pupils could engage the improvement trajectory as fully as possible.

[84]Basit (2003a, p. 61).

# Chapter 5
# Theorising Teacher Identity

## 5.1 Analytical Strategies

### 5.1.1 Processing Time

We have concluded our account of the 5-year process through which trainees become fully accredited, the 4 years of their training course and their first year as a teacher in school. Yet as we have indicated, we feel uncomfortable about drawing out a dominant story, beyond the sketches that we have drawn, as if a modal experience is more important than individual accounts. However, our attempts to pinpoint transitions for individuals in a graphic way were not very successful. As we have reached this stage of the book perhaps it is pertinent to spend a little time reflecting on our evolution in terms of our own understandings, as the researchers, of how we have sought to theorise our data. In creating an account of transition in the trainees' understanding of their future professional task we attempted to introduce Ricoeur's work on time and narrative, which we felt could provide an interesting and useful theoretical frame.[1] Time and our activities within it are a function of the stories we tell about it. But those stories are a function of our sense of temporal existence and how we experience life unfolding, and the objects that populate them move in and out of significance and change their compositions. This hermeneutic approach appeared to be a natural development from the theoretical analysis we brought to the first study,[2] as described in Chapter 4. A key point of entry was Ricoeur's idea of a temporality that defies phenomenology except at the level of narrative. For example, the process of history cannot be fully captured in the stories about it. We cannot agree on the existence of key characters, places or events, let alone the relationships between them. In teacher education we may *mythologise*[3] certain expressions or points of reference which contribute to socially constructed *phenomenologies* which serve as anchorages or frameworks for given communities.

---

[1] Ricoeur (1984), (1985), (1987).
[2] Brown et al. (1999).
[3] Barthes (1972), Gabriel and Žižek (2009).

So viewed, official languages become an imposed form of anchorage that taints the space people see themselves working in. Trainee progression is always conditioned by the discourses that surround it. There is not a singular story. "Progression", if it is such, can be discerned from a multitude of perspectives that are not necessarily commensurate. As researchers, there is difficulty in deciding which of these discourses to take seriously in attempting to pinpoint progression. Progression, improvement, development and transition are all ideologically tainted notions. Insofar as research points to policy implications, there is a need to establish how actors might position themselves differently as a result of research findings and which lever they might apply.

In tackling the problematics of depicting time we sought to follow Ricoeur's (1984) notion of *mimesis*, the imitation of action, which we have explored elsewhere.[4] How do we reify the passing of time into an explanation of it? We might, for example, see the trainee's early attempts at integration into course demands as involving reference back to the familiar pre-understandings they had of educational terminology (such as "teaching" or "learning") now again being confronted. Thus teaching and learning would be understood from the point of view of a child learning mathematics in school which then gets superimposed on initial attempts to grapple with issues of teaching and learning within a college of education. Later, they would enter what Ricoeur calls the realm of poetic composition. This could be seen as comprising the initial attempts at working with a new language in an as yet unknown situation. Trainees have to take chances with speaking in particular ways. Later, by means of this poetic refiguring of the pre-understood order, the novice teacher finally reaches the end of the training process. Yet their language usage is still prior to its routinisation in a place of work, post-college. We conjecture that trainees have a fantasy of how it will be when they become a teacher; a fantasy that is subsumed without trace after the transition has taken place. The imagery we have here is akin to Wittgenstein's anecdote about trying to untie a knot – you face a knot but when you untangle it you cannot recall where the knot was in what is now a straight piece of string.

The linguistic instability present here resists longitudinal analysis. Usage of terms does not have fixed meaning. For example, how does an expression such as "*mathematical investigation*" get introduced into the vocabulary of a student who, on entering college, has never experienced one? The meaning and usage of such expressions change through time for the individual but not necessarily in the way that the person detects or monitors. Words start off as placeholders for a superficially conceived notion. Perhaps they then go through a phase of being a useful working definition. Later, however, the term may be discarded as it becomes too much of a cliché without functionality. But in this fluid existence, the use of the word collides with other words being used. They get combined in sentences and impact on each other's meaning: group-work/investigation, problem solving/algorithms, learning by heart/drill, maths/number, teaching/explaining. At any stage, meanings result

---

[4]Brown and Roberts (2000).

from the signifier and signified being jarred into a fixed relation in a common sense construction that is currently being lived. Yet, in Ricoeur's model the introduction of any new word activates strains and stresses throughout the whole sentence and results in the meaning of all words being challenged in some sense.

Within our study, the basic intention was to develop an account of how students understood their own transition during their time on the course and how this connected with their own school experience and their perceptions of their own future task as a teacher in school responsible for teaching mathematics as one subject within the overall primary curriculum. Elsewhere,[5] we have explored how practising teachers can revisit earlier reflective writing towards building an account of their own transition. In constructing the interview schedules our intention was to provide students with similar opportunities to account for how they saw their own transition. Questions were also selected with a view to making comparisons between students' accounts of their understanding of mathematics and its teaching. These were designed to enable comparisons between students within a year and with similar students in other years. We postulated some supposed indicators of progress *inter alia*: developing use of professional language; developing pragmatic articulation; explicit reference to transition, development.

However, the whole notion of transition became problematic. There was no transition except in what we, as researchers, construed as transition and we could introduce a host of alternative indicators to monitor or construct it. Trainees providing an account of their own transition did so according to shifting criteria. As researchers, it became unsustainable to support consistent criteria of our own. Students could create their mathematical histories in a variety of ways. Many, for example, discussed it in terms of a history of pain. Others saw it in terms of a pragmatic agenda. In later years, students often filtered it through a story of transition into confidence in teaching the subject. Histories are mapped out from different perspectives. As researchers we could also seek to construct our own accounts of student transition but in doing this we needed to ask which version we privileged and for what reasons. We felt constantly torn between trying to make sense of how students saw their own transitions and acknowledging that this did not need to be any sort of linear trajectory, whilst trying to impose our own account of the transition. We also had the supposed transition the college was trying to effect and further the ways in which the inspectors judged this to have happened. How could we mark time? Whose markers of time should we choose?

Another issue for trainees conceptualising their own long-term histories is that there is a certain difficulty in projecting yourself back to when you were fourteen, ten, seven, or whatever, and imagining yourself as someone equipped to evaluate lessons where you were a pupil. Initial conceptions of what it is to be a teacher seemed not to be about evaluating mathematical achievement but rather much more to do with fear and the avoidance of it, or of being fun, or not being boring, where success was confirmed by statements such as "I understood it then because he put it

---

[5]Brown and Jones (2001).

over in an interesting way" or "the penny dropped". As such, the criteria the "trainee as child" used in evaluating their teachers were considerably at variance with the system of evaluation used in the professional discourse. But the students universally seemed to believe this background gave them the necessary insight into the task of being a teacher. Many people believe themselves to be experts in education simply on the basis that they went to school. This sort of mentality also seemed prevalent to some extent in the trainees seeking to find ways of expressing how painful memories of their own schooling tells them how to be a better teacher than the ones they experienced. The training programme, in some respects, sustained this naivety by offering child-centred education as the dominant model.

Yet, in many interviews we encountered a great reluctance or inability to make sense of school experience. This was especially poignant in one example of a first year student. It seemed as if she had not undertaken any significant reflection on her own experience of schooling as a basis for her future role as teacher. There was no articulation of what a good teacher was, or of how she might fit such a mould. There was little sense of any progress, from the outset of the course, in her understanding of mathematics as a subject to be taught. She lacked an ability to narrate her experiences, in particular, the transcript of her first interview showed little capacity for storying her professional learning journey – little imagining of a "victory narrative". The interview was marked by absences, and extracts from our field notes of the time reveal our struggle with making sense of what was said:

> Jennifer sees mathematics as a mere list of topics such as numbers, fractions, equations and algebra. It is a subject that scares her unless it is in the context of puzzles. To do it, she feels, you need to 'think logically' but there is a difficulty for her in developing around that observation. At school, maths was something that was written on the board and copied by her where she felt no interest. She felt her teachers were impatient but acknowledges that she may feel this because she didn't like maths and was not confident with it. By implication she seemed to be acknowledging that her sense of teachers hurrying her was consequential to this anxiety. For her the greatest skill for a teacher is patience and the need to recognise that students sometimes struggle with the subject. As a teacher herself she felt she would be able to empathise with students who were struggling. She expressed pleasure when describing a teacher who she had observed recently spending time with pupils on a one to one basis. She hoped that she would pick up such good qualities herself and not the bad qualities such as 'not giving children equal opportunities'.

In summarising our encounter with Jennifer, we are trying to give some representation to the significant number of students who were extremely reticent during interviews. In listening to Jennifer, the overwhelming impression was that she felt unable or reluctant to speak. Many of her answers were restricted to short clipped sentences, where she was "not sure" or "did not know", as though it was an unfamiliar style of conversation with which she could not engage. For us this pen-portrait involves someone unable to articulate mathematics except for the affective experience, and who sees teaching as primarily concerned with being patient and attending to individual needs. There is no development of mathematics per se except lists of crude categories. The teacher's role is not developed in terms of learning objectives but in terms of being a sympathetic mentor. The transcript was made up primarily of questions, prompts and encouragement spoken by the interviewer faced with a largely silent interviewee. The interviewee does not recognise or relate to many of the categories introduced by the interviewer. Many of her answers are single words seemingly shielding her self from painful memories or the pain of the current experience in the interview itself.

We compared this interview with one that we held with a fourth year trainee who seemed to be struggling in a number of areas of the course. There was quite a difference right from the outset in that mathematics was conceived more broadly and understood as a forum for alternative understandings. The transition she had gone through was demonstrated in terms of an increased level of articulation whereby she employs the discourse of the teacher/question poser, narrates herself through resolutions to difficulties and calls on more examples to anchor her thoughts.

Nevertheless, in our hunt for examples of emerging professional language and its specialist vocabulary there were fairly poor pickings to be found in either of these two trainees' accounts. The first year student showed a distinct absence. The fourth year student, meanwhile, revealed culturally informed ways of accounting for teaching and learning but very much at a procedural level. Transition was explained in vague terms such as improved "confidence" or "familiarity". We felt obliged to lower our sights. We looked through the transcripts of a stronger fourth year, where there were many thing to suggest that she had participated in a teacher education course and where substantial transition had been effected. There were clear indications of more articulate procedural language with more sophisticated use of examples, more differentiation of professional skills yet our overriding feeling was that she was atypical in offering the specific things that we had set out to find in assessing the quality of student articulation.

So, in short, we felt that we could monitor increased sophistication. That is, we could detect styles of speech more akin to college/school styles of expression in discussing teaching, its practice and its purpose. We could, in a relatively limited sense, glean information from the students on how they articulated their own progression. Within this we could to some extent examine students' capacity to reflect, evaluate and plan in respect of a particular lesson or in more general terms. In doing this we could seek to learn a little about the culturally dominant form of articulating progress (for initial training students, for children) and how trainees get initiated into this (or how they transgress this). Yet we found ourselves largely unmoved by the narratives that we were able to extract.

This intermediate but ultimately disappointing attempt at analysis nevertheless located the platform from which our more final attempts emerged. Whilst remaining convinced by Ricoeur's account of time and narrative, there were practical difficulties involved in pinpointing narratives as if issued by an individual person. Who was choosing the narrative? Were the researchers choosing or was it the trainees themselves? Or was it another case of ventriloquism with the governmental discourses defining the evaluative strategies? How might one choose to delineate these narratives? How would one choose the agenda? It was this sort of difficulty that caused us to step back a little to view our material slightly differently. The premise that an individual could construct his or her own history was also flawed as the account would always depend upon the viewpoint and perspective adopted. Rather than a self-contained ego "that is a biological result of the interaction of psychical and social relations" that can be objectively described, the ego we envisage "depends on the subject's relations with others" and "is governed by fantasy, and modes of identification, and introjection".[6] We had, for example, considered comparing our own analyses of how the trainees spoke at different stages of the course with their own accounts of those histories. Needless to say, the stages implicit in each of the two systems were quite impossible to compare with each other, especially given the paucity of many interviews. The shifting subject positions hinted at in both their accounts and our accounts made a consistent story difficult to achieve. This loosened our assumption that narrative was tied to tangible events and projected us in to a world where we had to acknowledge that these accounts themselves had a very prominent role to play in structuring reality.

## 5.1.2 The Truth of Interviews

But how might the status of such interview material be assessed in pinpointing the activity of mathematics classrooms? The activity is essentially seen through the filter of trainees' conceptualisations together with some further anchorage in the form of our own researchers' records of the context within which those conceptualisations took place. Ricoeur has examined the question of interpretation and proof in relation to Freud's theories, based as they are on the analysis of patients talking in psychoanalytic sessions. We shall be guided by this approach in establishing the "truth" of our data within the empirical enquiry. Ricoeur (1981, pp. 247–273) identifies four criteria for "facts" in psychoanalysis.

First, for a phenomenon to enter the field of analysis it must be something capable of being said. Second, it must be said to another person, which builds into it an element of inter-subjectivity. That is, it is said in a way that the patient supposes the doctor wants to hear and could understand. Third, the psychoanalytic material points to "psychical reality" (in contrast to material reality). A patient is guided in current actions by some sincere belief based on past events. The veracity of that belief is irrelevant in treating the patient now: "what is psychologically relevant is what a subject makes of his fantasies" (ibid., p. 253). Fourth, it is necessary for the material to insert itself into some story or narrative. Ricoeur (1981, p. 253) asks:

> But what is it to remember? It is not just to recall isolated events, but to be capable of forming meaningful sequences and ordered connections. In short, it is to be able to constitute one's own existence in the form of a story where a memory as such is only a fragment of the story. It is the narrative structure of such stories that makes a case a case history.

As we shall see shortly, this notion of story has some resonance with Žižek's use of the word "fantasy". For Žižek, fantasy is not opposed to "reality", or escapist. Rather, it is the subjective frame through which the individual is able to gain access

---

[6]Grosz (1990, p. 31).

to reality. Indeed it structures what we call reality. This supports Ricoeur's assessment that time is not a function of phenomena perceived by everyone in the same way. The individual can only access reality through her capacity to tell stories about it. This, inevitably, reflexively builds something of her into the reality she portrays.

In our account we have trainee teachers putting their thoughts into words, which are then offered to an interviewer. Further, they attempt to compose these thoughts into a coherent narrative. The trainees are guided in this more by what they think rather than by any notion of external truth. In seeking to verify the interview material, we assume sincerity from the trainee. Nevertheless, we acknowledge that, as researchers conducting the interviews the interviewees may have seen us as university representatives, for whom a particular "truth" was appropriate. The trainees use language that contains "psychic" material rooted in the trainee's specific understanding of events. Nevertheless, our key instrument in examining the credibility of our data is in looking at the way in which the trainees' utterances during interviews build into coherent stories.

Stories are shaped by their supposed context. Psychoanalytic sessions may, for example, be predicated on "helping the subject to overcome the distortions that are the source of self-misunderstanding".[7] Whilst our own interviews might be viewed as forums in which sense making takes place, it is the university course and the subsequent induction into schools where this sense making is played out for real. As suggested, any such narrative creation by the trainee entails a complex mediation of diverse demands, and a diverse range of ways of making sense. Any analogy of success on the course with psychoanalytical cure, however, would be more suspect. Trainees may not necessarily become "better" through the training process. It may be enough to perform in a prescribed fashion. Freud's work was shaped around the notion of cure, an end point at which resolution is achieved. There are, however, alternative ways of conceptualising psychoanalysis. Such an alternative, more akin to the work of Lacan, might see psychoanalysis as the construction of a reflective/constructive narrative layer that feeds whilst growing alongside the life it seeks to portray. For example, the reflective writing component of some training courses may provide a forum for building such a narrative layer.

Having introduced our empirical material, where have we got to in our broader discussion? Equipped with some information provided by the data, we shall again pick up our conceptual frame within which there are two journeys being followed by trainee teachers. Nevertheless, whilst maintaining for our discussion the potential dichotomy of individual and social, our own commitment to this model is weak. We are encapsulating our discussion across what appear to be two incommensurable perspectives. The personal journey is governed by factors such as emotion, professional satisfaction and social worth. This journey contrasts with the official journey, which seeks to provide a well-defined route through a sequence of criteria referenced demands. Nevertheless, these journeys intersect in individual people who need to find ways of dealing with this apparent conflict. We have questioned how the

---

[7]Ricoeur (1981, p. 265).

trainee teachers see this as a task of reconciliation. But we have also raised the possibility that this reconciliation may be partial with conflicts being partitioned away from each other in the trainees' conceptions of their professional tasks. Similarly, the demands lack consistency, yet mingle in a composite administrative discourse that shields these inconsistencies.

For the trainee building a sense of self, there is inevitably a gap between how she "is" and how she "might be". A resolution cannot be achieved without compromise in which certain desires will be re-routed. The best that could be achieved would be identifications with elements of any supposed unified structure. There are multiple stories of what it is to be a teacher to be negotiated. These stories do not necessarily lend themselves to final resolution in relation to each other. Conceptions may be both idealistic and unachievable in themselves and impossible to reconcile with other conceptions. The teacher may nevertheless experience this apparent need for reconciliation as a demand being made of her. She may feel obliged to respond to this demand with some account of her success in achieving reconciliation, or otherwise feel that she would be doomed as a result of failure. We shall now seek to pinpoint how this conflict manifests itself in the trainee's professional evolution, through providing some examples. This prepares the ground for a more prolonged discussion in the next chapter of how such trainees produce mathematics.

But in which ways would this account be offered? As Convery (1999, p. 139) reminds us "identity is created rather than revealed through narrative".[8] Perhaps, teachers

> feel that they are deficient in relation to their stereotype of how teachers behave, and conceal this inadequacy... by reconstructing a morally prestigious self-description that they can use for public display. However, in so doing we reinforce an unrealistic stereotype and become complicit in our own alienation. Such reconstructions may act as short term therapy for the individual, whilst contributing to a collective repression, to which the only response is this ultimately disabling palliative of further self reconstruction (op cit, p. 142).

Thus, the failure to reconcile alternative demands is understood as a personal failure and hence understood as a need to change oneself yet again. But we are also digging up sensitive history and touching on the role of teachers in early identity formation. Memories are activated through conscious and unconscious dynamics.[9]

A growing body of psychoanalytic educational research, through its emphasis on concepts such as the unconscious, phantasy, affect and sexuality has worked "to unseat the authorial capabilities of expression to account exhaustively for qualities of experience, to view history as a causal process, and to separate reality from phantasy".[10] This impacts on current self as well as on reportage of past selves:

> One key difficulty is that school memories do not just invoke relations with authority but also repeat one's own childhood helplessness, dependency and desire to please. This strange combination means that reflecting on one's learning seems necessarily to pass through these

---

[8]cf. Gergen (1989).

[9]Felman (1987), Britzman and Pitt (1996), Pitt (1998), Lather (2000), Britzman (2003a), (2003b).

[10]Pitt and Britzman (2003, p. 760).

unbidden repetitions of love, hate, and ambivalence that make the transference, reminding us of the very earliest scenes of education, learning for love, even as we encounter ideas and selves that seem far removed in time.[11]

The narrative layer can also be seen as providing a mask for the supposed life behind it, a life with attendant drives that will always evade or resist full description within the narrative, and a life that cannot know much of itself until later and then still only partially.[12] There is a real difficulty in pinpointing the subject being encountered in the research process. Poststructuralist research methods have heightened

the problem of verisimilitude embedded in such foundational concepts in qualitative studies as voice, identity, agency, and experience while still expecting to offer some contingent observations about how individuals – including the researcher – make knowledge in and of the world. This methodology offers a new tension to educational studies by bringing to bear on participant narratives the very problem of narrating experience and by asking what conditions or structures the narrative impulse.[13]

In the previous chapter we provided our particular framing of the journey which began for our trainees as they recounted their school days as mathematics scholars and followed them through transitions from school to university training courses and from thence to attaining their first teaching appointment as both new teacher, and "supposed" mathematics authority. We considered how their professional identity shifted in response to the different positions they adopted, as trainee or new teacher, and the different roles they assumed (learner, teacher, assessor, assessed, carer, employee). The trainee/new teacher may have felt the need to attempt a reconciliation of these various roles in order to have some account of her achievement and satisfy her desire to narrate a coherent narrative of self.[14]

For example, mathematics was a subject that filled many trainees with horror in their own schooling. Yet they were soon compellingly persuaded that "maths isn't just scary numbers" and as the training course progressed such anxieties seemed less pervasive, almost to the point of disappearing once the trainee had qualified to teach. How had this been achieved? Despite a history of ambivalence towards the subject of mathematics, they stopped presenting themselves as mathematical failures. Rather, they told a story that left out the issues that they preferred not to confront. They told a story in which the qualities they saw themselves possessing had a positive role to play.

Let us consider this in relation to students' comments about the skills they feel they need in order to be a teacher of mathematics: "I like to give as much support as possible in maths because I found it hard, I try to give the tasks and we have different groups and I try to make sure each group has activities which are at their level. Because of my own experience" (Yr. 4). Another student comments: "The

---

[11] Ibid.

[12] Jagodzinski (1996), Pitt (1998), Felman (1987), Britzman (2003b).

[13] Pitt and Britzman (2003, p. 756).

[14] Harre (1989), Sokefeld (1999).

first one that springs to mind which I believe that I've got and which I think is very important particularly in maths, would be patience" (Yr. 4). A new teacher is more expansive:

> Well I'm sensitive towards children who might have difficulty with maths because I know how it might feel and I don't want children to not feel confident with maths... I use an encouraging and positive approach with them and... because I think if you're struggling in maths the last thing you want is your confidence being knocked in it, you want someone to use different strategies in trying to explain something to you and use a very positive, encouraging approach and not make the child feel quite – Oh they can't do maths never... you know, so, yeah, I think my own experience in maths has allowed me to use a certain approach with children (NQT).

Such happy resolutions to building the supposed skills required to teach mathematics (being "sensitive", "patient", "supportive") it seems, can provide effective masks to the continuing anxieties relating to the students' own mathematical abilities. The evidence in our interviews pointed to such anxieties being sidestepped rather than removed since they were still apparent in relation to more explicitly mathematical aspects of our enquiry, or to a lesser extent, in relation to the Numeracy Skills Tests.

There is also a need to be cautious in relation to how we are reading our data. Which truth are the interviewees telling? In an informal conversation with Tony, Rom Harre described how he often asked a lot of neutral questions in the first half an hour of any interview he was conducting since he felt the interviewees did not really relax until then. However, can we be sure that the state of being relaxed would produce a better truth? Lacan's position on this on this issue was legendary. He was removed from the main international group of psychoanalysts for holding short sessions where the client did not know when the session would end, instilling great urgency into everything they said. In his view the tension created by this uncertainty was more revealing. If we inspect the interview extract above we might suggest that there are various forms of concealment evident. Apart from the masking of mathematical anxiety that we have identified, there is an uneasy mix of moral and causal explanations. In responding to Harre's (1989) work, Convery (1999, p. 137) suggests that "individuals use metaphors of struggle to create an impression of an essential self". The "truth" of experience is processed through a story frame in which the individual portrays himself as struggling. Our interviewee might be seen as producing a "preferred identity"[15] that uses moral platitudes to endorse a style of operation that she has been obliged to choose as result of her mathematical shortcomings. But how might we access the truth beneath? Clearly such a notion of a singular truth is problematic given our analysis so far.

As we have said, identity is constructed rather than revealed through such narrative processes. There is not an innate truth to locate. Identity is about *identification* with particular modes of making sense. So we are left with the question of how interviews enable us to access alternative versions of reality and what those versions

---

[15]Convery, ibid.

enable us to say and do. The content of our interviews is clearly touching on some personal issues yet the media through which these matters are accessed precludes any sort of neutrality. In a psychoanalytic perspective, the unconscious is pressing upon the things the interviewees say. Yet there can be no definitive manifestation of this unconscious. Successive stories are tried out for size as the interviewees negotiate the trust they feel able to offer to others and their preparedness to accept a particular version themselves. These stories, according to Žižek (2001), provide the subjective fantasies through which reality is structured. He discusses this point in relation to the work of the Polish film director Krzysztof Kieslowski, who started out his career as a social documentary filmmaker, examining the lives of people in Poland in the turbulent 1980s. Yet in touching on the emotional lives of his subjects Kieslowski was uneasy about the portrayal of these lives on film. Insofar as genuine emotions were revealed, his work as a filmmaker became intrusive. Such emotions need to be recast and read as fictive material and in a sense be made unreal to work in the filmic medium. Kieslowski's resolution was to move into fiction films rather than documentaries as the former enabled him to get at a better truth of the emotional content of lives that he wished to explore. Žižek (2001, p. 75) argues that for an actor in Kieslowski's documentaries, "he does not immediately display his innermost stance; it is rather that, in a reflective attitude, he 'plays himself' by way of imitating what he perceives as his own ideal image". In the case of our study, the emotional content of personalities was only partially accessed in interviews and that element then further needed to be fitted within a discourse (story frame) appropriate to the research domain. We found ourselves obliged to retain the limitations of the documentary form. There is a necessary distancing of the story told from the life it seeks to capture. The reality of that life can only be mediated through a subjectively produced fantasy of it. And as Žižek (p. 73) further advises, "the only proper thing to do is to maintain a distance towards the intimate, idiosyncratic, fantasy domain – one can only circumscribe, hint at, these fragile elements that bear witness to a human personality." The personalities that we are seeking to learn about can only be read against certain backdrops where we as researchers and they themselves seek to understand how personalities and research perspectives and backdrops and discourses and external demands and aspirations, and more come out in the wash.

## 5.2 Technologies of the Self

In Chapter 2 we outlined some alternative hermeneutic models towards providing a framework through which we could examine how humans can relate to language. We suggested that language does not provide a neutral descriptor of reality but indeed the world and the people within it are created and understood through this discursive apparatus. Our understandings of "who we are" are a consequence of how we describe the world. Yet in contemporary models there remains much controversy as to how language intervenes. There has been particular dissonance between critically oriented philosophers like Habermas and those of a more radical or poststructuralist persuasion, such as Derrida and Foucault, that continues through their heirs to this day. Žižek (1989) commences his survey of contemporary philosophy according to how human beings construct themselves as subjects, with an account of a well-known debate between Habermas and Foucault.[16] In a series of papers culminating in a book originally published in 1985, Habermas (1987) took on his poststructuralist rivals. Whilst more supportive of Foucault than he was of many others, his critique of Foucault led to a response and a rather short lived debate prior to Foucault's death in 1984.

As seen earlier, Habermas appealed to a set of universal principles that with sufficient work could be rationally achieved through social consensus. He sought to cut through the hidden exercise of force resulting from supposed ideological distortion to reach "Ideal" communication.

> Rationalization here means extirpating those relations of force that are inconspicuously set in the very structures of communication and that prevent conscious settlement of conflicts, and consensual regulation of conflicts, by means of intrapsychic as well and interpersonal communicative barriers. Rationalization means overcoming such systematically distorted communication (Habermas, 1991, pp. 119–120).

As explained, it was Freud who influenced Habermas in his understanding of how language sometimes has an uneasy relationship with the reality it seeks to portray. As with one of Freud's clients, Habermas' self-reflecting human subject sought to make things better from some supposed deficit position by locating and eradicating linguistic distortion. By assuming a critical distance this distortion is confronted by the human subject who then acts to remove it.

Foucault (1997, p. 298) rejected the possibility of this critical distance since in his formulation the human subject was a consequence of discourse. I am a bearer of social relations. I am a product of the words that are available to describe me. He also rejected Habermas' supposed consensus centred on universal principles as being utopian.

> The idea that there could exist a state of communication that would allow games of truth to circulate freely, without any constraints seems utopian to me. This is precisely a failure to see that power relations are not something that is bad in itself that we have to break free of. I do not think a society can live without power relations, if by that one means the strategies by which individuals try to direct and control the conduct of others. The problem, then, is not to try to dissolve them in the utopia of completely transparent communication but to acquire the rules of law, the management techniques, and also the morality, the *ethos*, the practice of the self, that will allow us to play these games of power with as little domination as possible.

We cannot adjudicate alternative versions of events by making reference to a "correct" version, "no given form of rationality is actually reason".[17] Foucault abstained

---

[16]See for example Habermas (1987, pp. 238–293) and Foucault (1998, pp. 440–448).
[17]Foucault (1998, p. 448).

from dealing with texts through commentary and gave up all hermeneutics, no matter how deeply it may have penetrated below the surface of the text. In his book *Madness and civilisation*, for example, he no longer sought madness itself behind the discourse about madness. No universal rules were to be located beneath the surface of human activity. Each individual was to be responsible for his or her own self-mastery.[18] Foucault (1997, p. 177) sought "to study those forms of understanding which the subject creates about himself". He coined the term "technologies of the self" in which individuals strive to "transform themselves in order to attain a certain state of happiness, purity, wisdom, perfection or immortality" (p. 225). Individuals were seen as being *subject* to particular discursive practices. And it is this idea that has fuelled the contemporary domain of *subjectivity* that has been influential in so many quarters.[19] Teachers and children are subject to an array of discursive practices that shape their participation in life.

Both thinkers, however, resorted to some sort of aspiration to makes things better. For Habermas a better life was to be achieved through greater rationality and living according to some agreed moral code. Foucault (1997, p. 298) aimed at a better more balanced life through personally resolving individual need with external demand with "as little domination as possible".

Žižek questions the possibility of achieving an ideal and the attendant supposition that this can shape current practice an argument that he contends is taken further in the works of Althusser and Lacan,[20]. Žižek who published his first book in English in 1989 and has published more than thirty since, has been largely responsible for revitalising interest in Lacan.[21] The impact of such writers on the field of education was slow in its arrival. Prior to the nineties they barely featured in educational debate with a few notable and impressive exceptions.[22] However throughout the nineties,

---

[18]This history of Foucault was outlined by Habermas (1987, p. 241) and Žižek (1989, p. 2).

[19]Tony Brown's book *Mathematics education and subjectivity* is to be published in Springer's Mathematics Education Library series.

[20]The work of Jacques Lacan emerged most notably in the fifties and sixties with a controversial career. He became famous for presenting regular widely attended seminars in Paris. His career criss-crossed the paths of other leading French intellectuals such as Althusser, Merleau-Ponty, Levi-Strauss, Ricoeur, Barthes, Foucault, Lyotard and a younger Derrida. A Lacan-centric history of these times has been provided by Turkle (1978). Derrida (2002, pp. 147–198) has also provided an account of his memories. The "movement" associated with these writers was widely known as poststructuralism but none of these writers labelled themselves as such. Lacan was especially keen to distance himself from writers such as Derrida where a rivalry between the two camps still remains (see Easthope, 2002). To many contemporary thinkers this group comprises some of the leading writers of present day philosophy, although many university philosophy departments seem to resist this idea with utter dismay and downplay contemporary Francophile points of reference.

[21]Many claim, however, that Žižek has reinvented Lacan by reading him against the German Idealist philosopher Hegel, whereas Lacan's own declared point of reference was Freud. See for example Myers (2003) and Kay (2003). Certainly Žižek promotes Lacan as a new left alternative to poststructuralism.

[22]See Henriques, Hollway, Urwin, Venn, and Walkerdine (1984), Felman (1987), Walkerdine (1988).

from small beginnings, references to his poststructuralist counterparts mushroomed impressively, although still generally giving mathematics education a wide berth. Lacan and his legacy, however, remained a fringe player in these moves, ill-befitting his growing influence in the wider spectrum. His work has appeared in relation to a more general interest in psychoanalysis and education emerging from a group of academics working in Canada.[23] There has been a sprinkling of engagements with Lacan in education research, specifically in mathematics,[24] art[25] and teacher practitioner research.[26]

Bearing in mind that our central task in this book is establishing the reality of mathematics and its teaching as a function of how it is enacted by people in the field, we need to understand how that enactment results from the individual's understanding of the situation. That is, how is human self-conception shaped by societal situations? Both Lacan and Žižek see the human subject as caught in a never ending attempt to capture an understanding of his or her self in relation to the world in which he or she lives. The metaphor of the client attending a psychoanalytical session points to an understanding reached through a process of talking about oneself in relation to this world. That is, individuals make sense of the world through talking about it. Successive sessions, and the perspectives they produce, are taken into the world to be tried out for size. In this sense, teachers sharing reflections as part of a process of professional development are renewing their self-identity. They are learning to identify with new ways of making sense of their situations. In the writings of Lacan the human subject is always seen as incomplete, never quite getting to a final resolution. Identifications of oneself are captured in a supposed image. That is, for Lacan, such *identifications* are privileged over any notion of an ultimate *identity* reached through a process of analysis. Through this route Žižek departs from any notion of social totality[27] or potential consensus as implied in Habermas, to a recognition that social perspectives are always partial and cannot be mediated by a "correct" perspective. In the case of a trainee teacher then there is not a final version of teacher identity. Rather the task is to analyse how identifications with alternative educational agendas (e.g. those encountered variously at university, in school, and in curriculum requirements) are mediated.[28] Lacan places particular emphasis on the child's early encounters with a mirror in which he recognises himself:

---

[23] Key writers in this group, who are centred more on Freud, include Britzman (e.g. 2003b), Pitt (e.g. 1998), Todd (e.g. 1997), Appel (e.g. 1996, 1999), Briton (1997), Jagodzinski (2001), and Robertson (1997).

[24] A playful move marked the territory in mathematics education (Brown, Hardy, & Wilson, 1993). See also Tahta (1993, 2008), Baldino and Cabral (1999), Walshaw (2004), Cabral (2004), Brown (2008a, b), and Walshaw (2010c).

[25] Atkinson (e.g. 2001a; 2001b; & 2002) has considered art education through a theoretical framework derived from Lacan and Žižek.

[26] Brown, and Jones (2001), England and Brown (2001), Brown and England (2004), England (2004), Brown, Atkinson, and England (2006), Brown (2008c).

[27] Laclau and Mouffe (2001).

[28] cf. Sokefeld (1999).

> We have only to understand the mirror stage as *an identification*, in the full sense that analysis gives the term: namely, the transformation that takes place in the subject when he assumes an image (Lacan, 1977, p. 2, his emphasis).

As an individual, I am forever trying to complete the picture I have of myself in relation to the picture I have of the world around me, and in relation to the others who also inhabit it. I respond to the fantasy I have of the Other and the fantasy I imagine the Other having of me.

We opened this book with a sketch of Clare, a new teacher about to enter the profession. What version of herself does she feel comfortable with? Or what version of herself justifies her feeling the way she does about herself? What fantasies does she have about herself, the place she will work in, the people she will work with and the broader social context within which this takes place? What story does she tell to justify her actions? In such a psychoanalytic perspective, rooted as it is in Freud (e.g. 1991), the *unconscious* resides in the background making us do things that do not always get expressed explicitly in the versions we tell. For Lacan this unconscious dimension is more powerful than the conscious and shapes the things that we say. Žižek's (1989, pp. 87–129) discussion of Lacan suggests that I notice what I do insofar as my actions inhabit my fantasy frame of who I am. As explained earlier, for Lacan a "fantasy" is a filter through which reality is structured. The bits that I do not to see consciously, however, haunt this version of events. At the same time I have to reconcile this with the image others seem to have of me and how the tasks I face seem to be framed for me by others. I am trapped in having to constantly ask the question: "Why am I what you (the big Other) are saying that I am?" (Žižek, 1989, p. 113).

The suggestion here is that individuals create an image of themselves that they can feel comfortable with. A trainee teacher who sees herself as an aspirational child-centrist educator determined to enable children in her class to enjoy mathematics might, for example, ask what personal needs are being soothed by her alliance with such educational objectives. She might provide an account of her past that makes sense of her current actions and rationalisations. Alternative accounts may be generated and considered. This can lead to attempts at building a firmer understanding of how such accounts are related to the events that they seek to depict. It may not always be easy, however, to express what one feels. This further leads to recognition that there is no final story. Rather there are stories that help for the present, as sense is made of the past, as movement nudges to the future. The analogy of a psychoanalytic session does not take the client to a supposed end point where the client feels at peace with the world. Rather the work is on going as a permanent aspect of self-realisation. It might, for example, be seen as reconstructing the past to create different scenarios for current or future actions.

It is through this route that Žižek offers a departure from Habermas and Foucault. Žižek points to alternative conceptions of the human subject as represented in the work of Lacan and the neo-Marxist writer Louis Althusser. Žižek suggests that the debate between Habermas and Foucault shields a more fundamental distinction between the works of Althusser and Lacan. The core issue, as Žižek sees it, relates to how supposed imperfections in present human practices provide motivations in shaping future practice, but unlike Habermas, Žižek does not suppose that these imperfections can be resolved. For Žižek, life as it is actually being lived is always at some distance from the supposed model of how it might be lived, or how we would like or imagine it to be. This failure of fit results in dissatisfactions that are seen as needing to be overcome. This locates, or activates, desire, a desire that can never be fulfilled.

As we have seen, Habermas sought to remove the distortions that have arisen in language. He supposed that we could get behind these distortions or ideologies to see truth. For Althusser, in contrast, we always occupy an ideologically derived position. We never have the luxury of speaking from outside an ideology. A particular example that Althusser (1971) offered was the schooling process. He described schools as an instrument within the "ideological state apparatus". For him schools were a device through which the preferred ways of the state were disseminated with general consent. For many pupils and their parents progression through school is an ideological movement to which they are readily mobilised, encouraged no doubt by such occurrences as the British government's proudly proclaiming that standards in school mathematics in England are rising.[29] We may ask, however, whether it is appropriate to see this as improvement in the quality of "mathematics" per se. Perhaps, rather it is indicative of success in the government's project of convincing the public that the government's understanding of mathematics is the correct one and that the content of the tests defines what mathematics is. Yet government are measuring a version of mathematics that lends itself to being measured in a particular way, rather than according to universally accepted criteria. Standards have not been raised as much as the criteria through which standards are understood have been changed. Trainee teachers, meanwhile, need to cope with many alternative conceptions of mathematics. These include, the "horrific" stuff some met at school, the investigatory activities they did at university, the regulated phenomena read about in government documentation, the practical administrative version they performed in their own teaching, or the "mathematician's" version of mathematics. Yet there is not an independent adjudicator offering the final word on what mathematics "is", nor to identify the forgeries. Analysis does not result in a "correct" conclusion. Rather, the trainee is guided by social necessity. This might be the need to get results through the course of least resistance, whether this means using the government framework as a creative spur, or using it merely to avoid reproducing their own bad school experience. Or, it might simply be that the framework "has had huge impact (and) shapes your teaching of maths,... you know 100%...". It is for the trainees to choose the route that seems to best suit their preferred mode of social participation. In short, within Althusser's model, individuals identify with particular social ways of making sense. As a teacher, I might feel that the National Curriculum does a good enough job of describing mathematics and reflects my personal ambitions as a teacher. So I go along with that programme, align myself with

---

[29]Strathern (2000) discusses the "audit culture".

it, and see myself as a teacher in those terms, and see mathematics in those terms. In this way I become integrated[30] into particular socially normal ways of participating in the world.

Lacan, however, suggests that the distance between 'life', and how we make sense of it, must not be obliterated. This very gap creates the desire that shapes and motivates life itself. For Lacan, in contrast to Althusser, individual identity is not just about mis-recognition of oneself participating in some social programme. Rather human identity is a result of mis-recognising oneself in a rather more fundamental way. The stuff of personal construction is an attempt to reconcile one's view of oneself with the views one supposes others have of you. For a teacher seeking to reconcile personal aspirations with social demands (such as in a government inspection) there is inevitably a gap between how she is and how she might be. As one trainee teacher in our study put it: "We are not this, this and this". For Lacan it is this gap that defines identity; it opens the space for subjective intervention, whether this is personal identity, social identity or professional identity. It provides the position from which the individual can view the world and produce a subjective account of it *as if* from outside it. I can see the possibility of stepping outside of the world and acting differently.

New teachers may need to believe that they are making things better for their pupils to be able to function in their professional roles. And they need a story that carries them through with that belief. New teachers may prefer to believe that they have a purpose beyond mere compliance. They need to construct their own professional identity in positive terms.[31] This personal need perhaps predominates over any actual externally imposed performative criteria, or any actual alignment with a collectively defined programme. There's more to teaching than getting it right according to the rules. The trainee does not need to reach a final resolution of such dilemmas and may happily work with many such notions variously activated according to demands made at different stages of his or her training. Lacan's (2006) conception of the subject is a fragmented self, where alternative discourses feeding through her practice fail to meet and be reconciled with each other.[32] The new teacher has multiple masters and mistresses and cannot please all of them. This can be regarded as an opportunity to make some real choices.

Žižek (1989) reminds us that people may still act on the assumption that they are moving towards their ideal even though they know that they will never get there. Even if they do not take things seriously, they are still doing them. Brown (2008d) has discussed this point in relation to educational policies. Lacan, we believe, assists us in examining how student teachers use language and how this locates their desires, their fears and their hidden motivations and how these govern their professional practice and how their social action might be seen as a function of the

---

[30] Althusser uses the term "interpellated".

[31] For example, see Povey (1997).

[32] Troman (1996), (1999), Stronach, Corbin, McNamara, Stark, and Warne (2002).

social discourses that guide their everyday practice. Žižek's work meanwhile develops Lacan's work in the context of broader social relations and a political project predicated on social improvement. A particular theme that we shall address later relates to so many actions seemingly supposing a trajectory to an ideal solution. How might actions be re-shaped in the light of knowing that this ideal probably will not ever be achieved fully? In the absence of a final truth that can be nailed down, Žižek (1989) argues that certain "quilting points" need to become operational in pinning down systems of rationalisation within the social sphere. Common sense needs to be draped over a more complex collection of rationalisations. For example, the overarching principle of "class struggle" governed Marx's project and Žižek argues that all of his sub-projects were shaped in relation to that basic premise. In contemporary educational analysis a notion such as "raising standards" assumes a similar sort of centrality for administrations defending their policies, as though there were a singular scale for measuring. Policies are often presented in the form of answers to the question of how you raise standards. There are, however, many other anchorages to such debates; for example, assertions of "professionalism" might also anchor the rationalisations of teachers' unions seeking to hold on to something by that name. In the new discursive order, "skills" as a notion has also gained widespread prominence in specifying educational objectives. Meanwhile educational research has been advised to be "interventionist" and, most importantly, "evidence-based".[33]

## 5.3  Regulating Consensus

Earlier we met with an idealistic Nathan working towards a harmonious account of teaching. Whilst we have now offered some theoretical support to such idealism we felt unable to sustain this approach. We have argued that individual can never finally pin down their identity since it is necessarily a function of identifications with disparate and often conflicting discourses. We cannot please everyone. The human subject is inescapably "fragmented" and cannot succeed in reconciling all the contradictory discourses that s/he encounters. The trainee is always torn between many demands that cannot ever be fully satisfied. In this section, we shall suggest that the official training discourse provides a cover story to conceal these difficulties, providing a camouflage for issues that seem to remain complex and irreconcilable. The trainees subscribe to various social programmes relating to the classroom. These, we suggest, enable the trainees to suppress some of the more difficult issues arising in their training. Whilst they do identify with many of the external demands that they encounter, their articulation of this engagement often seems to build the very gap that keeps them away from inevitable conflicts in building a coherent sense of selfdiscourses.[34] Any attempted resolution of the conflicting demands cannot be achieved without some compromises. We cannot easily aspire to a unifying structure

---

[33] McNamara (2002).

[34] "the disabling palliative of further self reconstruction" (Convery, 1999, p. 142).

upon which everyone will agree. Certain desires will always be left out. The only consensual frameworks that seem to claim a unifying agenda in English mathematics education at present are governmental policy instruments. Such instruments succeed in a forced consensus in that they appear to achieve governance through fairly widespread common consent. That is, the policies seem to be successful in making it appear that they account for the complete picture. All solutions to all problems, it seems, can be found within the apparatus. There is no outside to be mopped up, or to lead us astray.

A key example in our study, the Strategy, provided a pragmatic approach to facilitating the trainees' participation in the professional enterprise of teaching. Some trainees found it over-prescriptive but relatively few seemed to be wholly opposed. It was accepted as a centralised unifying structure given the relative weakness of any other frame. It had also become a generally popular social programme to which many could subscribe. Delusional or not, the trainee teacher perceived himself or herself as part of some social programme designed for the common good. This seemed to be based on some faith that if the National Numeracy Strategy were administered effectively then children would learn mathematics more effectively: "We had quite thorough training about the numeracy strategy, about mental maths, getting children to talk about maths, so maths and literacy were probably the areas where I was most prepared" (Yr. 4). The Strategy provided practical guidelines for effective participation in collectively conceived social programmes. Participation in such a programme was seen as a key aspect of professionalism. The supposition seemed to be that the programme had become a benchmark of "effective practice". If you followed the Strategy, you bought in to a specific trajectory that supposed a particular approach to improving mathematics for children. As we shall argue in the next chapter, the trainee's conception of mathematics was then a function of how they understood their social participation. Their conception of being a teacher was shaped by perceived expectations of this participation and one's success in complying with its demands.

As we have seen in the data, however, trainees were tugged in many different directions along the way as there were many agencies (e.g. university tutors, schools) seeking to mediate their agenda through the broader governing programme. Trainees, for example, were required to inhabit other government constructions of teachers and of mathematics, in which personal discourses and practices were squeezed into shape: "We are being (inspected) in maths, we are scared that if they come and see us and we are not, this, this and this" (Yr. 4). This also arose through prescriptive curriculum documentation regulating the training process:

> Where gaps in trainees' subject knowledge are identified, providers of ITT must make arrangements to ensure that trainees gain that knowledge during the course and that, by the end of that course, they are competent in using their knowledge of mathematics in their teaching.[35]

---

[35] Department for Education and Employment (1998b, p. 48), original emphasis.

University tutors concerned about their own inspections further added to this:

> She (the tutor) was probably exceptionally nervous, just like teachers are, I mean, you're being watched and, you know you're being observed and you're going to have comments made upon your teaching approach or teaching style, the level of teaching,... inspections are the same in schools, it's just completely false, you don't get a proper idea of the school and it's like when we were on school experience and the planning that we had to do for maths for numeracy and it was like rigorously checked and we weren't allowed to go into schools unless the plans were good enough and that was all for the benefit of (inspectors) (Yr. 4).

Students still in university demonstrated a keen awareness of the frameworks governing the course and their imminent accreditation. There was a strongly regulatory climate with a host of government initiatives supplementing the demands students faced in university and on school placements. The trainee's professional identity seemed to be a function of a partial reconciliation anchored in some assumption about what constituted correct behaviour, or practices that would result in their accreditation. As such, there was a sense of having to get it right according to official agendas although our data suggested that the partiality of the students' perspectives resulted in immediate tasks being privileged over any broader reconciliation. Our data, unsurprisingly, pointed to trainees being more anxious about the various requirements they faced prior to their accreditation, and being more concerned with achieving what was expected of them. Certainly for such students the external demands ensured a compliant attitude, but a compliance with an approach that was generally seen as supporting the common good, namely the generally accepted need for mathematics to be taught: "It's something we need to participate fully in life from a very early age". The grip of government policy would not appear to be easily displaced. It was offering one version of governance supported largely through popular consent, helped probably by the limits on the trainees' capacity to afford a critical purchase on policies with which they were obliged to comply.

Meanwhile, however, once released from university into the relative responsibility of being a teacher in school, there was a greater sense of autonomy with the individual teacher in the driving seat, governed more by personal motivations and ideals. Here the new teacher might more readily have recognised that the conflicts or antagonisms were irreconcilable but at the same time also recognised that looser interpretations could be sufficient as a more pragmatic attitude evolved. This offered more scope for making individual decisions. By the time they had started work as a teacher they recognised that the various demands could be met and integrated more with their own personal aspirations ("You have more autonomy"). As another new teacher put it: "You can be more spontaneous... even though you've got to follow the demands of the... numeracy hour". This then might be seen as a frame privileging the teacher seeking to recover his or her "own voice". Although a harmonious and complete social perspective may not easily be achieved, the individual, having negotiated entry in to the profession, can now seek to juggle the external demands from a position of greater assumed personal control. Nevertheless, the negative aspects do not stop there completely. Teachers much further into the profession experience similar pressures. Earlier, we encountered reports from the trainees observing nervousness in their university tutors. We include here a comment from a highly experienced school deputy head commenting on her feelings about the inspections:

> After one inspection I could not believe the actions both a pupil and I had taken. The child was feeling sick but continued with the work. She then vomited over the apparatus. I sent her to the toilet to clean up, wiped the desk and continued with the lesson. While comforting the child as she waited for the arrival of her parent to take her home I asked why she did not ask me to go home earlier if she had felt unwell. She said that she did not like to disturb me with the inspector there. I asked myself why I had not stopped the lesson and sorted her out properly. After another inspection the teaching assistant mentioned how different I seemed during an observation. She said that I seemed false (Chamberlain, 2004).

In line with our earlier analysis we might question the word "false". Rather, we might suggest, the deputy was playing a different self, according to the immediate demands she perceived. She continues:

> However, as team leader in a primary school I could not avoid playing a major role in this process. My professional responsibility was clearly documented and involved collaboration between the government and the school's management. The Performance Management Policy and procedure were statutory requirements, so I had to work within imposed limits that the government provided through the model of Performance Management Policy. This states that: 'the team leader and the teacher work together to ensure that objectives are discussed and agreed; regular and objective feedback is given; adequate coaching, training and development is provided and that the performance review takes place' (Chamberlain, 2004).

Earlier, we introduced a perspective on how a human constructs his or her self as a subject. This rested on the inevitability of mis-recognitions resulting from attempts at achieving resolution of disparate concerns. The assumption of such a perspective, we suggest, weakens any easy supposition that the transition from university trainee to full time classroom teacher incorporates a shift from compliance with external demands to a more "autonomous" state of affairs. Rather, it seems more realistic to suggest that in both environments the demands are so great that reconciliation is not possible in any actual sense. The trainee or new teacher's account provides a cover story for a situation that is complex and does not lend itself to clear representation. For example, it seems unlikely that the new teacher could juggle the various demands (e.g. meeting government requirements, enabling children to find mathematics interesting, maintaining classroom control, fitting into school structures, being liked by the children) in to a clear story. Earlier, we quoted a new teacher who put it thus: "What you teach and how you teach it and the actual set-up of the lesson is restricted to sort of government requirements and school requirements and LEA (Local Education Authority) requirements and inspection requirements and everyone else but you can still fit in your own style in that". Despite the optimism of this quote it seemed impossible for this new teacher to appreciate fully and then reconcile all of the alternative discourses acting through her. The statement might be seen as an image that the new teacher wants to have of herself. The teacher might buy into official story lines and see (misguidedly or not) her "own" actions in those terms. This does not have to be seen as a problem. But it may mean that new teachers like her subscribe to an intellectual package deal laid on for them, rather than see the development of their own professional practice in terms of further intellectual and emotional work to do with resolving the contradictory messages encountered.

Professional development more broadly was perhaps seen in terms of better achieving curriculum objectives that the new teachers seemed comfortable with for organising practice. It appeared that the Strategy provided the unifying agenda, at least partly because it had become the new orthodoxy: "I find the numeracy and literacy strategies quite useful but I've never known any different" (NQT). The trainee's capacity to be critical was limited by their need to comply:

> The thing with government policies is really whether you agree with them or not and you think they're beneficial or not, you've got to adapt and change to go with them, so it's just a case of experimenting with them, trying them out and then adapting them to suit you, so... I mean, you've got to use them, so if you can adapt it to suit you then it's going to be beneficial (Yr. 4).

The Strategy does appear to have provided a language that can be learnt and spoken by most new teachers interviewed. In this sense the official language spanning the Strategy and its policing through the inspection regime, seemed to have been a success. Many trainees appeared to see the Strategy as a pragmatic approach that facilitated their participation in the professional enterprise of teaching mathematics. One new teacher comments we heard from in earlier comments: "I think largely it's the way that it's structured – my own personal experience of maths since I left primary school has not been good,... it was never my most enjoyed subject so I definitely think it's the way that it's structured". Meanwhile another says: "I actually quite like the structure of the numeracy, the mental maths, the section at the end, the plenary I quite like that structure because it's quite sort of easy to follow". Any ambivalence towards the Strategy seems measured with an acceptance that others know better. After all: "Obviously somebody somewhere with a lot of authority has actually sat down and written this numeracy strategy, well a number of people, so they... it's not like they don't know what they're talking about".

Given the complexity of routes into the teaching profession, trainees paint a fantasy version of themselves that seems to do the job. Often, it involves borrowing from the official language to mask perceived personal deficiencies. It appears that the Strategy has become a generally popular social programme with which many can identify. This does, however, point to a need to find ways of adopting a critical stance in relation to the parameters of this discourse, discourse in which difficult issues are being suppressed rather than removed. For example, when confronted with mathematics of a more sophisticated nature from the school curriculum, the new teachers remained anxious. The Strategy and university training, however, had between them provided an effective language for administering mathematics in the classroom in which confrontation with its more challenging aspects could be avoided. If true, this points to certain limits in the teachers' capacity to engage creatively with the children's mathematical constructions. And perhaps further professional development in mathematics education for such teachers might be conceptualised in terms of renegotiating these limits.

Before closing this chapter, it might be pointed out that there were some differences of professional opinion expressed during the consultations leading to the creation of the National Numeracy Strategy. We argued in our literature review for the British Education Research Association that the government's claim of the initiative being informed by research lacked some credibility.[36] These differences of opinion were not entirely assuaged, yet the government message was that everyone had sung from the same hymn sheet in specifying the content of mathematics lessons. For new teachers, unaccustomed to previous administrations, these debates were concealed beneath the veneer of well-defined language shaping practices. As our new teacher posited earlier: "You have to do what they tell you to do". In this respect, it seems important that research in mathematics education targets itself at disrupting some of the cover stories that have been produced in seeking a more comfortable life.

---

[36]Brown, and McNamara (2001).

# Chapter 6
# The Shaping of School Mathematics

## 6.1 Introduction

The identity of mathematics itself cannot remain unaffected by initiatives of the sort that we have described. The apparatuses of mathematics teaching are part of the culture of mathematics and thus part of the mathematics itself. In some earlier work, pedagogical frameworks (e.g. the balance method for solving linear equations) were seen as inseparable from the mathematics being taught.[1] The pedagogical devices were shown to be cultural artefacts firmly rooted in the evolution of school mathematics and the way in which it was understood.[2] Here we are suggesting that the instruments of curriculum reform have also become part of mathematics itself – building in to the mathematics specific traits of the particular society, such as its mode of governance, attitude to school, teachers, children. The National Numeracy Strategy, for example, specifies the shape of mathematics activity and defines certain cultural norms as to how it should be performed and assessed. Similarly, teacher practices as understood generally in a primary school context provide the professional frame for mathematics and conceptions of how it is exchanged in social forms. Many such factors shape mathematics in the school context. These also include conceptions of professionalism, broader conceptions of teaching and of mathematics, the affective response to the subject, the need to comply with accreditation demands and the way it is assessed. The social conception of mathematics has become reified in the way in which it is understood structurally within the English reform agenda. It became clear to the trainees, as they proceeded through training, that there was a multitude of conceptions of what mathematics was, and how it might be taught, that perhaps needed to be reconciled in some way. The trainee may have supposed that by assuming a critical distance these alternative conceptions could be harmonised according to a set of rational principles so that some consistency could be detected in the divergent demands. Yet it seemed evident in our data that the trainees responded more to current demands one at a time, rather than seeking an

---

[1] Brown, Eade, and Wilson (1999).

[2] This point has been discussed more fully by Brown and Heywood (in press).

T. Brown, O. McNamara, *Becoming a Mathematics Teacher*,
Mathematics Education Library 53, DOI 10.1007/978-94-007-0554-8_6,
© Springer Science+Business Media B.V. 2011

overarching reconciliation. Or, perhaps, a language of reconciliation was borrowed from official discourses.

It may be difficult to achieve consensus on an ideologically free conception of mathematics teaching. Mathematics itself is susceptible to being portrayed through discursive apparatus and caught between alternative accounts. Mathematics is generally a function of the social agendas relating to the circumstances of its practice. In primary education it will be mediated through the discourses pertaining to this arena. To locate under the surface of these discourses, any sort of a "real" mathematics that might better anchor our understanding seems to be a spurious task. There is no ultimate object of desire in this scenario. In taking this perspective ourselves, we are not researching issues in mathematics education with a view to operating on the underlying mathematics. That is, we are not trying to distil mathematics from the social practices that embody it. Rather we are seeking to better understand the social practices that position and shape mathematics in its socially manifest form, in particular, those specific to the primary classroom. In doing this, we are seeking to explore the secrets of the forms of mathematics through which it arises in social practices. For this reason, we feel compelled to centre our attention on the social practices that embody the mathematics and seek to look in on it from outside, rather than working from mathematics out. In this way our research target is not to find ways of improving the techniques through which mathematics is taught but rather we seek to become more sensitive to how social practices more generally shape teaching practices specifically and hence create the social forms of mathematics.

Some social accounts of mathematics, which have been offered in earlier research in the field of mathematics education, seemed to us to be overly restrictive. For example, the work influenced by Shulman, addressing the notion of pedagogical content knowledge in relation to mathematics, was discussed in Chapter 3. This work analysed the pedagogical forms through which mathematics is encountered in schools. The discussion in such work generally pointed to the need to build a fuller conception of mathematics as understood through alternative representational forms that a teacher might utilise. Whilst we support the need for recognising the importance of mathematics being understood through different conceptual forms, we argue that much of this discussion is disembodied both from the individual people holding the knowledge and also from the societal derivation of that knowledge. That is, it is overly restricted to a purely pedagogical frame without sufficient attention to its broader social situation and the shaping derived from that. The mathematics that we seek to construct in this book is a function of socially normal primary school practices that in turn derive from broader conceptions of schooling. The mathematics we depict then is not so much an alternative form of mathematics per se but rather a microcosm of society's image of itself at a particular stage of its evolution, seen from a particular perspective.

There has also been a substantial amount of work addressing the social construction of mathematics under various banners (social constructivism[3], social practice

---

[3] Ernest (1998).

theory[4]). We question, however, how such notions of the social are constructed. Who decides how the social version of mathematics is arrived at? Which microcosms of the "social" provide the basis of such work? An issue that troubles the task of this book is that the trainees we interviewed were reluctant to talk explicitly about mathematics. They often preferred to remain silent in any account of what mathematics should be, or bury their discussion in accounts of how they organised their classrooms. But whose voice should count in the construction of mathematics in this domain? A key theme of this book is how trainee teachers contribute to the social account of what mathematics is in the primary school. Their voice is clearly an important one in the actual practice of mathematics in schools at this level. Yet it may be difficult for those with an emotionally charged history in relation to the subject to make their voices heard over those with a more confidently held view. Indeed, the research interviews upon which this study is based largely failed to penetrate teacher conceptions of mathematics except through a variety of administrative filters. But surely there is a need collectively to ensure the participation of such key players to avoid mathematics being defined exclusively by those external to the classroom. We cannot rely solely on others speaking for the trainees and new teachers. We contend that the classroom itself has to be a key site in which mathematics is generated and understood, rather than being a location where external conceptions are merely mediated.

This chapter comprises two main sections. In the first, we specifically outline how conceptions of mathematics derive from the curriculum infrastructure. In the second, we paint a more theoretical picture of how the *commodification* of mathematics as a school subject overly restricts the generation of mathematical thinking for pupils.

## 6.2   The Social Framing of School Mathematics

This section builds on the story told so far about how trainee and new teachers conceptualise mathematics in their teaching and learning. We endeavour to highlight and develop our understanding of how these conceptions of mathematics in the primary classroom are substantially shaped by norms of primary classroom practice rather than by mathematics defined in a more abstract sense. We further consider how these conceptions have become bureaucratised through being reshaped around new curriculum demands.

The narrow perspective afforded by reliance on interviews presents some difficulties in providing the mathematical content that would enable our work to fit less controversially in the domain of mathematics education research. But this is a crucial point: the practice of primary school mathematics generally does not fit comfortably around a priori conceptions of mathematics. It is shaped around a multitude of diverse social practices. The interview material that we have collected, however,

---

[4]For example, Adler (2001), Brodie (2009).

does avoid the research team's assuming some supposed expert perspective on actual classroom practice, although inevitably our mediation shapes the stories told.

We are concerned with understanding how teachers might change their practices. We are not, however, searching for new techniques for teachers but rather hoping to build new conceptions of how teachers understand and respond to social changes. As such, we see the data we have collected as providing information on how trainees receive and make sense of policy initiatives and how they might be responsive to adjustments to such policy initiatives. It's all very well having research-informed policy models that deliver better results but we need to be sure that changes in practice can be mobilised through credible teacher education processes. In the next section, we shall argue that the content of mathematics presents itself in *commodified* forms as outcomes of social practices. School mathematical teaching and learning is a function of social formation and of the social discourses that permeate that formation. How might we now pinpoint the specific influences on this formation? How do trainees locate the mathematical element in their practice? In a more limited way we consider how they talked about mathematical content more directly.

There are many influences on the trainee's conception of mathematics and we seek to examine how trainees experience some of these parameters. First, we briefly revisit the distinction that we made in Chapter 2 between phenomenological and official accounts of mathematics to consider how these alternative sorts of conception impact on student accounts of their work. Second, building on the last chapter, we consider in more detail how classroom practice in mathematics is shaped by the trainee's compliance with regulatory discourses and through caricatures derived from curriculum descriptions. Finally, we revisit some of the themes emerging in Chapter 4 capturing the trainees more directly describing the mathematical content of their classroom practice. We consider how the depleted memories of the trainees' own school mathematics underpin their conceptions of their mathematical work with children. We also demonstrate the limitations that some students experience in focusing directly on mathematics in this way.

## 6.2.1 Personal Versus Externally Defined Conceptions of Mathematics

From interviews carried out prior to the reforms, we traced the evolution of students' conceptions of mathematics as evidenced in their responses to the interview question *"What is mathematics?"* for students in each of the four years. Upon entering university, new students, many fresh from school, were not expansive in their descriptions of the subject. As we have showed, clipped, numerically oriented, responses predominated. Whilst they could say why they wanted to be a teacher, they could not say what mathematics was and how they imagined they would go about teaching it. Their accounts of mathematics were undeveloped and their conceptions of teaching were based primarily on their pupil perspectives of their own good and bad classroom experiences in their own schooling. As they proceeded through university, however, these conceptions of the subject were predicated more on a broader understanding of mathematical activity, embracing shape, data handling and other topics. It was also seen more as "exploring number, exploring shape, and all those sorts of things". Its rigid nature was questioned: "Although a lot of the time there might not be an answer or that the way you choose to get an answer might not be the only one". It was also seen as "a major part of everyday life". For students at the later stages of training, a conception of classroom mathematics shaped primarily by "good management skills", commensurate with good classroom organisation, has become predominant.

The mathematics of official documents and the mathematics often depicted during university training can be very different. Students were torn between these alternative conceptions, as they encountered changing demands as they progressed through their training: learning mathematics for the Numeracy Skills Test, appreciating mathematics pedagogically as a student teacher in a university, or fitting into conventional school practices when on a school placement.

Mathematics is constructed according to specific cultural, mathematical, pedagogical and political agendas, and its various features are a function of these diverse concerns. Trainee conceptions of mathematics need to be responsive to these alternative pressures. Yet conflicting phenomenological and official stories clouded the picture. In Chapter 4, we saw that the official version of mathematics was clearly evident for students earlier in the course, although it revealed itself a little obliquely in the students' accounts, primarily through the way in which they hinted at their anchorage in transmission methods. The teacher's task was seen as being to get the idea across, albeit using approaches that sought to soften the negative aspects of transmission. The importance of children's own conceptualisations revealed itself more within the accounts of students' discussing their own teaching later on in the course, most probably in the light of university input.

Trainees in the sample revealed harrowing memories of being recipients of transmission styles of mathematics teaching in schools. It seemed that this style of teaching accentuated any difficulties with mathematical learning. Yet their capacity to radically reconceptualise mathematics as a discipline, and its teaching, seemed limited to enacting a pseudo-transmission style where the approach was laced with motivational niceties. They thus attempted reconciliation but seemed to lack the critical capacity to combine the two dichotomised styles. Askew et al. (1997) associate this capacity with "effective" experienced teachers. For many in our sample of nonspecialist students this seemed to be out of reach in both conception and practice.

## 6.2.2 Compliance with Regulatory Discourses

We have somewhat artificially contrasted the teacher's personal aspirations with the regulations that govern the school curriculum and the professional competencies now specified for practising teachers. The regulations define practices and demand compliance. This administrative layer anchors the content of school mathematics according to its own terms of reference. As we have suggested, however, the trainees have embraced some of these demands as they progressed through training and their personal aspirations were married to these demands. More personal aspirations become expressed through the language defining the erstwhile demand. Both government and trainees then act according to these forms as though they deliver mathematics. We pursue this point theoretically later in this chapter. For now we shall take a further look at some of our data in the context of some of the regulative apparatus.

*The National Numeracy Strategy*

Until very recently, most regulative shaping of the primary classroom mathematics was derived to a large extent from this centralised source. Teachers differed as to whether the Strategy document was helpful guidance or excessive prescription. However, most new teachers interviewed regarded the Strategy as a "very useful" framework, supplementing the National Curriculum that merely defined content but not method:

> I think the Numeracy Strategy gives you a lot more examples. . . it gives you lots of practical things to try. . . I'm lucky because when I first started we were just looking at the National Curriculum but now, you know, it's changed, . . . I think it's a lot better. . . it's made me think. . . I think it's made everybody have more idea of activities and I mean it just gives you some good ideas where the National Curriculum you might look at something and think – Oh, how can I try and get that across, you know, and it'd take a lot of thinking about. . . I suppose you could say in a way it's made it. . . easier (NQT).

*Impact on individual school mathematics policies*

The National Numeracy Strategy superseded and rendered redundant individual school mathematics policies that had guided practices in the past. In general, school policies were no longer referred to and there was little mention of any on-going development of such policies. It seemed that the Strategy had achieved a fairly comprehensive grip that resulted in school based or more individually based conceptions of mathematics teaching being understood more through the centralised framework. In some cases, the Strategy was locally mediated by particular contextual factors such as the need for a supplementary scheme devised to assist speakers of English as an additional language. This was being administered in a school where all children came from communities comprising people who, in other parts of England, would be regarded as being from ethnic minorities. But even then the scheme was seen as commensurate with the national programmes:

> It's. . . specifically for the children who have English as a second language and it actually raises SATs (Standard Assessment Tasks) results as well. . . . That was the reason why it's set out the way it is. . . . Government policies and the numeracy strategy . . . sets off by you doing an oral starter then doing your bit of teacher exposition and then the children work and then like a plenary and the scheme we're using has that same format as well. . . (NQT)

*Alignment with other curriculum areas*

The new regime had realigned mathematics in relation to other National Curriculum subjects. Within this new scenario, mathematics as a school subject was lifted towards being fast paced and designed to activate mental alertness:

I'll be darting about the class and snapping questions at children in numeracy, so I think that the skills that I use in numeracy differ a lot from literacy – in the other way that I set the classroom up for activities as well, plan that I can do a lot more practical activities in numeracy than I can within literacy (NQT).

Mathematics it seemed was "fiery" and "snappy", whilst literacy was "slower and "calmer". This difference in style also leads this new teacher to feeling more confident with the activity orientation of numeracy than he does with literacy despite a history of ambivalence towards mathematics as a subject: "I could be . . . a little bit more confident at teaching maths than literacy – my own mathematical knowledge is. . . I'm not as confident as I am with literacy . . . but certainly with teaching it I feel a lot more confident somehow". Such sentiments were echoed in many of our interviews with trainees/ new teachers and with their tutors. The reassertion of a separate classroom identity for mathematics within a clear framework does appear to have made teachers more confident. It is less clear whether it will result in children becoming more confident. The changes have resulted in more teacher-led mathematical activity – a key source of anxiety reported among participants with regard to their own schooling.

*The shaping of the trainees' pedagogical discourse*

Such stylistic shaping of mathematical activity, it seems to us, is more than cosmetic insofar as mathematical content is located, observed and hence generated in a newly understood form of social activity. The Strategy provided a pedagogic discourse through which to conceptualise, articulate and share aspects of mathematics teaching and learning. This reshaping of mathematics appears to have increased its inclusiveness through redefining the way in which teachers and pupils could engage with it. Similarly, teacher practices, as understood generally in a primary school context, provided the professional frame for mathematics and conceptions of how it was exchanged in social forms. It was thus important to examine how trainees and new teachers conceptualised and represented mathematics, instrumental as they were in its generation in the classroom.

Students in the study overwhelmingly, as we have heard, subscribed to a view of mathematics as a utilitarian body of knowledge, a "life skill" that could be acquired most effectively through "hands-on" practical experience. The students, who could be ideologically characterised as "technological pragmatists",[5] held the beliefs that mathematics was "the study of numbers . . . taught in school to give children an insight. . . We use maths in everyday circumstances, shopping, housework, most jobs use numbers" (Yr. 4).

*Pedagogical materials as a proxy for mathematics*

Trainees put a great deal of effort into making mathematics resources for use in the classroom; these ranged from place value dominoes, to bingo to number fans. Pedagogical forms inevitably stood in for the mathematics itself and shaped the activity through which children encountered mathematics. Like the new teacher we heard in Chapter 4 thought:

---

[5]Ernest (1991).

It's impossible to teach place value without those arrow cards, they're superb because . . . the children can understand it so much easier when you can say – Look it is a ten 'cause the nought is hiding under the unit and you can explode it and they know that that's . . . the unit is sitting on top of the nought and it really helps them understand the nought's the place holder. . . I decided to use them and just to make the activity more independent. . . it means they're manipulating the numbers and they're then choosing the numbers they're using and reading them.

Here the arrow cards are used in an activity in which mathematical ideas are translated into particular pedagogical forms. The presentation of the activity seems to provide a way of locating mathematics, yet the activity seems to be clouding the teacher from alternatives. The pedagogical form becomes the mathematics itself such that it is otherwise "impossible to teach". The mathematical idea is supposedly pointed yet in the teacher's description it does not figure. The presentation of the arrow cards is a proxy for the mathematics. The practical features of the activities are very much in the foreground but the evidence of something more directly mathematical seems weaker. Such a conception of mathematical activity in the classroom seemed to result in the teachers feeling comfortable.

*The Numeracy Skills Test*

This test for intending teachers supplemented the school qualifications required for college entry. There was some sense of mathematics being regulated according to a particular social conception of mathematics suitable for aspiring teachers. It was interpreted as the government's doing something to raise school standards that the general public could understand:

I know a few people didn't pass it and. . . I certainly wouldn't have felt at all confident if the questions were much more difficult. I felt they were reasonable enough. . .. If you've not got the knowledge you're not going to be able to teach it very well and I go along with that in that if you as a teacher don't fully understand what you're teaching the children have got no chance. . . . So I can understand why the government have done that but at times I felt it was just done for the sake of trying to prove to other – to outsiders looking in that they were doing something to raise standards (NQT).

An enthusiasm for mathematics activated by earlier university sessions was blunted by pragmatic concerns in later stages of the course when training was more school-based. This resulted in the early successes university tutors had achieved in enabling students to overcome their negative attitudes towards mathematics being undermined a little. The Numeracy Skills Test further undermined these successes as a result of reactivating the trainees' unease about their own mathematical abilities.

*Government inspections*

An inspection of the university that took place during the study had a profound effect on university tutors and students alike, with mathematics in particular under the spotlight. University tutors could see their institution financially penalised if inspectors disagreed with the grades they applied. The inspectorial apparatus specified and regulated the features of trainee lessons that tutors were obliged to notice and evaluate. Trainees seemed less enthusiastic when it came to having their individual practices as teachers and mathematicians gauged against inspectorial definitions of what it is to be a teacher. One trainee complained: "I am not here to prove to (inspectors) that I can do maths. I am here to teach maths to the children and that made me angry, the fact that she was taking away the most important thing about teaching – the children – she was taking that away" (Yr. 4). It also shaped the delivery of mathematics sessions in university and significantly impacted on the way in which students prepared for their mathematics lessons in school placements:

> The worst experience to do with it was when we came back in September and were told we had to have our first half term… plans into the maths department and signed before they would let us go into school… We didn't know how it was going to work in reality. So we were giving in plans that basically we didn't really understand ourselves, because we hadn't worked that way before, and it was just – 'You get them in or you're not going into school… we want to see 4 weeks planning or else'… I knew that they were doing that because… (the inspectors) were going to demand that they'd done it or they wanted to be able to say to (the inspectors) – We've seen these students' plans, they are now alright to go in and teach the Numeracy Hour in schools (Yr. 4).

This activated some sympathy for university tutors administering the new university frameworks under (the inspector's) watchful eye:

> I found that because I was one of the ones that were chosen to be (inspected) obviously it had a direct impact on their jobs (the university tutors). And everything else and so they were very keen to really bring me up to scratch with the Numeracy Hour. So I felt quite special in that I'd had all that experience and it was beneficial in the end 'cause I got a 1. So I was dead pleased (Yr. 4).

Some students encountered inspectors directly. In the following example, we see how this impacted on lesson planning, the conduct in the lesson and the way in which the student evaluated her own lesson. It is also evident how the inspections are being used to monitor university practices. For this student it was a positive experience.

> It was a maths … inspection. So they actually came in and watched one of my maths sessions. They spoke to us very briefly beforehand, took a sample of the children's work to see what I'd been doing with them. They marked that. They marked my school experience file to see what I'd been writing about, stuff like that. And then they actually came and watched me teach. … Then I had an interview with them, but they were very, very nice, very friendly … And having to justify what I did was useful as well in an interview situation. Having to actually discuss why I did this and why it would be better next time if I did that and all the rest of it. So I found it a useful experience personally (Yr. 4).

In the school environment inspectors were similarly pervasive in shaping the forms through which mathematics was encountered. One student reported: "The school I've been working in have just had their own inspection and the word 'OfSTED' (inspectorate) instils fear in every teacher regardless of whether they're at university or in school, so I think they're all under pressure and that showed" (Yr. 4).

### 6.2.3  SOHCAHTOA, the Land Time Forgot: The Relics
###          of Mathematical Discourse

The reader may begin to suspect that the authors are resisting any sort of anchorage in "authentic" mathematical reasoning amongst our interviewees. Many examples of the trainees talking are seen in terms of participation in some sort of social discourse or another. We have seen students "talking the talk" without connection to content. Meanwhile, many display compliant tendencies following narrow paths as specified in regulatory apparatus. This section will not provide much relief to the reader intent on finding more mathematical anchorage.

As part of our study we sought to examine how content knowledge contributed to the skills base of trainees in terms of their ability to articulate their professional task and the skills they needed in support of this. We tried to get the students to talk about mathematical content directly as mathematical topics in themselves. Our strategy entailed asking the students to identify some topics on the curriculum with which they felt some familiarity. We then asked them to discuss common features of particular topics, for example, percentages and fractions. We were generally disappointed insofar as we sought stand-alone mathematical discussion. It was not a language in which they felt at home. They did not possess a reflective language in this regard despite much explicit work on this during university training. To give a flavour of these interviews, offered here, is an example in which a student was asked to identify one of the topics she remembered most clearly from her own school examination work completed 4 years earlier. This interlude followed a discussion of some mathematical topics she had taught to children recently. The student could be described as more confident in her mathematical learning than many, and more articulate in talking about it. She was interviewed as she approached completion of her second year on a 4-year course. Our intention was to encourage her to describe certain aspects of mathematics from her own schooling in as much detail as possible in an attempt to capture how she made connections in her own mind to the work that she was now doing with children.

> Q. You presumably took GCSE (*end of school exams*) fairly recently. Can you think of a topic within the GCSE that comes to mind now?
> A. Trigonometry.
> Q. ... can you draw any links between trigonometry as you remember it and the topics you've mentioned here? (*notes from the preceding discussion*)
> A. Yeah! Fractions. Well it's all about one thing over the top of another.
> Q. Shall we unfold that, what do you remember of that?
> A. I'd have to write it down. Silly Old Harry Caught A Herring Trawling Off America. So it's O plus A equals an H. Is that right? I can't remember what any of the letters stand for – Opposite, Adjacent, Hypotenuse? (*She writes S=O/H, C=A/H, T=O/A – (SOHCAHTOA).*)
> Q. I can see clearly how that connects with fractions. You've got S equals O over H, C equals A over H and T equals O over A. Now what sort of meaning do you bring to those?

A. It depends on what shape you're working on doesn't it? Triangle.

Q. Can you remember what any of the letters stand for?

A. Opposite, Adjacent, Hypotenuse. I don't remember anything else about what they mean though.

Q. So what do you know about the triangle?

A. It's got three sides. It's got a right angle in one corner. Don't ask me for the names of the triangles because I can't do those.

Q. So you've got a right angle one. What does this mean? (*pointing to S=O/H*)

A. Sine equals opposite over hypotenuse – is that what you mean?

Q. Yes. What does that mean on the triangle?

A. I don't know, I don't remember what sine is – I don't remember why they have any relevance.

Q. No memory of what sine and cosine are? Put in the hypotenuse, opposite and adjacent.

A. That's opposite and I am not sure about these – is that adjacent? You'll have to help me out.

Q. If I tell you the hypotenuse is the side opposite the right angle does that help?

A. That one? Why's it called opposite – that's silly.

Q. So opposite to – what do you think it means?

A. I have no idea. I would have assumed that – (pause)

Q. Side is opposite to. . .?

A. It can be opposite to anything. It can be – that one (some exploratory drawing follows).

Q. And which one do you think is adjacent?

A. That one, because it's next to it.

Q. So what do you suppose the sine is then?

A. The angle – no?

Q. What does it say here? (*pointing to the equations she had drawn*)

A. Oh! sine equals opposite over hypotenuse so that one maybe. No, I don't know. I don't want to make a guess in case I'm wrong.

Q. OK. You told me what the sine is. What's the cosine?

A. Oh – this one – that one? Adjacent over hypotenuse. So that's one and that one.

Q. So if I had a triangle like that where I know that was of length 3 and that was of length 4, what can you tell me about the angle?

A. That it's about 45%.

We stress that we are not wishing to criticise the memory of this student. We are pinpointing a shift in how she conceives mathematics, away from the once familiar pathways of her schooling, and how she has moved on to new concerns. Much "learning" would surely disappear for most people. An intriguing feature of this interview is the way in which a key component of the student's school mathematics experience seems to have been remembered through a placeholder such as "SOHCAHTOA". The student believed this acronym located some associated mathematical knowledge but closer examination revealed a disconnection. The point of anchorage had dissolved. The relics of school mathematical learning have been depleted into signifiers with only hazy memories attached.

Here an interviewee (Yr. 4) is relatively expansive in her discussion of the possible connections between time and number:

A. You've got to have an understanding of number to be able to develop on to time and the same with money, but it's a different type with money because with time you're working to a base 60 and money you're working with a base 10 or 100.

Q. Is that confusing?

A. Yes, very. I look at this dial and I think how did I ever learn anything.

Q. Right so those two are connected, anything else, any other connections, any other mathematical concepts that are brought in when you talk time or when you talk money?

A. Well you've got fractions based in that and I suppose to the same extent you could have fractions built in with money like 50p is half of a pound and the children worked very much on those sort of scales. Because if you don't know that a circle cut into four and you don't know what four is then you've got no concept of either of them have you? I suppose really they could fit into fractions as well because you've got to have an idea of rotation and – so that's time as well isn't it because of quarter pasts and half past, the hands are moving round the clock aren't they? And you've got place value and you have to have –

Q. Where was place value?

A. That was with the money, but it's also connected with numbers because you've got to know the value of tens, units, hundreds.

Such discussion seems to point to the way in which so many aspects of primary school mathematics are tied in with specific pedagogical forms (e.g. fractions seen as partitions of a circle and thus a link to rotations).

Some students pointed to their own difficulty in communicating mathematical ideas and pointed to this in relation to a transmission conception of the teaching task.

I find it hard to explain it ...because I've known something so long it's ... just the way it is like say division and multiplication are inverses – I just know that, I just know it and I find it hard actually explain to them what I mean by that... I sometimes think – Oh am I confusing them? ... And I wish I could do that better (NQT).

In the second study we sought to focus on the language the trainees used as teachers in describing the mathematical content in their own classes. Our intention was to discuss the mathematics lesson in terms of the mathematics but the administrative pedagogical filter never seemed far away. It often felt that we were cornering the students so that they did not have the option of talking about anything other than mathematics.

The following male new teacher, who had identified maths as a problem at school, nevertheless displayed most mathematical insight in his discussion of his work with children. Let us take the following interview extract from a lengthy discussion:

> I'm trying to get the children to see that 6 × 4 would produce the same answer as 4 × 6 because that's work of the lowest ability group so that, I mean, we moved on actually to breaking it up into 3 different parts so we might have a 2, a 5 and a 3 in the box – would the answer be the same as if we had 5, 3 × 2? . . . because a lot of the children at that time, their concepts would (be) that it would have to be a completely different answer . . . I think that's what it was, you know, the reversing of the multiplication does the answer still work out? (NQT)

This provides an example of what we were seeking to target in the interviews but generally did not manage to get. What is contained in this extract? He clearly holds a concept of commutativity and associativity and sees these as concepts to be shared with children. There is some residue of classroom management concerns in the assigning of mathematical tasks to particular ability levels. Similarly, there is an assumption of mathematics being seen in terms of being ideas that you try and get children to see. In this case commutativity and associativity are the concepts being identified on the curriculum and activities with Multilink cubes are being constructed to introduce children to these concepts. The Multilink activity leads to visualisation of a particular form – the apparatus shapes the conception – the mathematics is a function of the pedagogic device. The new teacher continued expansively in a similar fashion in relation to some number patterns a child had generated:

> This child actually needed quite a lot of help to complete this one, but he's got the first couple given to him. 1 × 9 is 9. 2 × 8 is 16. And you can see it as a pattern that has emerged here. He's not used the blocks in a kind of a haphazard fashion. He's seen the pattern 1 × 2. He's broken it up into a 3 × 7, got the answer 21, got the 4 × 6 and then he's got 5, 6, 7, 8 – 5, 4, 3, 2 – so he's gone up and down to get his answers and same when we worked down here. He's worked independently but he's not done too much. As I say it took him quite a long time. It was quite interesting this one actually in that he worked out, for example, he broke his cubes up in this first one into 4 × 4 × 2 so he had a 4, a 4, a 2 so you need to do the 4 × 4 × 2 and he's actually worked out what 4 × 4 is – 16 × 2 gives him that answer so he's found it easier to work out the first bit and then work out, you know, the final bit. . .

Although mathematically unsophisticated, this interview demonstrated a trainee's capacity to analyse pupils' work in terms of its mathematical content that seemed absent in so many of the other interviews conducted.

## 6.3  The Secrets of the Forms of School Mathematics

In this book, mathematics as a notion is formed in the social space of the English primary classroom. This section focuses on some theoretical issues relating to mathematics as a subject to be taught and considers how it might emerge from the battle between the trainee's individual and social space. We begin by reviewing some of the discursive layers that have housed mathematical learning in the preceding

chapters. We then argue that it is important to see mathematical activity in relation
to other social activity, rather than just in relation to the mathematical ideas it is
designed to conjure. It is further argued that the commodification of mathematics
as a school subject in certain pedagogical forms overly restricts the generation of
mathematical thinking for pupils.

### 6.3.1  The Discursive Layers of Mathematics

*The consensual domain of mathematics*: In reading the interview transcripts as psychoanalytic materials there is no ultimate truth to be unearthed beneath the layers of
interpretation. Yet the way in which the trainees talk about their teaching is likely
to have some impact on the way in which they teach. We now wish to pursue the
more radical conjecture, namely, that this is also the case for mathematical activity
more generally: that there is nothing beneath the discursive layers of mathematics.
Nonetheless, the discourses themselves have a tangible effect, as an approach to
formatting or organising our thoughts, on our understanding of mathematics.

Before moving on with our assertion that we are unlikely to achieve consensus about the constitution of mathematics, we ask what sorts of things we might
want to insert into this totality, were it possible. Insofar as we are engaged in a
research enterprise designed to improve the practices of mathematics education,
what sorts of features may contribute to an aspired consensual domain? We might
address this by first asking what sorts of things may have been in this consensus until
now. Traditional aspirations in the domain of mathematics education research have
included an understanding of mathematics anchored beyond social particularities.
To abandon this would surely involve a painful sacrifice for many anchored to conceptions of humans with specific mental facilities relating to mathematics. It might
also cause discomfort to those seeing mathematics as a particular quality of the lived
world. We may add to this, problems for those with conceptions of teaching involving "correct" approaches and research strategies predicated on "improvement". In
this way conceptions of teachers and research have been centred on a specific conception of mathematics. How might we proceed if we have elected to drop anchor in
a social totality centred on mathematics? We pursue our concern with what constitutes mathematics in the trainee's mind. We ask what structures house the trainee's
conceptions of mathematics? How is mathematical learning a function of this edi-
fice? We are not seeking to locate mathematics as a definitive thing in itself rather
we seek to understand how it results from the interplay between, on the one hand,
the individual trainee's perception of it and, on the other, reifications of mathematical understandings as manifest in social institutional forms. We review and extend
some of the examples we have offered of how school mathematics is shaped.

*Mathematics as a function of pedagogical discourse*

School mathematics is a function of the educational domain in which it is encountered. How we see the salient features of mathematical learning depends on where
we are positioned in any educative process. The structure and content of school

mathematics is also a function of the learning theory that we choose to apply in observing it happen. It seems inescapable that pedagogical discourses relate to the enterprise they support and govern the choice of teaching devices, which in turn condition the mathematical learning. For example, in an analysis of a teaching scheme, mathematical tasks designed for less able students were found to be of a different nature to those given to their more able peers.[6] For any given topic, the emphasis on the instruction varied between the texts, and it seemed to result in exclusion for the less able from the real business of mathematical learning as understood in more abstract terms. Instead, they were caught in the discourse of "less able" mathematics. The analysis identified at least two levels of mathematics, each characterised by a discourse with associated styles of illustration, questioning and assumed perspectives. But clearly there are many such discourses operating in mathematics education. Moreover as with the distinctions between mathematics designed in the schemes for less or more able students, differences between these discourses are swept over. In many situations, this is a consequence of outcomes being seen primarily on a register of mathematical content, independent of the processes that led to them. Nevertheless, each of these discourses misses the mathematics it seeks to locate. Each is characterised by some sort of illustrative approach that simultaneously serves as a teaching device, but this arguably draws us away from the mathematics.[7] This, of course, is also true of the mathematical tasks designed for the more able students following a scheme where situations are couched in more overtly mathematical forms. Each of these discourses is predicated on some sort of mathematical objective. This might be tied down to performance in a specific discursive frame, such as the solving of a linear equation or more transcendental mathematical claims such as abstraction, the noting of generality or intuition. School mathematics is mediated and articulated through many teaching devices. These devices, however, should not be seen merely as a means to an end, since such embedding is crucial to the constitution of the ideas being studied within "school mathematics". Such constructions of mathematics, however, also result in associated constructions of the students working through mathematics construed in this way. That is, the student is seen as "high" or "low" ability, at a particular "developmental stage", "ready" for a particular style of teaching; "mathematically intuitive", an "interpreter" of mathematical ideas or a "doer" of mathematical procedures.[8] These terms predicate particular learning theories and assessment strategies, and the particular characteristics they value. We shall return to the example of ability shortly.

   Earlier, we briefly discussed the transformation of "subject knowledge" into "pedagogic content knowledge". This repackaging of mathematics necessitates facility with the representations, illustrations, examples, explanations and analogies

---

[6]Dowling (1996).

[7]The educational strategy of getting analogies to fit the ideas being taught is also well trodden in science education. See, for example, Heywood and Parker (1997, 2010).

[8]cf. Sfard and Linchevski (1994).

that make mathematical ideas comprehensible to others. We feel that the separation between pedagogical form and mathematical content is misleading, however, since all learning can be seen as representational, as can all mathematics. The practice of primary mathematics as observable in schools is, however, subordinated by an organisational discourse that further distances classroom practice from more overtly mathematical forms. Teaching mathematics is, for many primary teachers, the implementation of government requirements played out through commercially produced schemes. Specialist attention to mathematics teaching within university courses and even school placements is weak, and struggles to compete with basic issues of survival in the classroom judged through organisational criteria.

## Conceptions of the Curriculum

We have sought to examine how curriculum-based conceptions of mathematics redefine the mathematics being tackled. The attempt to describe mathematics in a curriculum inevitably results in a caricature of traditional understandings of mathematics as a discipline. However, this caricature can be viewed variously. For example, as a serious but imperfect attempt to describe mathematics to guide school teaching *or* a cynical ploy to make teachers and children more accountable according to specific institutionalised accounts of mathematics *or* a reconfiguration of mathematics itself to meet contemporary needs. We do not need to reach a final resolution of such dilemmas. For example, a trainee may happily work with many such notions variously activated according to demands made at different stages of his or her training. As we have seen Lacan talks of a fundamental mis-recognition in personal identity construction. The self with whom the individual identifies is a fragmented self threaded through with alternative discourses of practice that fail to meet and be reconciled with each other. Interpretations of the curriculum, rather than facts about the curriculum, govern the trainees' sense making but these interpretations evolve as they are reconciled with new experience.

## Regulative shaping of mathematics in trainees' minds

We have considered how mathematics is held in place by official regulation or normative practice in schools. Recent reform in initial teacher education in England has resulted in mathematics being bureaucratised to a much greater degree. How might we understand this change and its effects in terms of the social constitution of mathematics? How does this modify existing conceptions of mathematics? Or rather, how does mathematics get repositioned with regard to earlier aspirations relating to professional discourses? The bureaucratic shaping of mathematics changes mathematics itself and the way it ultimately supports the social activity that it targets. That is, the substance of mathematics becomes oriented around certain commonsensical accounts of what mathematics is, for example, a particular set of skills specified according to certain criteria. This bureaucratic grip extends to trainees following the official line because they feel ill equipped to develop, conceive or follow anything more personal. Or indeed they may see it as their personal approach, steeped as they are in the social apparatus. Job entry requirements are specified in terms of the attainment of skills specified in such ways. The trainees then understand their professional aspirations in these terms.

*Reluctance to participate in mathematical discourse*

Mathematics does not slip smoothly off the tongues of some trainees. Their nervousness in relation to the subject prevents more fluent articulation about the nature of the subject, even if mathematics were to have a more fulsome social discourse attached to it. The result of this, we suggest, is that teacher discourses about mathematics that might be evident amongst teachers working with older students, are relatively undeveloped among primary teachers. They have many subjects to teach, and for many trainees mathematics is not the topic through which they choose to develop their broader professional discourses. We offered some examples earlier, but there was not much of a directly mathematical nature. Against this backdrop, there is also the individual trainee's personal need to build a conception of professionalism around her sense of her own professional worth. In part, this professional worth is understood by trainees in terms of effective participation in socially constructed programmes designed to improve the quality of mathematics taught in schools. Collective programmes may provide motivation for new teachers by offering a framework against which these teachers can build a conception of their professional functionality in relation to their evolving personal definition of what it is to be a teacher. This definition, however, is often the result of a suppression of the teacher's anxiety as to the nature of mathematics, and their capacity to learn the subject. But further, seeing mathematics purely in terms of administering a curriculum surely cannot be seen as being sufficient. Such a limited perspective on teaching risks depriving the new teacher of assuming curriculum responsibility shaped around their personal aspirations and sense of ownership of their professional task. For any development of mathematics, we might at least hope for some expression of professional integrity on the part of new teachers drawing classroom mathematics towards their more personal conceptions of teaching the subject. It would seem, however, that such conceptions, at least as insofar as they require explicit discussion of mathematics, are often expressed in relative silence.

*Mis-recognition of participation in emancipatory[9] enterprises*

It appears evident from our data that many conceptions of teaching are apparently based around an accentuation of a teaching role predicated on critically progressive aspirations. Child-centred conceptions of teaching, for example, figure prominently in our student interviews. Many conceptions of teaching displayed within those interviews are predicated on some sort of idealism in which the trainee has a key role to play:

> I like having young children and being able to love them, you know... I feel it's important to catch... them young and to... instil the right values into them and I feel that I can do that and I think that they respond better at a younger age, because they've not had as much input and they're a bit more open to different values, but I think when they get older I think you

---

[9]The term is typically associated with Habermas.

get more set in your ways and it is a bit harder to break bad habits and things like that. . .
really break things (Yr. 4).

In Althusser's terms, trainees are guided by mis-recognitions of themselves following a particular social programme – whether that be the official programme aimed
at raising standards or a more liberatory education predicated on personal enlight-
enment in a broader sense. The potential for individuals to make things better in
some absolute sense is dampened as a result of mathematical learning's becoming an aspect of social compliance. A transmission orientation to teaching seems
more likely insofar as mathematics is seen as a subject needing to be taught rather
than generated anew by the learner: a potential reproduction of the practices that
seemingly gave rise to anxieties about mathematical learning in the first place.
Liberatory education, meanwhile, appears to be on the back burner in England,
except in fuelling an occasional attempt at critiquing the new regime. This has
sometimes led to a backlash in the form of initiatives predicated on promoting
creativity to re-motivate lost souls.[10] The trainee teachers we interviewed specified their professional identities in terms of affinities with official discourses, and
transgressions were generally shaped within this frame. Idealism did, nevertheless,
shape the trainees' conceptions of their professional selves albeit in a constrained
way. And the government teacher recruitment publicity material certainly played up
to this: after all, to quote a high-profile teacher recruitment campaign, "everyone
remembers a good teacher".

### 6.3.2 The Productivity of Discourse

School mathematics is held in place by a variety of discourses and interpreted variously by trainees according to perceived need and ability. We have urged a move
away from universally supposed conceptions of mathematics and practice designed
to nurture them. Rather, the cultural specificity of particular curriculum formulations of mathematics should influence the styles of teaching that go with them. Yet
no matter how much analysis we carry out we will never get to the bottom of what
mathematics really is. Mathematics, as a way of thinking, is situated amidst a multitude of discursive layers, none of which pinpoint it. If we strip away all the layers,
we are not left with the essence of mathematics. We are left with nothing. Nothing,
that is, apart from the psychic and material effects resulting from the discourses;
the people and places that have been affected by the existence of mathematics. But
mathematics itself has no material existence.[11] We suggest that it is necessarily the
discursive layers that teach us what mathematics is. These discursive layers need to

---

[10]ESRC *Creativity in Education Seminar Series*, 2003–2005; BEAM conference *Promoting Creativity in Mathematics*, 2005.

[11]This is consistent with the contemporary philosophy of Badiou (2007, p. 7) who declares that there are no mathematical objects. Brown (2010), discusses this in relation to the renewal of knowledge in mathematics education contexts.

be seen as part of the stuff of school mathematics. We have seen how mathematics is reified in the verbal consciousness of the trainees themselves, caught as they are between many alternative discourses. We have examined the sorts of mathematics and the sorts of teachers that drop out of this struggle. We have questioned how the trainees' and new teachers' accounts pull at the reality they face. Now we ask how we might learn from what we see as necessary failures in fitting models (of teaching, of mathematics) to our analysis. Our next step is an attempt to pinpoint the ontological basis of our endeavour to fit such models.

So to emphasise the point: mathematics as such does not exist in any material sense.[12] Nevertheless it produces tangible effects in psychic, social and physical activity. It formats reality. This notion is akin to Foucault's poststructuralist understanding of discourses. Discourses do not have a positive existence yet, nevertheless, produce effects. They shape our lives, by impacting on our creation and reading of events, even though they do not have any content as such. Mathematics does not impact on our lives as mathematics *qua* mathematics but, rather, through the social practices that take up mathematical ideas into their forms. There are, however, many social practices and their associations with mathematics are varied. The effects are a composite of many social forces, where any specific conception of mathematical shaping might not be privileged.

Contemporary hermeneutic understandings of discourse see interpretation as being integral to the discourse itself. That is, discourses comprise a seamless layer of text that extends into specific interpretative approaches. The interface between words and action is softened. In Gadamer's hermeneutics "there is more truth in the later efficacy of a text, in the series of its subsequent readings, than in its supposedly 'original' meaning".[13] This is perhaps the key theoretical point of this book. The idea of, and the ideas of, mathematics have effects on what we *do* as action. And it is that *action* relating to mathematics and accounts of that action that lend themselves to interpretation.

Any linguistic account of the properties of mathematics is necessarily restrictive, a reduction that inevitably misses much of that which it seeks to describe. In many situations, however, it is this very constraint that activates the mathematical thinking itself. In this book we have sought to emphasise the word "education" in the term "mathematics education" towards privileging its status as a social science, susceptible to social scientific analysis. Mathematics, as practised in schools, entails participation in a socially defined practice and is held in place by a range of social discourses. Husserl (1989), in his classic work on phenomenology, in struggling to get at the truth of geometry, spoke of how intuition "very quickly and in increasing measure falls victim to the seduction of language".[14] Thus we argue our analysis of school mathematics should focus on the functioning of these discourses. We cannot focus on the functioning of mathematics in its own right. Symbolic forms can

---

[12]This has been discussed in relation to the Lacanian philosophy of Badiou by Brown (2010).

[13]Quoted by Žižek (1989, p. 214).

[14]See also Brown and Heywood (in press).

point to key aspects of mathematics but cannot be synonymous with them. There is always a gap. It is this gap that guides us here. In particular, we need to ask what attitude we should have towards it.

In a poststructuralist-oriented analysis, such as that offered by Foucault, we could recognise that no discursive account specifies mathematics as such. This framework, however, does not assist us necessarily with the undeniable qualities and properties of mathematics, which do have real psychic effects in more abstract mathematical analysis. There are also highly significant material effects in practical enterprises such as building bridges, the effective analysis of economic models, or everyday finance. Trainee teachers are involved in many discourses, more or less obliquely mathematical, in relation to their task of teaching mathematics in the primary school. There are properties in mathematics itself, which guide but do not fix these discourses. Mathematics introduces polarities around which the discourses flow. For example, our descriptions of ourselves moving around may draw on geometrical or spatial terminology, which provide a structural filter on our movements.[15] Our movements and, in many respects, our sense of how our bodies move physically are understood with reference to such terminology. Or more generally, mathematical modelling of real life situations is shaped around mathematical concepts. The discursive flow results in actual impact on the physical and social world. Actions follow from instances of mathematical modelling. In schools, however, it might be argued that it is a *commodified* version of mathematics that has taken the lead. The institutionalised markers of the polarities have taken on a life of their own. That is, mathematical language itself points to a style of social interpretation, social practices, or ways of understanding the teacher–pupil relationship. The reifications of mathematical entities replace the mathematical entities themselves in guiding thought. As we saw earlier "it's impossible to teach place value without those arrow cards, they're superb because ... the children can understand it so much easier". But this sort of issue becomes more serious when a curriculum enshrines a method as one that all students should follow. Yet more serious is the tendency for international comparisons to conceptualise mathematics more generally as specified types of performance in a particular set of prescribed skills.

Mathematics underpins social practice. This practice is subject to multiple interpretations. But mathematics is itself more than a social practice. There is something more significant that needs to be accounted for. The assertion of mathematics as knowledge influences, or even creates, that which it is trying to locate. By acting as if the statement were true, in a sense, it becomes true, and the actions become a reification of that truth. They stand in for that truth, and in a certain sense become that truth. If mathematics is seen as being about learning multiplication tables, the emphasis on mathematical tables becomes part of the commodification of mathematics and the way it is understood more broadly. But more generally the statements that seek to locate mathematical phenomena so often become the statements that

---

[15]Ibid.

police its boundaries.[16] Such fluidity of meaning marks the on-going historical formation of mathematics in the context of social practices. Mathematics is both an assertion in the text but also a denial that such assertions in the text locate mathematics. It has no positive existence yet functions as though it did have. Nevertheless, social objects are generated through which mathematics is understood. The guarantor of the identity of an object is *"the retroactive effect of naming itself. It is the name itself, the signifier, which supports the identity of the object".*[17] The name "mathematics" alone remains in the intersection of all the descriptive features that we may assign to mathematics. The name holds the place. All other descriptive features of mathematics fall short of locating mathematics itself.

Yet for Lacan there are psychological drives that escape regulation through our attempts to pin things down in clear terms. Desires are re-routed as a result of our unsuccessful attempts to satisfy them. The elements left out of any description come up to haunt the elements that have been included. And there will always be elements that escape the grasp of any description. There is a delinquent in all of us who does what s/he pleases, what he enjoys, outside of the framework governing our actions. For someone engaged in mathematics, the symbols within which one is immersed activate mental dynamics not quite captured in the symbols themselves. For the trainee teacher following government prescriptions within their training, there may be a perverse pleasure involved in gauging one's actions against these rules and seeking to comply. And as we have argued in the earlier parts of this chapter conceptions of mathematics derive from these attempts to follow social rules with educational contexts.

Yet the regulation in educational contexts is defined through precise language. Teachers are very often given very prescriptive directions that fail to activate rich educational experiences:

> Pupils should be taught to understand addition and use related vocabulary; recognise that addition can be done in any order; understand subtraction as both 'take away' and 'difference' and use the related vocabulary; recognise that subtraction is the inverse of addition; give the subtraction corresponding to an addition and vice versa; use the symbol '=' to represent equality; solve simple missing number problems [for example, $6 = 2 + ?$ ] (National Curriculum).

Similar detail is provided in advising how this might be achieved and the standardisation across teachers sets norms of practice that translate as regulation. In this way mathematics gets to be defined as a set of skills, procedures and competencies that partition mathematics in to so many discrete components. That is, mathematics manifests itself as so many commodities exchanged in the educational marketplace.

---

[16]cf. Gattegno (1963), Freudenthal (1978).

[17]Žižek (1989, p. 95), original emphasis.

The term "commodity", however, requires some unfolding.[18] A social form mediates the desire, or stands in for it. Similarly, mathematics is desired by society. This desire to have mathematics gets expressed as a demand for something more specific, such as a set of particular skills, or a curriculum of a certain form. What is concealed in the forms of mathematics crafted as commodities? Or rather what is embedded in the materials and practices through which people encounter what is called, "mathematics" in the classroom? What are the dominant commodity forms in primary mathematics education and how do they govern our practices and our analyses of those practices?[19] Similarly, what are the secrets of the form of a teacher as a commodity? That is, in our social construction of "primary mathematics teacher", what do we include? And how do societal desires to incorporate mathematics in life get translated into teacher training programmes of the forms they currently take? What desires are being expressed in teacher training guidance provided for universities and their students?

We propose that mathematics *as it is manifested in primary classroom activities* is a symptom of other things. That is, it is not only a symptom, for example, of a higher mathematics of the sort a university academic mathematician would suppose. It is, perhaps, more significantly referenced to social practices. For example, primary mathematics may be crafted to be consistent with the wider primary curriculum and models of classroom organisation, valuing other things such as quality interactions between pupils, activities that keep children quiet, pupil autonomy and appropriate classroom behaviour. Nevertheless, the influence of a more traditional conception of mathematics remains strongly present in the sense that this mathematics provides the system against which the correctness of school mathematics is judged. The point in our analysis here is not to target the underlying mathematics as the ultimate quest but rather to question why mathematical activities in the classroom have assumed the social forms that they have. That is, why have they become commodities with a given form? We are seeking to reduce the emphasis on the *metaphorical* association between mathematical activity and mathematical ideas. Rather we propose a *metonymic* association between mathematical activity and social activity more generally.[20] This entails linking the mathematical activities (seen as activities governed

---

[18]Žižek makes a rather curious analogy between the notion of commodity in the work of Marx and dream in the work of Freud. He sees both as being symptoms of something else. With both commodity and dream we should "avoid the properly fetishistic fascination of the 'content' supposedly hidden behind the form: the 'secret' to be unveiled through analysis is not the content hidden by the form (the form of commodities, the form of dreams) but, on the contrary, *the 'secret' of this form itself.* The theoretical intelligence of the form of the dreams does not consist in penetrating from the manifest content to its 'hidden kernel', to the latent dream thoughts; it consists in the answer to the question; why have the latent dream thoughts assumed such a form, why were they transposed in to the form of a dream?" (Žižek, 1989, p. 11) Similarly, in relation to commodities, Žižek argues that capitalist economic analysis suppresses alternative understandings of the value of labour.

[19]Williams (forthcoming), discusses theoretical conceptions of "use" and "exchange" values of mathematics education within our "audit" culture from a Cultural Historical Activity Theory perspective.

[20]This develops an idea first explored elsewhere (Brown, 1987, pp. 171–174).

by certain procedures, rules, performance criteria, etc) with other social discourses, including those specifically related to mathematics. The meaning of the mathematical discourses thus becomes a function of their relationship with the other discourses with which they are entwined.[21] This softens any assumption that the activities are anchored in specific mathematical concepts. Rather, we need to attend to the reification of such supposed concepts as they unfold in alternative discourses. This would move us away from any universal conceptions of what mathematics should be about but instead alerts us to the historical and social processes that generated classroom mathematics in the forms it now takes.

As an example of how discourses work, we shall return to our earlier brief discussion of the way in which teachers' conceptions of the child's ability shape the mathematics offered. Here a new teacher differentiates between pupils:

> They were each given a set of digit cards and they had to generate initially a two-digit number. ... The lower ability had a pile with the 1 and 2 in and then the rest of the cards and they could only make a number up to 30, and the higher abilities moved on after doing a few examples ... to using the 100 s and they made the number. And then they had to write it out. To meet the objective they had to write it out as a word as a number and then how many tens, how many units.

It would appear that the teacher's conception of the mathematics is a function of how she understands children's ability. The composition of the lesson results from how the teacher makes this assessment. The bureaucratic discourse of children's ability is constructed in particular ways. For example, the perceived teacher-learner relationship between a teacher and a high ability child may be predicated on the teacher's assuming that the child can perform certain skills prescribed in particular ways, at a fast pace, without any help. Meanwhile for the slower child the teacher assumes that the skills need to be prescribed differently and that they will take the child longer to perform. Both content and style of learning are adjusted according to the child's ability. Explicitly mathematical concerns appear to be getting squeezed out or transformed by administrative technology, such as classroom organisation setting learning parameters for different pupils. Activities are being created according to the respective needs of higher or lower ability students. Teaching objectives are being shaped around the particular demands of the curriculum. Mathematical work is targeted at revision for tests. Mathematics is thus commodified against a register of particular social discourses. In this sense the child's performance is a function of the learning theory being applied.

Yet we cannot assume consistency between children as to their apparent readiness to occupy new understandings and that this readiness is not straightforwardly associated with broader mathematical ability. Sfard and Linchevski discuss a child whose preference for considered interpretative assessment of meaning slows him down against a peer more amenable to unreflective implementation of techniques. It is this example which gives rise to their distinction between "interpreter" and "doer". They characterise the students' respective motives as follows:

---

[21] Presmeg (e.g. 2002) discusses this issue further.

> the meaningfulness. . . of the learning is, to a great extent, a function of student's expectations and aims: true interpreters will struggle for meaning whether we help them or not, whereas the doers will always rush to do things rather than think about them. The problem with the doers stems not so much from the fact that they are not able to find meaning as from their lack of urge to look for it. In a sense they do not even bother about what it means to understand mathematics (Sfard & Linchevski, 1994, p. 264).

This muddies the water in any attempt to draw clear distinctions between mathematical and cognitive domains. On the one hand, there are unreflective performances of mathematical procedures. On the other, there may be more sustained attempts to understand mathematics more deeply which can work against performance at least in the short term. This disrupts any straightforward attempt to correlate cognitive ability with mathematical performance. The preferences of interpreter and doer seem conflicted. Their mathematical progression is in different ways dependent on, among other things, chosen teaching strategies, or the assessment instruments applied. These in varying degrees impact on the student through the way in which they perceive their work being evaluated. Also learning theories used in explaining this progression might be seen as partisan, prejudicing against particular learners or against certain capacities or potentialities present within all learners.[22]

Consequently, any supposed discourse of mathematics gets meshed with a discourse of ability that points to particular ways of organising the classroom and constructing the content of any lesson. Yet in so many educational situations it is the latter that assumes prominence and takes the lead in shaping classroom activity. Mathematics gets defined as a performance of skills as specified in a discourse of ability, a commodification of mathematics that can be read off on a register of the child's ability.

In our analogy of the market place, commodified versions of mathematics would be exchanged. The signifier dominates the supposed signified. The word is more stable than the idea it holds. For example, a mathematics activity designed for a less able learner replaces the mathematical idea being sought. And signifiers respond to and shape other signifiers. An account of mathematics for the less able replaces mathematical thought per se. The commodified versions create the illusion that there is something more tangible beneath. These commodified versions however comprise the currency used to measure and classify mathematical thinking. The need for accountability in mathematical learning results in specific transformations of the mathematical teaching and learning around commodified forms. This might be seen as akin to the hermeneutic process described earlier where continuous understanding is processed as discrete explanations. The criteria-referenced account of mathematics manifested in international audits seems like an obvious example in this respect. The original desires for including mathematical ideas in our everyday lives, it seems, are being rewritten, to meet a specific caricature of mathematics. This caricature is produced in order to assess mathematical activity for the purposes of making international comparisons within a particular skills-based framework. In

---

[22]This is discussed more fully elsewhere (Brown, 2001). See also Even and Schwarz (2003).

this example, mathematics is being defined around specific reifications of intellectual processes. School curricula respond by increasingly emphasising skills rather than deeper appreciation. Such packaging of mathematics points to fantasies of what mathematics is "really" like, they provide particular ways of structuring reality. In this sort of process mathematical learning is reduced to the acquisition of specific forms of skills akin to mere commodities in a market. This defines value in a specific way and only takes account of certain measurable features. But in turn those measurable features come to be seen as mathematics itself, or at least condition this mathematics within the particular environment. In the sense that economics reduces things to commodities understood in terms of price, the assessment of mathematical learning is similarly reduced to context independent measures. International test criteria are culturally insensitive insofar as they are specified according to a supposedly universal cultural conception of the subject.

For example, in a number of countries with regional disparities of economic development, the promotion of mathematical learning according to international test criteria does not necessarily meet local employment needs. Indeed exam credits specified in terms of the criteria often lead to the students leaving their local community, and moving to more developed parts of the country or beyond. In certain rural areas in Sri Lanka, there are difficulties retaining high quality students in the tea industry as exam success in school mathematics is specified in terms of international understandings of mathematics. Such success leads to careers in the cities. Further, the curriculum is not generally shaped around the needs of the relatively homogeneous local economy. As with capitalism, mathematics gets created as a set of commodities and circulated as if one size fits all (Brown, 2003b). The dominant ideology of what school mathematics is gets to be circulated to all corners of the globe as though it is equally applicable everywhere. Resistance to this takes many forms, some of which we have examined and not least the remarkable capacity of trainee teachers to create a discourse of mathematics teaching with almost no explicit mathematical content.[23]

Our own memories as students of university mathematics, however, point to another example. So much of the substance of our lectures and the examinations that followed them comprised reproductions of classic results, e.g. "State and prove the Bolzano-Weierstrass theorem". These reproductions so often felt like the empty signifiers such as SOHCAHTOA failing to locate the excitement behind the work that led to their original production by others many years before. There is much variation between the commodified forms of "mathematics". Mathematical thinking is understood through such forms yet each fails in different ways.

We have highlighted the differences between first, the mathematical content or idea, second, its manifestation in a culturally located pedagogical form, and third, the desires that bring us to these phenomena in the first place.[24] Desire might

---

[23] See also DeFreitas (2004).

[24] For Freud the dream has a "structure (that) is always triple. This comprises the *manifest dream-text*, the *latent dream content* or thought and the *unconscious desire* articulated in a dream" (Žižek,

be associated with, for example, the excitement of mathematics to those who are mathematicians, the administrative control issues for those in government, or the relationship with children for young teachers. The underlying desires for many trainees teaching mathematics, we here claim, are largely unrelated to overt forms of mathematical activity. The *form* has usurped the *content* as a result of *desire* mistaking its object.

For a trainee teacher setting a mathematical task, there is the activity as performed by the child according to the curriculum demand, the mathematical concept supposed to underlie it, but then also the more unconscious desires being mediated by those forms. For example, desire may be expressed as wanting children to participate in some form of mathematical activity of the sort the teacher finds exciting, controlling the class effectively, being liked by the children, or meeting curriculum targets. Desire confronts an amalgam of social forces acted out in many conflicting ways and representing a multitude of alternative discourses. The unconscious desire may be the reconciliation of all these forces through one teacher. The mathematical activity and supposed underlying mathematical concept are conflated to suppress an amalgam of alternative forces. From an educational standpoint we need to analyse this attempted reconciliation, not the supposed delivery of the mathematical content in the mathematical activity. We are not looking for the true meaning of the mathematics, but rather we need to analyse how the social arrangements reveal our desires beyond. This comprises an exploration of the metonymic plane. The process through which mathematics has been bureaucratised has, in this analogy, become *mythologised* into particular social forms where signifier and signified get jarred in to a fixed relation.[25] And those forms clearly do shape public conceptions of what mathematics is and support intellectual and other activities in particular ways. The *commodification* of mathematics provides the social forms that enable mathematics to be circulated in support of social activity, whether as exam credits for professional advancement or in support of practical enterprises such as civil engineering projects or accountancy procedures. Yet this commodification can hinder the release of more futuristic conceptions of mathematics and how it might be learnt.

## 6.4  Conclusion

In this chapter we first sought to identify different types of trainee speech to see how these were revelatory of trainee understandings of mathematics in the specific social contexts of the classroom. Nevertheless, we felt that many trainees closed the discussion down or, at least, showed some disinclination or inability to develop their points. As such, these interviews did not lend themselves to transcription. The

---

1989, p. 13). We could regard the mathematical activity, or teaching device, as analogous to the manifest content (the *form*). The latent content is the supposed mathematical *content*. Yet the *desire* at work is constituted through a host of contributory factors.

[25]Barthes (1972), Gabriel and Žižek (2009).

trainees generally circumnavigated such mathematical difficulties in their accounts of their mathematics teaching, or found it difficult to say anything at all. This is not to say that the trainees are not effective classroom practitioners in mathematics. It may be that this sort of reflective capacity is not essential for effective classroom functioning. Our empirical enquiries, however, had sought to examine the degree to which trainees could articulate more fully the rationale underpinning their actions. Teaching, we felt, was governed by policies that (sometimes) assumed more than mere instrumental interpretation. The key purpose of our study was, after all, to see how trainees made sense of their own actions with regard to their mathematics teaching. Our findings, nevertheless, point to mathematically oriented discussion being undeveloped in trainee and new teacher accounts of their own classroom practice.

We have argued that a more mathematically oriented perspective resists insertion into the discursive practices of the trainees we are concerned with here. We have considered a dual perspective of (a) locating mathematical ways of thinking within social practices and of (b) assuming mathematics and then constructing social practices through that lens. We have, however, privileged the former rather than the latter on the grounds that we cannot locate a singular perspective from which to assume mathematics. We have argued that the commodification of mathematics as a discipline is a symptom of social desires expressed through certain social assumptions about the nature of mathematics and the way it addresses those desires. Further, mathematical culture has become more directly a function of its commodification, not the desires that led to this commodification.

For example, mathematics in English schools today has become a function of the audit culture that emerged in the 1990s. The mathematics we are coming to know is a function of the prevailing ideology. The original desires for including mathematics in our everyday lives have been rewritten. In many contemporary contexts, mathematics has come to be defined as *an end result* of an intellectual process rather than as *the process* of getting there. School curricula now emphasise skills rather than deeper appreciation, "doing" rather than "interpreting". University mathematics has so often become a survey of end points rather than a re-generation of mathematical experience. The symbolisation teaches us what we already know but introduces reification, and thus a commodification, and in due course mummification. This packaging of mathematical activity is a function of the supposed fulfilled fantasy of what mathematics really is.

We have suggested that an administrative language of how teaching should be conducted has replaced a more direct focus on the mathematical content of the children's work; and the reference offered to the child's ability might be read in this way. They can be seen as an alternative discursive apparatus that releases the teacher from needing to be more explicitly mathematical in describing the children's learning. Yet this apparatus can, nevertheless, shape classroom activity in mathematics, and hence shape the way in which children understand mathematics. The name "mathematics" locates something that is more than the sum of alternative descriptions of mathematics. For a teacher setting a mathematical task, there is the activity as performed by the child, the mathematics supposed to underlie it but then also the more unconscious desires being mediated by those forms. These desires shape mathematics and in that sense these desires are part of mathematics. Such desires could, for example, result from attempts to reconcile alternative demands, such as the teacher wanting children to do mathematics in a particular way, or meeting curriculum targets, or following other externally imposed rules.

In fact, trainee accounts of how they teach mathematics never catch up with them, but that should not stop them from trying. And these misses can nevertheless be informative. Perhaps it is possible to change attitudes to these apparent gaps. The gaps after all are responsible for continued motivation. In building a sort of inventory of what mathematics "actually" looks like within trainee discourse they can aspire to, but not succeed in, presenting a full picture. Mathematics will always exceed specific manifestations of it. Yet, this surplus over such manifestations points to a disappointment that it is not possible to be more precise. But it is this surplus, or gap, that results in motivation, or desire. There is a sense that there should have been more to it than has been pinpointed. We have argued that the *unity* of any given "experience of meaning" in the primary classroom is illusory. This supposed unity is supported by the name "mathematics". But in this location "mathematics" serves as a "'pure' meaningless 'signifier without the signified'" (Žižek, 1989, p. 97). The name "mathematics" that has been used liberally and variously throughout this book locates something that is more than the sum of descriptions of it. Yet in a sense it disappears as a socially accessible entity when these descriptions are removed. It has proved quite impossible to adopt a consistent perspective on what mathematics "is". Mathematics has the quality of "a pure signifier that designates, and at the same time constitutes, the identity of a given object beyond the variable cluster of its descriptive properties".[26] In the student accounts that we have offered, "mathematics" is only being accessed indirectly through descriptions of the activities taking place around it. And the sum of those aspects is not the whole. Or is it?

---

[26]Žižek (1989, p. 98). Žižek cites Kripke and his notion of a "rigid designator".

# Chapter 7
# Implications for Practice

## 7.1 Introduction

As this book draws to a close, we shall summarise its empirical basis and theoretical intent before building some further arguments based on our discussion. We commenced with a brief examination of how the teaching of mathematics in primary schools might be better understood. We looked at how some primary school trainees and new teachers conceptualised their professional challenge and how this understanding was a function of the training process and of the curriculum frameworks they encountered. The interviews that we carried out provided a way of accessing this emergent understanding whilst at the same time gaining some sense of the trainees' personal aspirations with regard to their chosen career in teaching.

There was a range of concerns where we felt this empirical analysis might assist us. We wished to develop an understanding of what it is to be a new teacher and build a picture of new teacher identity. In doing this, we also sought to develop theoretical apparatus for more broadly understanding teacher identity, an area that has attracted wider interest in mathematics education research and more extensively across the social sciences in recent years. This concern with teacher identity is often centred in how training might mobilise adjustments to wider practices. Teacher educators meanwhile need to confront their own role in policy mediation as their professional and academic autonomy has been eroded. We considered how we might better define the balance in initiating teacher development between personal enrichment and setting policies that explicitly prescribe the practices of individual teachers. We sought to examine trainees' responsiveness to policy initiatives so that we might better understand the effects specific policy adjustments have on the process of teacher training. These issues were examined in relation to a group of trainee teachers for a number of years spanning their university training and their first year of teaching in school. We were able to gain some perspective on the training process and gain some insight into how the trainees responded to different aspects of this process.

In carrying out this empirical analysis, we introduced some theoretical apparatus drawn from contemporary research in psychoanalytic theory. This provided a perspective on how we might understand the identity of trainee and new teachers as caught between personal, professional and social agendas. This enabled us to

T. Brown, O. McNamara, *Becoming a Mathematics Teacher*,
Mathematics Education Library 53, DOI 10.1007/978-94-007-0554-8_7,
© Springer Science+Business Media B.V. 2011

examine how trainee and new teachers construct themselves in language as individuals mediating the various personal and professional demands they face. Moreover, this theoretical perspective allowed us to read our empirical material with regard to understanding how mathematics is created between the official guidance and the trainees' own conceptualisation and enacting of this in the classroom. We attempted to pinpoint the trainees' styles of mediation of the mathematical discourses as specified in curriculum materials. In this way, we sought to locate and describe mathematics as it was understood by trainee and new teachers and presented to children.

In this concluding chapter, we identify key strands and build some arguments out of our findings towards considering how practice might be re-thought across these strands. First, we focus on how centralised policies shape teacher development. Second, we summarise the social constitution of mathematics in the primary classroom more generally. Third, we gather our thoughts on how mathematics in the primary school derives from centralised policies. We then consider the function of research in mathematics education in supporting work in these areas. We envisage that readers of this book will define their own practices in relation to each of these themes. Each theme derives from particular socially specific constructions where individuals mediate these constructions from their individual professional locations. The individual role as a stand-alone actor is generally compromised through his or her location within social trends and practices. As a consequence, the individual can never be too sure about his or her individual and social boundaries, and of how the professional landscape might be assessed in terms of what the individual might be able to do. In this final chapter, we explore alternative takes on critical practice that might intercept some of the newly dominant constructions that have compromised the professional agency of teachers.

## 7.2  Implications for Teacher Development

Educational policies are presented to individual teachers who filter them through their own agendas, and through quite a few other agendas besides. Policy statements often comprise a hardening up of multiple attempts to make sense of complex situations or assertions of speculative causal relationships. The common sense of the media or the simple stories that fuel political manifestos can often shape teaching practices, curriculum apparatus or research contracts. Policy mingles with other factors in the trainees' frame of reference, as part of a fuller story of how trainees pass through their training. But whose story are we seeking to tell and from which perspective? Clearly trainee teachers are a diverse group of people and our survey focused on a small sample at one university. There were many differences between the trainees and their understandings of what it was to become a teacher. Further, the group were entering teaching on a crest of major new initiatives in English schools, redefining classroom practices during the period of their training, and of our own studies. This period straddled two conceptual eras in terms of how teaching mathematics was understood. Our intention in the research was not to provide an account of what students were saying in any absolute sense. The task was seen more in terms of better understanding the process through which their views were formed, so that this understanding of the process might better inform the actions of teacher educators or policy makers. This formation of views happened at the intersection of personal aspiration and external demand, as they adjusted to new conditions. There were, however, common themes that emerged within our sample that suggests consensus in certain areas. Our analysis pointed to issues of more general concern.

As researchers, we felt obliged to gather our thoughts and shape our findings into a more coherent account. Our task required building a research perspective on the data we collected, a taming of some 200 hours of interview data. As researchers telling our stories, and for trainees telling theirs, information management was key. Somewhat akin to the government supposing causal relationships on a complex backdrop, researchers and trainees alike create stories to understand experience and to guide their movement. But this was not mere participation in neutral discourses. Certain psychological drives motivated each of us, the government, the trainees, and the researchers, to please, respectively, the electorate, the university, and the funding agencies/research audience. Each acted according to what they felt was required of them by a host of external demands.

As researchers, with the sample we examined, our basic taming of the data goes something set out as below:

Students often leave their own school with an image of mathematics largely confined to their affective experience of it. In particular, the majority of the trainees we interviewed reported being nervous about mathematics as pupils in their own schooling. Mathematics only enters conversational space, if at all, through the way in which it makes the trainee feel or in relation to the school grades they achieved. Such anxieties cloud their entry in to university. Yet they soon became convinced by pupil-centrist orientations of mathematics components of their initial training that were common in universities at the time. There was a spell during which mathematics was seen as fun. University sessions provided a version of mathematics that did not activate their anxieties. This provided an effective blueprint for their future teaching.

Later during the course, however, this input became a distant memory as such mathematical work was confined to early stages of the course. Nevertheless, it continued to flavour the student's attitude to the subject in a positive way. Major policy changes were effected during the course of their training but the positive regard for the subject apparently stayed intact. Its impact, however, on practical teaching approaches seemed less obvious. Issues such as survival in the classroom and fitting into school were more compelling. A key feature in their construction of their own professionalism during their training related to their assuming some empathy with the children they encountered in schools. That is, they felt that since they had suffered with mathematics in their own schooling they would have some success in sympathising with children when they encountered their own difficulties in mathematics. Our data pointed to the trainees understanding this as a problem resulting from transmission oriented approaches to teaching.

However, despite this approach's being identified as the problem, the sophistication of the trainees' conception of teaching did not develop sufficiently for alternative styles to be effectively implemented in their own teaching.[1] Rather they sought to achieve a less severe version of transmission, a delivery of mathematics but with an attempt to make it more enjoyable. These approaches, however, were not as pupil friendly as the students seemed to imagine, especially if they were mixed with a struggle to manage the class effectively. Practicality was seen as a saviour but this often failed to connect with the more formal styles of mathematics, which appeared to be required to ensure pupil success in assessment procedures. The organisational procedures evident in the National Numeracy Strategy became the standard approach.

Throughout their training, trainees perceived themselves to be overloaded at both university and school with alternative accounts of what teaching was. Our data pointed to different influences becoming prominent during different phases of the training. There appeared to be deficiencies in the overall reconciliation they achieved of the many conflicting discourses. The resulting partiality of accounts in many aspects of their training often led to the desire for quick fixes in attempts at reconciling alternative perspectives. Given the large variety of discourses available it seemed that those to do with immediate pragmatics were privileged. This led to an emphasis in interviews on talking about the administration of mathematics in the classroom rather than the mathematical ideas underlying classroom practices. It seemed that the choice of discourses was taken as an opportunity to sideline the version of mathematics with which they felt discomfort. Their anxieties remained latent, as evidenced in responses to the Numeracy Skills Test and interview situations focusing explicitly on mathematical content. Nevertheless, in their everyday task of teaching, both in school placements as part of the university training and in their work as new teachers in school, they could proceed without encountering these troublesome aspects.

Mathematics was subsumed within broader conceptions of teaching. In many respects the introduction of the National Numeracy Strategy was commensurate with this construction of mathematics. That is, as a set of procedures to be administered. The initiative succeeded in re-asserting an identity for mathematics after it had spent some years in the thematic wilderness within broader primary education practices. Nevertheless, so many aspects of the initiative emphasised procedural approaches rather than mathematical content. It was popular, as it appeared to be organisationally effective and enjoyable. It was commensurate with the mainstream discourse of administration prevailing in primary education. It was also a highly accessible structure where it seemed the majority of new teachers felt confident working to the specified framework. Further, the performance of it had the advantage of assisting the teachers to conceal any remaining latent anxieties they had with regard to the subject.

---

[1] Nolan (2010) reports similar difficulties of trainees moving from traditional to inquiry methods.

Despite the diversity of students, this broad account held for the majority, as evidenced in earlier chapters. Our research was shaped around how the students themselves constructed their rationales against the backdrop of a complex situation. They needed to embrace an amalgam of complex demands and live a life responsive to them. But it may be that we need to ask in what sense does it matter what the trainees think since, as we have shown throughout this book, conceptions of teacher development appear to be shifting, at least in the context of English schools. Mathematics teacher development is now seen less by the government in terms of person-centred mathematics development. This development is more top-down, about teachers being told what to do in ever more detail and with ever more regulation. The personal voice of the trainees has become diluted almost without trace with the felt need to meet others, such as more experienced teachers and teacher educators, in some shared agenda, defined by an imposed terminology. Most pervasive of all, the National Numeracy Strategy became a success, despite claims that it downgraded the importance of teachers' own voices. Mathematical ideas outside of this frame no longer seemed to feature prominently in trainees' accounts of their own teaching.

Professionalism came to be defined more in terms of compliantly implementing the curriculum. Personal aspirations were re-routed through the official language that had come to filter how the new teacher understood her own more personal aspirations of being an educator. The working week that teachers experienced was filled with tasks resulting directly from the new policy initiatives. Lesson planning was prescribed in detail in policy documents and structured by on-line planning tools such that teachers generally had much less scope for their own input. The teachers' intellectual space had been squeezed. As seen, demands for trainees had included: meeting school requirements; meeting university requirements; being popular with children; pleasing parents; building an enjoyable conception of mathematics; performing adequately on the Numeracy Skills Test; achieving personal aspirations; following the National Numeracy Strategy; getting through inspections, minimising teacher and pupils' anxieties relating to mathematics; and, not least, teaching up to ten other curriculum subjects. The trainees' accounts of who they were and how they identified with mathematics were built out of attempts to speak to these multiple agendas, with more or less commitment. Thus, their accounts of who they were as teachers were built out of their answers to the questions of how they were meeting these demands. Trainees and teachers spoke the ideologies within which they were immersed without necessarily being aware of this immersion. Seen in this way, there was no space for them to have their own say within this or to reflect on themselves as subjects. They were held in place by the ways in which they were described within the symbolic network. Teachers were externally defined as "this, this and this" and were recognised only to the degree to which they complied with these role determinations. How should we resist this state of affairs? This side of the account does not seem to bode well for longer-term teacher initiated professional development? Yet there are limitations to this account. Or there is another side to it.

We introduced this book with a supposed dichotomy between the trainees' personal aspirations and their compliance with external demands. But in the last section we conjectured that external demands, such as policy initiatives, are less precise than their initiators claim. The control technology is not reliable in terms of building mathematical achievement, no matter how strenuously it is applied. We questioned the analogy of personifying policy as an individual's intention. We concluded that policy implementation is far more complicated than that. Butler argues that the operation of power through the individual's immersion in particular discursive practices is paradoxical.[2] Individuals can only define themselves in relation to the constraints they see themselves as having accepted.[3] As an individual moves into a new discursive space, she understands who she is differently. For someone entering into training her sense of agency is modified, understood differently, against an emergent understanding of a new environment and of how he or she will be received. This entails a tricky meeting of a newly conceived agency rooted in personal aspirations encountering new conditions and an expectation that he or she will be told how to teach. Thus, the trainee's agency mingles with dependency and gets shaped by the form of the external demands encountered.[4] And there may be a perverse pleasure achieved through performing correctly within a given regulatory frame. As we have discussed here and elsewhere, the new reforms elicited positive responses from teachers across all age/experience/expertise/ teaching year groups. "Interesting ambiguities in interpretation emerged which depicted the Framework not just as a series of contrasts between 'autonomy' and 'constraint', 'flexibility' and 'focus', 'freedom' and 'prescription' but as being read in terms of both. For example, they saw freedom from uncertainty ("teachers like to be told what to do"), as well as coercion".[5] A specific task related to the trainees' taming of the beast of mathematics was that they actively reduced their emotional range in their dealings with it. They confined it to certain linguistic modes that kept it in check as a threat to their psyche. The regulation implicit in the National Numeracy Strategy appeared to be positively enjoyed in what might be seen as its substitution or straight-jacketing of the teachers' own professional integrity. The subordination gave rise to a particular form of agency.[6] The Strategy provided the parameters that shaped the teacher's sense of self as a mathematics teacher.

---

[2]"To be dominated by a power external to oneself is a familiar and agonising form power takes. To find, however, that what 'one' is, one's very formation as a subject, is in some sense dependent upon that very power is quite another. We are used to thinking of power as what presses on the subject from the outside, as what subordinates, sets underneath, and regulates to a lower order. This is surely a fair description of what power does. But if, following Foucault, we understand power as *forming* the subject as well, as providing the very condition of its existence and the trajectory of its desire, then power is not simply what we oppose but also, in a strong sense, what we depend on for our existence and what we harbor and preserve in the beings that we are" (Butler, 1997, pp. 1–2).

[3]See also Bordo (1999, pp. 173–191).

[4]Devine (2003) discusses such conceptions of subjectivity in relation to pedagogy.

[5]McNamara and Corbin (2001, p. 273). NB. The National Numeracy Strategy later became known as the National Numeracy Framework.

[6]Butler (1997, 2005).

The account of blinded immersion also fails to capture the flow of emotion or conscience activated in the trainees' efforts to comply with the demands they face.[7] There are drives that motivate more or less successful participation in a multitude of discourses. In Lacanian terms, the ego is an inauthentic agency working to conceal any apparent lack of unity. And teacher identity comprises a fragmented self, mediating diverse demands. Earlier we noted that "personal development may be characterised as change in the questions it is urgent or essential to answer".[8] At this stage of their lives there is no shortage of questions to choose from. Yet as we have argued, the trainees' subscription to the overarching official line, and its semblance of invincibility, can work as a cover for this multitude of conflicting demands. And the gap between the cover story and demands is a potential site for resistance where a more autonomous individual identity could be asserted. Crudely, the demands faced by the individual can be played off against each other under the cover of the bigger story. But, for this to be achieved, it is necessary to find ways of enabling trainees to see outside the frame. Recent government policy has seemingly provided a comprehensive picture that makes a wider perspective difficult and alternative ways of understanding education can seem peculiar against this all-encompassing backdrop. Yet these alternatives must be given space in the teacher education programme if the programme is to be more than mere training for a given regime. Curriculum packages have a limited shelf life, as has been demonstrated clearly by the demise of the National Strategies in England, almost forgotten within months. It would be worrying if all training were directed at conforming to just one current model, resulting in a proliferation of teachers and other professionals of a time-specific governmental truth, ill-prepared for adjusting to later changes. Policy initiatives must promote improved practice that transcends the conceptualisations embedded within the latest plan. Ways need to be found of keeping alive the debates that negotiate the boundaries of mathematical activity in the classroom and how those boundaries might reshape in response to even broader evolving social demands such as economic and intellectual necessity. It would be unfortunate if the prevailing conception of teacher development reached further towards the preference of providing new rules, with the teachers understanding their own professional development in terms of following those rules more effectively. Teacher biographies are typically characterised by engagements with a number of teaching approaches throughout any one career. Each shift from one to another entails mathematics being framed in a slightly different way that perhaps results in a different teaching style and, perhaps also, in a different conception of mathematics. Elements derived from each phase feed into composite experience and contribute to that teacher's mode of practice and emergent, and perhaps convergent, professional identity. These elements might be attributed variously to fashions in school practices, learning theories, assessment preferences or career phase of the individual teacher. The shifts in teaching approach would normally be locally negotiated on the basis of some supposed improvement

---

[7]Butler (1997, p. 107).
[8]Schafer, quoted by Felman (1987, pp. 99–100).

on the previous model.[9] The term "improvement", however, can be understood in
many different ways and resists stability across time, space and circumstances.

Teacher education must be seen in terms of teachers developing their own voice
and building their own professional rationalisations. "Professionalism ... cannot
thrive on performance indicators. It has in the end, to rely on positive trust rather
than be driven by performance ranking".[10] Effective implementation of the National
Numeracy Strategy is one thing. But we need to guard against this restricting the new
teachers' long-term professional development. After a few years in school, teachers
might want to rejuvenate their personal aspirations. Teacher education must enable
the development of intellectual capabilities to be responsive to successive changes.
Policy initiatives need effective teacher mediation. And for now this may require
teacher educators to reflect on their own complicity in policy changes that reduce
their educative role. Schoolteachers must be enabled to share the creation of mathematics in the classroom, rather than being mere conduits for a curriculum received
from above. Faith must be placed in the teachers and their capacity to execute the
policies and the associated curricula. They must hold on to their own professional
voices so that they can participate more fully in curriculum evolution.

## 7.3  The Future of School Mathematics

The twentieth century left a legacy of techno-scientific control governed by the
"ideology of 'real' social forces".[11] As we settle in to the second decade of a new
century, where such rationalistic aspirations have been re-routed in so many areas
of theory, it seems disappointing that the dominant premises of mathematics education research so readily hold on to those earlier instrumentalist tendencies. As
the broader task of social theory gets on with adjusting to newer orders, research
in mathematics education often continues to relate to two terms tenuously waving
to each other from disparate conceptual domains/eras. Mathematics understood in a
more general sense often continues to reside in a mythology in which it is conceptualised as a discipline beyond social discourses. Meanwhile education as a field,
within England at least, resists conceptual immersion in the broader social sciences
as it finds itself increasingly susceptible to government regulation and definition.
School mathematics has been bureaucratised within this legislative structure and has
arguably parted company with both more traditional markers delineating mathematical activity, and possibly newer styles of thinking that might pay dividends into the
future. Thus, current conceptions of education and mathematics are restrictive and
not conducive to evolving understandings of these disciplines, nor of the composite
field of "mathematics education". Cultural studies and the broader social sciences
meanwhile have developed apparatus that could potentially unite understandings, or

---

[9]Brown, Hanley, Darby, and Calder (2007), Hanley (2010).

[10]Stronach et al. (2002).

[11]Lather (2003, p. 259).

redefine the limits, of the two domains. Yet presently this apparatus falls between the two stools of incommensurate understandings of mathematics and of education.

The more intellectual rewards and benefits associated with the discipline have been increasingly swamped by the demands of standardised testing. The response to this apparent crisis of mathematical identity is to read mathematical achievement in schools through a register of *commodified* procedures, in a one size fits all model, spanning diverse nations and communities. This counters post-modern rhetoric that insists that we resist such grand narratives. And indeed the coherence of activity held together by the name "mathematics" has been weakened under the weight of so many demands being placed on it. A fragmented subject indeed! It seems necessary to adopt an attitude to school mathematics that accepts its diverse social contingency as part of its on-going formation, where mathematical learning is hitched to different styles of engagement. School mathematics as a discipline needs to be responsive to different domains of practice and theory. This very diversity, however, undermines clear definition and has opened the door to assertive governance in some quarters in the absence of broader professional or intellectual consensus.

Mathematical learning cannot be understood except as a function of the individuals who engage with it, governed as they are by an array of social agenda. Yet constructivist theory that has dominated mathematics education research for the last 20 years has generally been predicated on individual human subjects reconstructing existing social knowledge. Whilst "inquiry" methods permit greater learner autonomy and newer conceptions of mathematics, the overarching conception of "individuals" acquiring or producing "mathematical knowledge" has been maintained. Meanwhile, teachers are increasingly externally defined through legislative documentation and recognised through the filter of their compliance with this role determination. This formulation reifies mathematics as a list of concepts or procedures and specifies teacher role in terms of delivery. The formulation restricts teachers' autonomy through limiting their capacity to reflect on themselves as subjects and to assume agency in choosing the agendas governing their professional practice. Yet the newer conceptions that we have explored of the human subject and of mathematics can enable conceptions of "learner" and "teacher" more responsive to environmental change and the multiplicity of social demands.[12] These alternative conceptions open approaches to conceiving mathematical learning that are not locked into time-dependent conceptions of learners, teachers and mathematical knowledge.

Throughout the book we have adopted various perspectives on how mathematics is understood in the classroom. Two particular perspectives have been highlighted.

First, we have outlined the external perspective, either of the mathematics expert detecting the formation of mathematics in classrooms or of a government official concerned with administering schools and the standards they achieve according to some "economy of performance".[13] The professional environment in certain

---

[12] Brown (2003a, 2008a, 2008b).
[13] Stronach et al. (2002).

locations is increasingly governed through ever more visible surveillance instruments, such as high profile school inspections and testing. This makes demands on teachers and pupils alike and sets the terms through which researchers and teacher educators observe such activity. These demands have become reified in an environment of supposed or intended control technology. Such apparatus serves the view that there is one correct and centralised version of mathematics.

Second, we have considered classroom mathematics, as seen by participants within the classroom, as an "ecology of practice".[14] Here the trainee teacher sees mathematics from a pragmatic organisational stance, looking at things in terms of what they, personally, can do. We have suggested that empathy is a key factor governing motivation among trainees. The trainees' own memories of suffering mathematics leads to a belief that they can now empathise with pupils struggling in their own lessons and that this will prove effective in motivating and encouraging their pupils. Through these empathetic motivations, teaching and learning of mathematics becomes a particular strategy for social participation, one in which mathematics has been anchored in affective accounts of what it is. That is to say, mathematics is what you feel about it and what you have felt about it and what you feel others could feel about it. Meanwhile, children are obliged to oscillate between declaring what they do see and what they think they are meant to see.

Neither of these two perspectives, however, is entirely satisfactory yet each specifies particular views of what mathematics is. These views cannot be trumped by a correct overview, since they are true for the people holding them. The hermeneutic model that we outlined offered an approach to broaching the apparent divide between these two alternative conceptions of mathematics. The divide we suggested could be effaced by emphasising the circularity of moving between hard-edged results and interpretations of them. In line with the practices on the university course described, a conception of mathematics could be constructed that is more harmonious alongside the more traditional conceptions of mathematical topics, but without the associated assumption that this implies a particular pedagogical attitude to these topics. To use the terminology that we introduced earlier, it may be possible to have a Mathematics 1 attitude attached to a Mathematics 2 curriculum. For example, "connectionism" addressed this in its insistence on valuing alternative individual perceptions of key core ideas. Such an approach seems a promising direction for mathematical studies within initial training courses, although our results seem to suggest that such an approach might be beyond the current intellectual and performative capacity of many non-specialist students.

The social situation of mathematics as a discipline needs to be recognised and individual perceptions of mathematics cannot divorce themselves from the social frames in which mathematics is generated and understood by others. As mathematics education researchers, we cannot restrict ourselves to telling individual teachers about strategies for improved practice in some absolute sense. The curriculum framework decides the meaning of so many of the terms. But conversely, policy

---

[14] Ibid.

makers cannot assume custody of the right to decide how this social framing is constructed. A more sophisticated account of the normative practices through which mathematics comes into being is required, and of the stories that support those practices. Many of the features prominent in the courses we have examined have fostered a more positive attitude to mathematical learning. Such approaches, however, should be more specifically targeted at accommodating (both critically and compliantly) the social filters (such as curriculum documents and associated classroom practices) through which mathematics teaching is increasingly being understood. There does seem to be a need to ensure that school-based work features specific attention to mathematics as well as other curriculum areas if these are to rise above the surface of an overly organisational concept of primary practice. This seems essential if mathematical ideas are to be generated rather than merely administered in the classroom. Teaching has to be more than an implementation of some external definition or compliance with current practice. Moves, however, often seem to be in the opposite direction.

Our empirical analysis has been predicated on locating the mathematics that is to be found in the social discourse of the trainees. This discourse results from a mediation of centrally defined requirements relating to the teaching of mathematics. Classroom mathematics is a function of the classroom teachers' interpretation of curriculum guidance and administrative procedures. We have argued that trainee and new teachers' grappling with the perceived social demands are formative of mathematics as an area of thinking. In an important sense, school mathematics is what schoolteachers say it is. This formation is important as an understanding of both mathematics and teacher professional development in mathematics. This, however, is problematic if the external definition always retains the upper hand. It is the insistence on an externally accountable version of mathematics set within a restrictive register, which counters the success of universities that have succeeded in providing a version of mathematics that positively engages future teachers. Meanwhile, the weight of the accountancy apparatus squeezes out the possibility of more autonomous professionalism. There appears to be a slightly ironical situation, if our own results are to be believed. It would seem that the most successful initiative in England relating to mathematics in recent years could place its success on the shoulders of reducing the need for trainees to develop their discursive capabilities in relation to mathematics per se. Despite amassed efforts of the government and its entourage of 'field forces', trainees have pulled off a remarkable coup; substantially removing mathematics from an initiative designed to build it.[15] When asked what skills they needed to be a mathematics teacher in the primary school, the responses from trainees seemed not to emphasise skill in mathematics itself. They seemed to speak mainly about empathy with pupils and classroom organisation in administering the scheme.

---

[15]Mathematics was also downplayed in earlier conceptions of English primary school mathematics, e.g. thematic approaches and published mathematics schemes.

Our theoretical analysis meanwhile has been centred on the way in which social desires relating to the teaching of mathematics in schools have become commodified in specific social forms. Learning outcomes are dependent on the learning theories and assessment instruments being applied. The ultimate story of *what mathematics is* remains undecidable – so particular accounts are asserted to mark this "void". For example, the pedagogical devices used in teaching have often become naturalised as if they were the mathematical content itself. And in some senses they have indeed become that, since mathematics gets to be known through material caricatures of mathematics; such as particular results through standard methods. Through the jarring of habitual conceptions, school mathematics as a notion has been mapped out into a set of procedures, but as understood within outmoded conceptions of practice. These anchor mathematics yet do not open up mathematics as a subject that can be easily talked about. It is the social forms that have tangible effects on classroom practices and the prescriptions set in respect of them.

Throughout, we have been keen to insist that our conceptions of mathematics are heterogeneous, socially derived, situated and, inevitably, ideologically motivated. Our principal argument in this regard is that the activities of primary school mathematics have a strong association with the organisational and philosophical discourses of primary education more generally and that the link with a more explicitly mathematical discourse is increasingly squeezed out as the teacher proceeds through her training on this course. School mathematics has been bureaucratised and is held in place by administrative regulation. Thus, as teachers, teacher educators and as researchers, we should operate on these social practices and their metonymic link with other social practices as well as on the metaphorical link between mathematical activities and the "mathematics" supposedly underlying these activities. The former can perhaps make mathematics more accessible and perhaps more supportive of other human endeavours. The accountancy procedures trainees and teachers face, however, are privileging the latter. We argued that poststructuralist analysis (Althusser, Foucault) missed the mark in our earlier examination of mathematics itself since the analysis of individuals being immersed in discourses squeezed out more subjective perspectives. That is, people could not report on the experience of being immersed in discourses since they did not notice that they were immersed. In the psychoanalytic perspective that we favoured (Lacan, Žižek) mathematical discourses succeed by suggesting rather than pinpointing the intellectual flows they seek to activate. Mathematics operates through stories perhaps in the guise of pedagogic devices. But the reality of mathematics for humans is seen through subjective fantasy frames that need to be brought alive in stories. The excitement mathematicians feel is predicated on emotional flows circulating around the various accounts they provide of what they are experiencing subjectively. We need to understand how these stories work rather than supposing that mathematical content can be perceived directly. As we have argued throughout this book, mathematical content is a function of its social housing. However, this housing can obscure the supposed content.

This poses for us an interesting question. Should mathematical content, be made a bigger part of an already crowded initial training programme given that it activates renewed anxieties among the trainees without apparent benefit in terms of classroom functionality? A conjecture that we have explored centred on trainees not developing a particularly sophisticated discourse of mathematics prior to entering university. Talking about mathematics is not a significant feature of the school pupil's world. As they learn to talk about it in the university environment, mathematics is not seen independently of the discourses of teaching it. They do not become more sophisticated in discussing mathematics itself. Mathematical content knowledge derives from an alternative discursive frame. This jars with the language of mathematics that they learn in university, a language that has enabled them to shield their anxiety in relation to the subject.

Mathematics has many faces where the effectiveness of any teacher education initiative targeted at the enhancement of classroom practice is dependent on how the style of training is matched to the specific professional and administrative needs. Training in mathematical content as such may well not be sufficient or even useful if it is not understood in terms of pedagogic need and the administrative structure that supports it. For example, the Numeracy Skills Test, designed to lift standards for teachers in England, triggered anxiety among trainees, undermining the successful image work that had been achieved by universities in re-casting mathematics as a subject that could be enjoyable. Similarly, the content orientation of the National Numeracy Strategy put teachers back at the front of the class to re-adopt the didactic styles of teaching in schools that had triggered so many of the anxieties that had blighted the school experience of so many of the trainees we had interviewed.[16] Nevertheless, the curriculum guidance did appear to be effective in allowing teachers to get on with the job, in a curriculum where numeracy had regained some prominence after a period of downgrading in English schools.[17]

## 7.4   The Research and the Policy Environment

Trainee and new teachers invariably encounter and respond to the wider policies that define their practices in schools. These policies have a marked impact on the discursive patterning shaping the conceptions the trainees have of their own teaching and of their actions in the classroom. To some extent practice will be in line with wider

---

[16]In some recent research carried out by Manchester colleagues into children learning mathematics there was a rather startling conclusion that if certain procedures were followed the children's performance in tests could be improved, surely good news if we have clearly defined targets, but unfortunately this was not the whole story. The study also concluded that if these procedures were indeed followed, in particular transmissionist teaching to the test, there was also a negative consequence in the form of children being switched off mathematics, Williams (2008). More recent work suggests that they are also less prepared for university (Williams, in conversation). One interpretation of these findings, which can claim a large sample, is that longer-term facility with mathematics, enjoyment of mathematics, and exam success, are not necessarily commensurable ambitions. In the short term at least we may need to make a choice comprising fewer than all three.

[17]This downgrading had been partially a result of thematic approaches combining work across subject areas, arguably undermining mathematics as a subject in its own right – an earlier administrative sidelining of mathematical content within the school curriculum.

policy intentions. An underlying question in our analysis has been concerned with how an educational authority or government conceptualises and articulates educational policies for mathematics and the associated training of teachers. We can only offer interpretations of how the political task is conceived through articulations of this made in the public domain. Yet we might nevertheless question the extent to which the effectiveness of any such policies might be supposed by the government itself. How much in control does the government perceive itself to be? more generally how might we understand the capacity of large-scale policy initiatives to effect change according to a prescribed vision? Setting policies is not an exact science. Neither is the retrospective analysis linking causes to effects. Definitive analysis of whether mathematics abilities have indeed improved, and if so how much, is difficult to achieve. And this lack of definition provides an arena in which claims and counter claims can compete. In this section we examine some of the apparent mechanisms through which a rhetorical political linguistic layer parts company with more empirically grounded claims relating to mathematical performance.

It is in the nature of policy directives, that those who have issued the policies are required to stand by them in the name of political consistency, once the policies have been enunciated. For a politician to change his or her mind too readily, there is a risk of this being seen as indecisive, a characteristic unbecoming of true leadership. Policy statements, however, can be more stable than the situation that gave rise to them and can become more influential in shaping the actions that ensue than the original or new situation. The British government has pursued a high profile strategy of taking charge of school practices in England through a multitude of regulatory devices. We have taken this as a case study that may shed light on how wider policies impact on the professional practices of teachers and thus how research might intervene in understanding and influencing practices. But, as importantly, it might enable us to think more productively of how teacher educators mediate policy and how they hold on to their own professional agency as policies become more centralised. The policies in question have been widely disseminated and provide detailed criteria through which mathematics has been understood and teacher performance has been shaped and judged. They have been held in place by a hard-edged publicly available language defining moves towards better mathematical achievement. Detailed prescriptions of mathematics subject knowledge came in three strands: *Knowledge and understanding required by trainees to secure pupil's progress in mathematics*; *Effective teaching and learning methods;* and, *Trainees' knowledge and understanding of mathematics.*[18] In this way, the content of school mathematics, modes for its delivery and teacher characteristics were defined. The suggestion by the government that these policies were informed by research is questionable, if only because wide-scale research has been controversial or does not exist. Policies, however, do not function in isolation. Training procedures are in the hands of university tutors and placement schools more or less susceptible to government demands. This filters policies with different styles and enthusiasms. These

---

[18]Department for Education and Employment (1998b), Annex D.

agencies are trustees of the teachers' development. Notwithstanding, as we have heard in Chapter 4, the inspectorial apparatus and annual self-evaluation system has strictly regulated policy implementation to discourage any outbreaks of more radical interpretation.

Such official prescription directed at education professionals was encircled by a public debate conducted through the media where the government further expanded on its intentions. The government's armoury was also reinforced by some oft-cited tenets underpinning the policy directives. For example, the National Numeracy Strategy had been successful in raising standards, assertive government educational policies did make a difference, whole class teaching was more effective than other styles, poverty was no excuse for poor academic performance among children, and so forth. Additionally, teacher shortages and an attendant high-profile publicity campaign to attract new teachers, from the United Kingdom and overseas, pointed to teaching quality being a function of teacher supply, recruitment and retention.

In observing this debate and the official apparatus that went with it, what might we surmise as to the government's underlying intentions at the time? We wish to consider, albeit speculatively, how the rational premises of such policies and supporting rhetoric might have emerged and then functioned. Let us begin by asking the question: what was in the mind of the Minister of Education who introduced the first policy framework?[19] Various options seem possible:

- The minister wanted to improve mathematics by whatever means as part of his quest to provide an education as a basic human right – any rationalisation of how he achieved this was secondary to that basic desire.
- The minister saw pursuit of the improvement of mathematics as a good ploy for re-election – his only real concern.
- The minister sincerely believed that the implementation of his policies would bring about improvement in mathematics in the way he had suggested.
- The minister was himself aware that policy setting is not an exact science but instinctively believed that a simple and insistent presentation of his policies would achieve for him the best possible outcomes in some way or other. This might have been through, good participation amongst teachers, quantifiable improvements in test scores, an image of a government taking charge, or more negatively, the demotion of mathematics as a political issue in the public's eye.

Which account best described the minister's perspective? Perhaps all of them do, despite apparent mutually exclusive aspects. Maybe it depended on what mood the minister was in. After all in Lacan's terms even ministers are fragmentary subjects responding to multiple demands that cannot be fully reconciled. It seems impossible to attain a "real" version of events. The options above merely provide alternative fantasies through which reality might be structured, where a final interpretation would

---

[19]cf. Žižek (2000, pp. 61–62).

not be achievable. To personify the implementation of policies with a clear association between one person's rational action and its effect risks oversimplifying the broader concern. We have argued in this book that so often individual intentionality does not explain particular modes of action. Rather, individuals are subject to particular discursive regimes that shape their actions according to normative practice, but where occasional bursts of individuality seep out. The effects of policy implementation are probably too complex to be encapsulated as being choices by individuals. Such is the nature of policy setting. Life is a complicated affair. But sometimes, in order to communicate, the path through life is presented as a set of choices that can be clearly understood. The government cannot explain all of the complexities underlying its chosen policies. Those complexities might overwhelm the very people who the policies are meant to convince. Yet, conversely if the government conceals information that appears to contradict its advice then it may be accused of deception. It is necessary to steer a course between these two poles. This, however, presupposes that the government itself has some sort of overview with more complete information. The scope of such an overview, however, could well be rather limited. The government like most other people in the account that we are providing only have a partial view of themselves and of the world that they occupy. And as we have repeatedly emphasised, this means that those governed by the policies, such as teachers and teacher educators cannot have emphatic control over their own professional environment.

What kind of discursive interplay is at work in setting and defending government policies relating to mathematics teaching in schools? And also in the research perspectives shaping and responding to those policies? Some research carried out around the time of the policy changes and the public response to it highlighted some of these issues. We shall briefly examine some aspects of this debate in building a broader account of the environment within which teaching, and research into it, is understood. The research itself and the way in which it intervenes in the public debates, we suggest, conditions the way in which research in mathematics education is read more generally. In this respect, any message emanating from our own research needs to be read against this sort of backdrop. There cannot be a clear message as any message is necessarily a function of the way in which it is pigeon holed by those reading it.

The government report underpinning the introduction of the National Numeracy Strategy presented by David Reynolds, the Chair of the Government Task Force[20] claimed that its methods derived from firm evidence. The international evidence, collated into an annotated bibliography of research,[21] supported a case for greater pedagogical prescription. Margaret Brown, also as it happens a member of the Task Force, carried out two separate research studies with her team at King's College, London. The research was governed by two key questions: What makes an effective

---

[20]Final report, Department for Education and Employment (1998c), see also Muijs and Reynolds (2001).

[21]Department for Education and Employment (1999b).

teacher of mathematics? Which factors improve mathematical attainment? The first question was the basis of a study funded by the government[22] before the introduction of the Strategy. The second question motivated a major study funded by the Leverhulme Trust,[23] which coincided with its implementation. The latter analysis points to pedagogical factors being an overly emphasised factor in determining mathematical performance. The Leverhulme report contests Reynolds's account on a number of points:

- the evidence for the effectiveness of whole class teaching is much less strong than is claimed, and may equally increase the negative effect of lower quality teaching;
- mathematical achievement is a function of social circumstances, although such circumstances do not seem to impede improvements;
- there is some doubt about the claims that teacher effectiveness can be reliably assessed by classroom observation, either by inspectors or by head teachers.

According to the Leverhulme Study, by far the biggest research programme in mathematics education in the United Kingdom, no one really knows what constitutes a good teacher of mathematics. The teacher questionnaires used in analysing a range of variables across years 4 and 5 (pupils aged 8–10) of primary education[24] were analysed "with respect to biographical data (e.g. level of mathematical qualifications, years of experience, appointment to co-ordinator post) and to pedagogical factors including frequency of access to calculator, and frequency and type of homework set". The authors concluded "No variable has been statistically significant across both years, and only a handful have reached significance in either year". The report echoes a message from an international audit of student performance (TIMSS) conducted around the time "'there is no simple answer' – while each (variable) probably has an effect, none by itself made a major difference" (Beatty, 1997, p. 8).

Additionally, conclusions from our own study suggest other ways in which government policies may be undermined:

- policy apparatus can counter development of autonomous professionalism among teachers;
- policy is compromised by affective consequences of policy administration (e.g. fear activated by Numeracy Skills Tests);
- a return to teacher centred styles of teaching potentially risks a re-emphasis on the transmission mode, a source of some anxiety for our trainees.

---

[22]Askew et al. (1997).

[23]The final report comprises four books published by Springer: Millett, Brown, and Askew (2004), Baker, Tomlin, and Street (2006), Askew, Brown, and Millett (forthcoming), Brown, Askew, and Millett (forthcoming). See also Brown et al. (2002) and Brown, Askew, Millett, and Rhodes (2003).

[24]Brown et al. (2002).

The specific concern with mathematical attainment in England that led to the introduction of the Numeracy Strategy was triggered by accounts of England's relatively poor performance in the subject internationally. The increasing prominence of international comparisons of performance (e.g. Trends in Mathematics and Science Study and Program for International Student Assessment) has caused various governments to reflect on their policies and justify them in terms of improving performance against such testing criteria.[25] The debate points to some implicit assumptions as to what counts as mathematics and how it should be measured. For example, the criteria used to assess mathematics (where England performs less well) appear to be regarded as more important than the criteria for practical problem solving (where England does well[26]). It might be arguable that skills in problem solving are more important to both economic performance (the apparent underlying incentive) and pupil motivation to learn, than the potentially more abstract skills of mathematics itself as conceived within the comparative tests. Policy makers in England, however, may not be overly preoccupied by high performance in "problem solving" since, in public perception, "mathematics" per se is seen as the more prestigious indicator. After all it may be that for the wider electorate, government policies on mathematics might simply be a minor indicator of a wider ability to effectively implement policies and hence of a government in control and deserving of re-election.

The search for supposed key variables, however, distracts us from our main concern of how mathematics is conceived and evolves as discursive material; the proliferation of which is a symptom of the impossibility of holding an overview. One more story, to cover over the fact that no one story is ultimately convincing. Nevertheless, the discursive belt and braces governing professional practices and the conceptions of mathematics that they point to so often get meshed in a language of control technology. That is, mathematics as a notion is constructed as a phenomenon that extends into a conception of its own implementation. Mathematics is wedded, or perhaps welded, to a notion of pedagogy. The mathematical material is specified in such a way that it points to particular styles of teaching. Unfortunately, the control at work here appears to be rather diffuse. The discourses are many. They often conflict and do not lend themselves to easy categorisation within a mechanistic model. Nevertheless, the account that is declared publicly in government documentation, for example, mops up any underlying conflict of intention in relation to these discourses. The statement of a definite policy stands against a largely indeterminate backdrop. Yet the policy statement makes us read this complex backdrop through a specific ideological lens. Further, having made a specific policy choice, the minister must now be governed by the declared story, rather than by the original conception, if that could ever have been pinpointed, that led to the creation of this story. The demands on politicians to be consistent generally make it necessary for the minister to give the appearance of believing his own story, indeed being so wrapped up in

---

[25]Muijs and Reynolds (2001).

[26]Organisation For Economic Co-operation & Development (1999).

its presentation and its reification in action, the minister may begin to believe it. The story takes on a life of its own with a widening gap between the story and the reality it originally purported to represent. Further, useful frameworks, designed in good faith as resource guides to good practice, can function differently when they are reinterpreted as regulatory frameworks.

The game of exploring what was going on in the government's thinking is maybe seductive but inevitably misleading. It panders to the beliefs of researchers, governments, teachers, and the public alike, that someone is in control in a mechanical sense and that the characteristics of this control can be specified and operated on. Complex situations are apparently being interpreted as though they are dominated by distinguishable causal relationships that can be adjusted to specific requirements. This does not appear to be the case. There are too many factors at play and it is rarely possible to be precise. Nevertheless, professional roles and professional worth are defined in terms of activating such control, or at least being able to effectively implement centralised prescription. But how much is it possible to believe in such control technology? In what circumstances does this control technology work? The Secretary of State for Education at the time of the introduction of the Numeracy Strategy appeared to believe his own story or at least was prepared to offer his resignation if it appeared not to work. More cynically, it may be that such public expression of belief in his own effect was the best strategy to ensure his promotion to his next job, which he later secured. But might sincerity have been acquired as the minister started to believe his own message, whether or not it delivered results interpretable as being consistent with success? Politics routinely enters the territory of re-writing history to explain and justify current actions. Living the story can become the new "reality", with the story imprinting itself on reality. This sort of backwardly looping rationale characterises the psychoanalytical perspective that we have taken. The discursive patterning that results from this can shape subsequent life and perceptions of it. And in turn new mappings of this emerge and so forth.

We started out, however, with a question of whether policy should be targeted at maximising autonomous professionalism amongst the teaching force or at providing an easy to follow framework that guides trainee and new teachers through territory in which they are susceptible to anxiety. In conclusion for the latter, we suggest that policy demands cannot assume the behaviourist response their initiators may wish to harbour. It would be wrong, however, to assume that the complexities are subliminal and defying all analysis. It does seem that the expression of such policies results in a shaping of new teacher practice. But the task of analysis is more complex and cannot be predicated on the assumption that clear solutions will be found. It is not easy to locate simple causal arrangements. This, however, does not stop people claiming them, or others believing them, or, at least, acting as if they believed them, and perhaps in that way making the causal relationships happen. The government asserts a clear, simple, accessible story to explain its policies. Inevitably, such a story is an oversimplification yet perhaps more digestible than the complex, but more accurate, alternative. The government had chosen to emphasise a story that the National Numeracy Strategy worked, and that its success depended more than anything on how teaching style was adjusted. Is it legitimate to offer this sort of over-simplification in the name of clarity and the success of a policy that is having some sort of impact? What could be an alternative? The truth of the success of the National Numeracy Strategy as the key policy instrument is less clear. Does it warrant such an assertion? Headlines, such as the following from the Times Education Supplement, however, perhaps have more impact than any underlying story, true or otherwise:

> A £400 m failure. The national numeracy strategy has made very little difference to pupil attainment, research shows. The flagship government programme to transform maths teaching in primary schools has done little to raise standards despite costing £400 million. -The scores of the least able were actually worse (Mansell & Ward, 2003, p. 11).

Are we now to be governed by such headlines, or the research underlying those headlines, or the supposed truth underlying that research? Or does research merely offer yet another truth to cloud the overall picture? An overview with a clear consequential strategy would be an unlikely result of such research investment. The picture simply is not a clear one. It depends on the particular slant and power dynamics pertaining to the given discussion.

Another option may be to focus attention elsewhere. The other possibility we have put forward would be to highlight a story that best supports professional agency, rather than one in which trainee and new teachers are supposed to need explicit governmental support. Many teachers, it appears, are leaving the profession as a result of workload pressures from implementing the new policies. Encouraging teachers to stay in the job longer to gain experience, trusting and nurturing teacher professionalism, may have greater longer-term benefits than prescribing how they might do the job better within the current framework that is of dubious merit. To pursue this option, however, initial training may need to be more than enabling trainees to fit a particular mould.

How then might we conceive of research designed to confront the conception and implementation of policy? Research is sometimes commissioned with a view to its contributing to public debate. Sometimes, research is produced with the objective of developing curriculum material. Chapter 3 has demonstrated it can be difficult to build a clear picture from the diverse and dispersed research findings. Research is occasionally used in the service of developing teacher education models. Yet so many of its models suggest the possibility of an elastic supply of teachers hearing, and able to comply with, its recommendations. New teachers, especially those in primary schools, are guided in their practices by many factors, and research in mathematics education is not always high up the list. Similar things might be said for many teacher educators whose agency has suffered in the climate of centralised policy and the erosion of opportunities to follow higher degrees.[27]

To suppose that research can in some sense be factual in an unambiguous way seems untenable in the light of the preceding discussion. It can only seek to impact on people's beliefs. A core thesis of this book has been that it is impossible to extract

---

[27]This year the English government announced that it would only fund newly qualified teachers undertaking a masters degrees under its direct control (the Masters in Teaching and Learning).

mathematics and its teaching from such socially derived parameters. Research can only intervene in ideological exchange by providing empirically or theoretically supported arguments. We have argued that there are difficulties in inspecting policy initiatives as products of individual politicians' imaginations. There is always a gap between conception, declaration and implementation, opened up by the complexity underlying any supposedly causal relationship. Research statements, meanwhile, are accredited to individual names. Yet, generally, such statements have a more restricted circulation than government statements. They can be ignored or re-contexutalised to a realm of insignificance. Rarely does such work get exposed in the wider media. Such statements rely for their effect on how they are utilised in some rhetorical exchange. That is, their impact is a function of their contribution to discursive effects. On very rare occasions these effects include legislation designed to actualise research recommendations (albeit usually with some compromises). Our discussion in Chapter 3 highlighted how in many countries large-scale research does not exist. The United Kingdom has large numbers of small-scale reports where transferability from the specific research site is often an issue. In countries like the United States, where much more research does exist, there is still disappointment as to how much information it provides in support of changing practices across populations.

Any supposed dialogue between policy discourses and research discourses nudges towards artificiality in so far as the two discourses emanate from incommensurable linguistic domains. This is evident in recent high profile discussion. As seen above, policies presented by the government were backed up by a claim that these policies were consistent with research findings. Some researchers contested these claims. Meanwhile, there has been such a shortage of research in the area (in the United Kingdom) that not enough is known to be able to make definitive claims. How might this impasse be negotiated? As a public expression of a policy instrument the government claim – that its policy strategy was supported by research – was designed to achieve particular effects; which might include an assertion of effective management, a defence of a particular policy requirement or to activation of a specific response among teachers and the electorate. As such, it was presented as a *performative*,[28] where the linguistic meaning of the statement may not be in the same order as intended or actual effect. The research community however, responded to it as though it were a factual statement, a *constative* to be supported (as by David Reynolds) or questioned (as by Margaret Brown).

The dialogue between researcher and government often comprises posturing for some intended rhetorical effect. This comprises the story frame through which sense is made. For Žižek these stories appeal to the subjective fantasies through which reality is structured. These stories are aimed at the benefit of some variously defined audience. For example, teacher educators might be governed according to a particular interpretation of the exchange. The empirical research carried out at Kings[29]

---

[28] Austin (1962).

[29] Askew et al. (1997).

followed standard research conventions and is valid within these structures. Yet, it was shaped in response to the government posed question: what makes an effective teacher of numeracy? The government funding the project on that question succeeded in drawing the debate in to its own chosen domain. As a policy maker the government sought a clear unequivocal message. They wanted to know "what works?" It was the task of teachers to improve their teaching so those children achieved better results in mathematics. Teacher education was understood, funded and monitored in these terms. Teacher educators were supposed to conduct their work on this basis.

In their later Leverhulme funded work, the King's team argued that the situation was much more complex.[30] Although such teacher characteristics, as identified in the earlier study were a factor (when pupil and school effect were controlled), it was difficult to identify the components that made teaching more effective. Such a view would cast doubt on policies predicated on adjusting teaching styles and most certainly the Leverhulme research suggested that the effectiveness of whole class teaching was much less compelling than the government had claimed. Adopting such a stance may, however, so result in researchers in mathematics education being told that their services are no longer required, insofar as their task is defined in terms of advising how mathematical attainment could be improved within the model in question. The language of control technology often seduces researchers. To learn that pedagogical style was a minor factor would surely be disappointing news to researchers in the area. In this way, the domain of researchers in mathematics education gets to be defined fairly restrictively. The dialogue between researchers and government seems to become even more tenuous. The government only sponsors research and evaluation within specific guidelines and, apparently on occasions, we are given to understand, only reports on the findings if the research is consistent with what the government needs to back up its "clear story". The parameters of mathematics education research in England are shaped around these sorts of public debate. Thus, researchers themselves are drawn into this domain to join with the government in the alleged debate, not least because researching pedagogical style is the home domain with which many such researchers identify themselves. And being recognised within this debate, fraught as it is, brings with it a certain prestige, audience and indication that one's research is hitting the mark. Bordo (1999, p. 24) argues that academia is often susceptible to mediatising its image.

> Academics sometimes use the accessories of theory (for example, specialised forms of jargon, predictable critical moves, references to certain authors) less in the interests of understanding the world than to proclaim themselves members of an elite club. In the process they create caricatures of themselves and of those who don't belong, peopling the scholarly world with typecast players and carving out narrow theoretical niches within which all ideas and authors are force-fit. Certain theoretical preferences, moreover, run throughout disciplines like incurable diseases, often carrying invisible racial and gender stereotypes and biases along with them.

---

[30]Example Brown et al. (2002).

A more charitable interpretation might be that academic fields get to be learnt through caricatures as it would be too overwhelming to do otherwise. Nevertheless, the impact of Bordo's comments seems to hold in educational research. The "production of educational theory and research is itself a site of ideological and political struggle".[31] This, however, is not necessarily self evident or consensual. Such views are clearly issued from within an ideological standpoint. This present manuscript is quite clearly ideologically motivated. We believe that it could not be otherwise, yet this very conviction falls foul of certain perspectives on what constitutes research. We include here two extracts from some extensive and helpful comments from referees commenting on earlier drafts of this present book.

> The strongest parts of the manuscript are those that argue against the political control of mathematics education. This is achieved in a way which is beyond and above the popular views expressed in the daily news and this is very important.

> While any work that seeks to make explicit social impacts on knowledge must necessarily describe the social contexts in which that knowledge emerges, the authors must take care to make their tone politically neutral. As a reader of *research*, I don't care or need to know about the authors' politics or opinions and to insert that in the tone lowers the credibility of the research.

We align ourselves with the line of the first referee insofar as we are making a political case. We reject the choice that the second referee seems to be supposing, that we could choose between ideology and neutrality. Neutrality is not an option available to us. Empirical research is always set against an ideological backcloth more or less visible to those involved. As we have indicated, ideologies can only be inspected from within other ideologies. But often our own ideology is at least partially invisible to us. We only have a limited perspective on our own individual and social boundaries.

Undoubtedly, there will be divergence between the views of different agencies, namely, governments, schools or universities, as to what education is trying to achieve and how it might be improved. Yet divergence also arises between mathematics educators. Many would hold particular conceptions of mathematics and see their task in terms of guiding activity towards the achievement within that conception of mathematics. Others might conceptualise maximising the intellectual capacities of the children more generally and find mathematics that exercises those capacities. There are those who might see their objectives in terms of meeting the demand of externally defined audit. Meanwhile the research agenda of primary schools is not always down to specialist researchers in mathematics education but rather directs itself at more general needs in primary education, as perceived by a range of stakeholders. Each of these research perspectives would be associated with specific discursive practices and be governed by particular operational objectives, measurable against some sort of commodified criteria.

---

[31] Britzman (2003a, p. 68) citing McCarthy & Apple. See also DeFreitas and Nolan (2008).

Nevertheless, one might imagine that consensus would hold amongst researchers in mathematics education that research should primarily be seen in terms of benefiting the needs of children in our schools, or the economy. It is less easy to agree on how that might be best achieved, or of how the task might be conceptualised. One commonly acknowledged factor also seen as being more important in determining mathematical performance than pedagogical style is the socio-economic background of pupils. Against this backdrop, views may vary as to what mathematics in school seeks to achieve. Given the different levels of achievement, should schools in deprived areas, for example, have their mathematical objectives defined in the same way as those in more affluent areas? A convincing argument might be that a level playing field is created if all children face the same tests. Such a scenario, it might be thought, would enable less affluent children to demonstrate that they have the same skills that might be assumed of more affluent children. Yet this denies the profound and wide ranging consequences of social and cultural capital.[32] And also, it is posited, there is a need to enable children to adopt a more critical attitude to their education. It is not enough to simply train them in basic skills.

Two tutorials with Manchester primary school teachers addressing mathematics education within the context of practitioner-oriented higher degrees alerted one of the authors to this issue in an immediate way. Both teachers were preparing their classes for imminent national tests. One of the teachers was working in a school in an affluent area that, as a fee-paying school, was not obliged to follow the National Curriculum or the associated testing. The school, nevertheless, chose to take the tests as past experience indicated that the children performed well and their participation in the activity confirmed their academic success specified in those terms. The second teacher, meanwhile, was working in a deprived inner city area. Her first task was to ensure that children attended school for the tests, which in this case were obligatory. She, however, had some ambivalence to this as past experience had shown her that the tests merely labelled most of the children in her class as not succeeding within this frame. On the morning of the test in question, she drove to the house of an absentee 11 year old to pick him up. She found him drunk from a party the night before celebrating his father's release from prison. She further wondered what purpose the exercise served for the children in her class. It is schools in such areas that frequently are identified as having lower levels of achievement, providing a base line against which more successful schools can assert their achievements. Such tests feed into published league tables and hence influence the school's capacity to attract pupils and associated funding. This contrasts with some countries like New Zealand where schools in poorer communities and achieving lower scores might attract more financial support. This alternative reasoning was captured in a humorous note on a television programme: "The lower the marks you get in these standardized tests the more funding the school gets, so don't knock yourself out" (Edna Krabappel, teacher in *The Simpsons*).

---

[32]Christensen, Stentoft, and Valero (2008) discuss how mathematics teaching practices can confer power differentially.

To specify mathematical targets in the same way for both teachers seems to be problematic. There is a not a simple administrative solution that suits all in their educational needs. The supposition that mathematics is the same across the board is not tenable. The "clear story" does not include the needs of these children in its remit. It seems unhelpful to define achievement in such a way that many children in certain areas have publicly declared academic failure added to their list of woes. To be in a class where most do not succeed does not feel like sharing the same playing field as a class where most succeed, and if it is, one is always in the losing team. To say, as did a former Chief Inspector of Schools, that poverty is no excuse for poor performance and that attention should focus primarily on pedagogic style seems to be missing the mark in assisting teachers in meeting immediate demands in their professional life. It is defining education, and mathematics education in particular, too narrowly. Pinker (2002) meanwhile, widening the spectrum of political interpretation to include a psychological angle, attributes more importance to hereditary and peer group factors than to either pedagogical or social factors.

Even if we were to suppose that a dialogue between government and researchers is in some sense meaningful, it seems unlikely that a mathematics education researcher could tell the government to do something about poverty to improve school mathematics results. And on the basis of the diverse research reports of the sort summarised in Chapter 3 what would a researcher be able to say? The government would generally only sponsor and respond to mathematics education researchers within the limited domain it supposes they inhabit – that is in the realm of adjusting pedagogical style to improve mathematical attainment. In this respect the dialogue is largely one-sided.

We may well ask: who will fight for education if it amounts to no more than compliance with narrow government agendas? The answer, it would appear from our discussions with many new teachers, is "quite a lot of people". This echoes Žižek's claim that we inhabit a culture of cynicism where, even though we know it does not make sense, we do it all the same. Teacher working practices are increasingly framed in a project apparently designed to dismantle the force of our teachers' contributions to these very practices, yet still they participate and seem to enjoy this participation. Recent resistance to school testing belies the fact that most policies are being followed compliantly.

It seems necessary, however, for researchers to resist the apparent narrowing of their specific domain. To restrict the focus of such work to a domain centred on current conceptions of mathematics seems inadequate. Mathematics education is a social science and needs to broaden its resources to reflect that. This needs to be achieved by drawing on existing resources in the more broadly defined area of the social sciences. So long as mathematics education research sticks to the restricted palette it is more susceptible to government definition of its role. Much of mathematics education research remains predicated on control technology shaped against an externally defined map of how we live. It has often been carried out in narratively restricted forms, answering questions within a domain that goes unquestioned. For example, pedagogical influences on mathematical learning are slight compared to socio-economic factors. Yet for how long have we supposed that research in the area through such means has led to significant improvement in our teaching of mathematics or, at least, resisted deterioration? What evidence might we offer to claim any success? Research, predicated on "improvement", seen primarily as comprising predictive devices guiding the delivery of "mathematics" to "individuals", will probably continue to be disappointed with its general impact. Such an attitude would be a manifestation of Freud's notion of the death drive: "going through the motions", enjoying this repetition, avoiding innovations that might disrupt existing routines and habits. One almost imagines an elderly colleague repeating lectures for years on end and resisting any institutional changes with a weary cry of "we tried that before". Fukuyama's (1992) notion of The *End of History* caused a theoretical stir two decades ago and might well be seen as an example of such a tendency. The book supposed a final model of human society had been achieved and there was no need for further structural renewal to the liberal democracy that had already arrived and proven itself to be the most resilient of political arrangements. Further, changes could, according to Fukuyama, be seen as mere fine-tuning. A research model understood as a model that had got it right would be replacing the life that it had previously sought to capture. Or perhaps the researcher's investment in the model might be seen as brushing aside evidence that works against this. In this mode, work would be undertaken as though the model really was a full account of the reality we are supposedly seeking. There is no gap. Reality is reshaped to fit the model.

Large research projects in mathematics education are rare and with Leverhulme the results have proved ambiguous in terms of possible strategic implications. Also, the constructions of such overviews, as in England, can lead to policies that tell teachers what to do without involving them in the decision. Meanwhile, there has been an apparent failure of major policies to have a clear impact in England. We might question the purpose of this control apparatus as an effective approach to improving mathematics teaching, at least in the terms that were intended. The policies have not worked well in terms of changing results and the cost seems high in terms of teachers being left out of the decision-making process. Suppose, however, hypothetically, that we were to get an accurate picture of how mathematics teaching might be improved in schools. Could we implement such an approach? To succeed would surely also suppose that teachers would understand it in the required way and that they could make the necessary changes to their practices. Perhaps, however, teachers have their own views and would prefer not to understand it in the required terms. They may also require a big helping of training with some insistence on the side to make substantial changes to their practices.

Is it helpful to see the process of our collective development in terms of grand solutions that can be applied universally? We might always be disappointed with the results of a process so defined. Raising educational standards has been a recurrent mantra of successive governments, but what evidence is there that we have made progress whatsoever? Are we better now than we were in the forties, the sixties, the eighties, or the nineties? Does anyone actually know? And if so what do they know? Certainly the features that we seek to compare are constantly changing. The mathematics curriculum is different – our needs are different. Mathematical skills and their relative importance are constantly being revised. For example, key school components in the sixties are not seen as so important now.

But control is also the fantasy that mathematics education researchers often have of themselves and their role. Although most researchers would see their brief as extending beyond responding to government initiatives, many would also want to see themselves as having control and define their space in terms of its potential for control. Research is often seen in terms of guiding improvement in practices. Much research in mathematics education, however, does not present itself as a response to governmental assertions. The "standards" debate does nevertheless persist beyond this domain. Researchers are concerned with "standards" as well. Mathematics education research is often predicated on the failures of classrooms to meet supposed ideal versions of mathematics through supposed ideal versions of teaching. For example, can we speak in terms of "dismal results achieved in algebra in our secondary schools"[33] (and how schools and teachers within them need to improve), as though there were some universal against which to measure? What other sorts of presupposition underlie claims of this sort? Apparently deficit models predicated on terms such as "dismal results", "failure" seem to have strong appeal in motivating research (as they do in motivating government policy initiatives). Such demands for improved standards result in a retreat into accountability and the kinds of mathematics that is more easily assessed. Whilst many of the demands placed on school mathematics are regulated within a more restrictive domain (e.g. of getting sums right), broader concerns surely must extend into the quality and appropriateness of experience provided. Test scores can be a poor measure of these.

Perhaps applied researchers inevitably delude themselves as to the nature of their impact: research agendas are often shaped around supposed control of researchers' own cover stories. Yet often research findings, and recommendations, where made, are not implemented beyond the research site itself, and sometimes not even there. The debate over whether research should drive, underpin or merely inform policy and practice is fundamental here. There is also a need for researchers to protect their professional integrity. Professionals need to construct a social purpose and perhaps try to shield their complicity with the more oppressive elements of their own practice. They may act in good faith in seeing themselves as part of some social movements and resistant to others. But perhaps such participation relies on misrecognition. They can only suppose that they are pursuing a specific social purpose. Everyone needs aspirations to shape their actions, a fantasy frame through which they inspect the reality of what they are doing. The "ideal", however, only exists insofar as it imprints itself on the story of trying to get there. In which senses is mathematics education research governed by behaviourist conceptions of change? One particular concern in generating research relates to the success of its own dissemination and implementation. The trainee teachers we interviewed were generally not readers of research journals in mathematics education. Indeed, the nature of their discussion of mathematics would point to a different set of concerns. Mathematical

---

[33]Herscovics and Linchevski (1994, p. 59).

objectives among such trainees were set modestly. There seems to be little point devising research statements if they do not reach teachers. Similarly, there is no point devising such statements that new teachers do not understand or cannot apply. Through which routes then might more sophisticated findings be disseminated? The training process is the obvious route. As we have shown, however, the route is already busy. Further, recent changes in England have squeezed university tutors' capacity to keep up to date with research, if they ever did, while ever more training has been relocated in schools, beyond the reach of university influence. The result is that the training is directed at compliance and not is so much an educational experience targeted at building judgement.

In asserting particular understandings of mathematics, whose interests might be served and how? Mathematics teachers are all more or less concerned with the child's needs to participate in a key social skill. For many, it is important to share with children the intrinsic pleasures of mathematics as a discipline in its own right. Yet the perceived prestige of school mathematics is also a function of its perceived practical importance in supporting economic activity and the social integration of our children.[34] School mathematics is funded and accommodated on that basis. The teacher's professional purpose is often specified in terms of such objectives. Similarly, researchers often construct their own social purpose in terms of high-lighting possible improvements towards these objectives, whether this is through promoting a more satisfying conception of mathematics or through successfully raising of basic skills. Mathematics education research objectives are often seen in terms improvement over many years but in which ways might actual improvement be quantified? Mathematics education research is predicated on supporting ever-changing forms of life. Skills are a function of an ever-evolving context and do not always apply to the next generation.

What then is the research enterprise in mathematics education? What task does research face in stimulating educational change? Aiming at ideals in this area has a poor track record. The gap, between how things are and how they should be, points to a supposed permanent deficit. This, however, is just one reading of events, but a reading that does seem to provide something to aim at, no matter how illusory. As research continues to transform our practices, there is a need to continue to undertake research that inspects how stories are produced to cover complexity. But likewise the complexities of much mathematics education research would surely be lost on many of the teachers that we have interviewed. How would the findings of research such as the studies mentioned in Chapter 3 feed into the practices of those teachers, or inform their trainers, even if clear messages could be extracted from such instances of research? It may be that researchers need to produce their own clear stories to cover over the complexities of their work if the work is to stand a chance of influencing mainstream discourses governing school mathematics practices.

---

[34]Skovsmose (2008).

There is a need for a different language that does not trap us within restrictive styles of analysis: one that troubles certainties rather than produces them. In the task of exploring alternative framing strategies, and their "reality effects", how might such strategies disturb each other into the future? There is no endpoint to be reached in a perfect set of guidelines. In fitting a research or scientific model, reality cannot be fully accounted for through a structural filter. Successive attempts to revise the filter merely alert us to alternative failings. Researchers tell stories of the world and these stories shape the world, but also teach us about it, both through their poignancy, and through the ways in which they seem to fail us. In the Lacanian account that frames this book, the task is not so much concerned with getting the story right (to effect a cure/resolution) but rather to focus on what can be learnt through making successive substitutions of the stories told. How might new opportunities opened up for inspecting the present and future be understood in relation to alternative readings of the past as "we carry on with patience the endless work of distancing and renewing our historical substance"?[35] Research activates the future as well as representing the past. It produces language that results in people living differently. Looking back over what has been achieved how would the results be evaluated? How would history be told? And how does that history shape and explain how things are done now? How can overly simplistic solutions be resisted, whilst still ensuring that things get done? As Lather (2003, pp. 261–262) argues:

> cutting edge educational research will be produced out of and because of the paradoxes of projects that develop a better language to describe a more complicated understanding of what knowledge means and does than by re-inscribing the idealized natural science model ... as we move to a future which is unforeseeable from the perspective of what is given or even conceivable within our present conceptual frameworks.

---

[35]Ricoeur (1981, p. 246).

# References

Adler, J. (1996). Lave and Wenger's social practice theory and teaching and learning school mathematics. In *Proceedings of the twentieth conference of the international group for the Psychology of Mathematics Education* (Vol. 2, pp. 3–10). Valencia, Spain: University of Valencia.

Adler, J. (2001). *Teaching mathematics in multilingual classrooms.* Dordrecht: Springer.

Adler, S. (1991). The reflective practitioner and the curriculum of teacher education. *Journal of Education for Teaching, 17*(2), 139–150.

Ahmed, A. (1987). *Better mathematics: A curriculum development study.* London: Her Majesty's Stationery Office.

Alexander, R. (Ed.). (2009). *Children, their world, their education: Final report and recommendations of the Cambridge primary review.* London: Routledge.

Alexander, R., Rose, J., & Woodhead, C. (1992). *Curriculum organisation and classroom practice in primary schools. A discussion paper.* London: Department of Education and Science.

Althusser, L. (1971). Ideology and ideological state apparatuses. In *Lenin and philosophy and other essays.* London: New Left Books.

Ambrose, R. (2004). Initiating change in prospective elementary school teachers' orientations to mathematics teaching by building on beliefs. *Journal of Mathematics Teacher Education, 7*(2), 91–119.

An, S., Kulm, G., & Wu, Z. (2004). The pedagogical content knowledge of middle school teachers in China and the US. *Journal of Mathematics Teacher Education, 7,* 145–172.

Andrews, P. (2007). The curricular importance of mathematics: A comparison of English and Hungarian teachers' espoused beliefs. *Journal of Curriculum Studies, 39*(3), 317–338.

Andrews, P., & Hatch, G. (1999). A new look at secondary teachers' understanding of mathematics and its teaching. *British Educational Research Journal, 25*(2), 203–223.

Appel, S. (1996). *Positioning subjects: Psychoanalysis and critical educational studies.* Westport, CT: Bergin and Garvey.

Appel, S. (Ed.). (1999). *Psychoanalysis and pedagogy.* Westport, CT: Bergin and Garvey.

Apple, M. (1982). *Education and power.* London and Boston: Routledge.

Argyris, C., & Schon, D. (1974). *Theory in practice: Increasing professional effectiveness.* San Francisco: Jossey Bass.

Aronowitz, S., & Giroux, H. (1985). *Education under siege.* London: Routledge.

Ashby, P., Hobson, A., Tracey, L., Malderez, A., Tomlinson, P., & Roper, T., et al. (2008). *Beginner teachers' experiences of initial teacher preparation, induction and early professional development: A review of literature.* London: GTCE/TDA/DCSF.

Askew, M. (2008). Mathematical discipline knowledge requirements for prospective primary teachers, and the structure and teaching approaches of programmes designed to develop that knowledge. In P. Sullivan & T. Wood (Eds.), *Knowledge and beliefs in mathematics teaching and teaching development. The international handbook of mathematics teacher education* (Vol. 1, pp. 13–35). Rotterdam: Sense Publishers.

T. Brown, O. McNamara, *Becoming a Mathematics Teacher,*
Mathematics Education Library 53, DOI 10.1007/978-94-007-0554-8,
© Springer Science+Business Media B.V. 2011

Askew, M., Brown, M., & Millett, A. (Eds.). (forthcoming). *Teaching and learning about number: Interactions in primary lessons and pupil progression*. New York: Springer.

Askew, M., Brown, M., Rhodes, V., Johnson, D., & Wiliam, D. (1997). *Effective teachers of numeracy*. London: King's College.

Atkinson, D. (2001a). Assessment in educational practice: Forming pedagogised identities in the art curriculum. *International Journal of Art and Design Education, 20*(1), 96–108.

Atkinson, D. (2001b). Teachers, students and drawings: Extending discourses of visuality. *Discourse: Studies in the Cultural Politics of Education, 22*(1), 67–79.

Atkinson, D. (2002). *Art in education: Identity and practice*. Dordrecht: Kluwer.

Austin, J. (1962). *How to do things with words*. Oxford: Oxford University Press.

Badiou, A. (2007). *Being and event*. London: Continuum.

Baker, D., Tomlin, A., & Street, B. (Eds.). (2006). *Navigating numeracies: Home/school numeracy practices*. Dordrecht: Springer.

Baldino, R. R., & Cabral, T. C. B. (1999). *Lacan's four discourses and mathematics education*. Paper presented at 23rd conference of the International Group for the Psychology of Mathematics Education, Haifa, Israel, pp. 57–64.

Ball, D. (1988). Unlearning to teach mathematics. *For the Learning of Mathematics, 8*(1), 40–48.

Ball, D. (1990). The mathematical understandings that prospective teachers bring to teacher education. *Elementary School Journal, 90*(4), 449–466.

Ball, D., & Bass, H. (2003). Towards practice-based theory of mathematical knowledge for teaching. *Proceedings of the 2002 Annual meeting of the Canadian Mathematics Education Study Group* (pp. 3–13). Edmonton, AB: CMESG/GCEDM.

Banks, B. (1971). The disaster kit. *Mathematical Gazette, 391*, 17–22.

Barrett, E., Whitty, G., Furlong, J., Galvin, C., & Barton, L. (1992). *Initial teacher education in England and Wales: A topography*. London: Goldsmith's College.

Barthes, R. (1972). *Mythologies*. London: Paladin.

Basit, T. (2003a). Changing practice through policy: Trainee teachers and the National Numeracy Strategy. *Research Papers in Education, 18*, 61–74.

Basit, T. N. (2003b). Manual or electronic: The role of coding in qualitative data analysis. *Educational Research, 45*, 143–154.

Beattie, M. (1995). New prospects for teacher education: Narrative ways of knowing teaching and teacher learning. *Educational Researcher, 37*(1), 53–70.

Beatty, A. (Ed.). (1997). *Learning from TIMSS – Results of the third international mathematics and science study: Summary of a symposium*. Washington, DC: National Academy Press.

Begle, E. (1979). *Critical variables in mathematics education: Findings from a survey of empirical research*. Washington, DC: Mathematics Association of America and the National Council of Teachers of Mathematics.

Bekdemir, M. (2010). The pre-service teachers' mathematics anxiety related to depth of negative experiences in mathematics classroom while they were students. *Educational Studies in Mathematics, 75*(3), 311–328. DOI: 10.1007/s10649-010-9260–7.

Bennett, N. & Carré, C. (Eds.). (1993). *Learning to Teach*. London: Routledge.

Bennett, N., & Turner-Bisset, R. (1993). Case studies in learning to teach. In N. Bennett & C. Carré (Eds.), *Learning to teach* (pp. 165–190). London: Routledge.

Benton, P. (Ed.). (1990). *The Oxford Internship Scheme: Integration and partnership in initial teacher education*. London: Calouste Gulbenkian Foundation.

Berliner, D. (1988). Implications of studies of expertise in pedagogy for teacher education and evaluation. In The Educational Testing Service (Ed.), *New Directions for Teacher Assessment*, Proceedings of the 1988 ETS Invitational Conference, Princetown, NJ.

Beyer, L. (1984). Field experience and ideology and the development of critical reflectivity. *Journal of Teacher Education, 35*(3), 36–41.

Bibby, T. (2001). *Primary school teachers' personal and professional relationships with mathematics*. Unpublished PhD Thesis, London, King's College.

Bibby, T. (2002). Shame: An emotional response to doing mathematics as an adult and a teacher. *British Educational Research Journal, 28*(5), 705–721.

Bibby, T. (2009). How do pedagogic practices impact on learner identities in mathematics? A psychoanalytically framed response. In L. Black, H. Mendick & Y. Solomon (Eds.), *Mathematical relationships: Identities and participation* (pp. 123–135). London: Routledge.

Bibby, T. (2010). *Classrooms and their discontents: Education and psychoanalysis.* London: Routledge.

Bines, H. (1994). Squaring the circle? Government reform of initial teacher training for primary education. *Journal of Educational Policy, 9*(4), 369–380.

Bird, T., Anderson, L., Sullivan, B., & Swidler, S. (1993). Pedagogical balancing acts: Attempts to influence prospective teachers' beliefs. *Teaching and Teacher Education, 9*(3), 253–268.

Black, L., Mendick, H., &Solomon, Y. (Eds.) (2009). *Mathematical relationships: Identities and participation.* London: Routledge.

Boaler, J., Wiliam, D., & Brown, M. (2000). Students' experiences of ability grouping – disaffection, polarisation and the construction of failure. *British Educational Research Journal, 26*(5), 631–648.

Bolin, F. (1990). Helping student teachers think about teaching. *Journal of Teacher Education, 41*(1), 10–19.

Bordo, S. (1999). *Twilight zone: The hidden life of cultural images from Plato to O.J.* London: University of California Press.

Bottery, M., & Wright, N. (1996). Cooperating in their own deprofessionalisation? On the need to recognise the 'public' and 'ecological' roles of the teaching profession. *British Journal of Education Studies, 44*(1), 82–98.

Bramald, R., Hardman, F., & Leat, D. (1995). Initial teacher trainees and their views of teaching and learning. *Teaching and Teacher Education, 11*(1), 23–32.

Bratman, M. (1992). Shared cooperative activity. *Philosophical Review, 2*(101), 327–341.

Brisard, E., Menter, I., & Smith, I. (2005). *Models of partnership in programmes of initial teacher training: A systematic review.* Edinburgh: General Teaching Council of Scotland.

Briton, J. (1997). Learning the subject of desire. In S. Todd (Ed.), *Learning desire: Perspectives on pedagogy, culture, and the unsaid* (pp. 45–72). London: Routledge.

Britt, M., Irwin, K., & Ritchie, G. (2001). Professional conversations and professional growth. *Journal of Mathematics Teacher Education, 4*(1), 29–53.

Britzman, D. (2003a). *Practice makes practice: A critical study of learning to teach.* Albany, NY: State University New York Press.

Britzman, D. (2003b). *After-education.* Albany, NY: State University of New York Press.

Britzman, D., & Pitt, A. (1996). Pedagogy and transference: Casting the past of learning into the presence of teaching. *Theory into Practice, 35*(2), 117–123.

Brodie, K. (2009). *Teaching mathematical reasoning in secondary school classrooms.* New York: Springer.

Brown, M. (1999). Swings of the pendulum. In I. Thompson (Ed.), *Issues in teaching numeracy in primary schools* (pp. 3–16). Buckingham: Open University Press.

Brown, M., Askew, M., Baker, D., Denvir, H., & Millett, A. (1998). Is the National Numeracy Strategy research–based? *British Journal of Educational Studies, 46*(4), 362–385.

Brown, M., Askew, M., Millett, A. (Eds.). (forthcoming). *Teaching, learning and progression in key numeracy topics.* New York: Springer.

Brown, M., Askew, M., Millett, A., & Rhodes, V. (2003). The key role of educational research in the development and evaluation of the National Numeracy Strategy. *British Educational Research Journal, 29*(5), 655–672.

Brown, M., Askew, M., Rhodes, V., Denvir, H., Ranson, E., & Wiliam, D. (2002). Magic bullets or chimeras? Searching for factors characterising effective teachers and effective teaching in primary numeracy. Paper presented to the conference of the *British Educational Research Association.*

Brown, S., Cooney, T., & Jones, D. (1990). Mathematics teacher education. In W. Houston (Ed.), *Handbook of research on teacher education* (pp. 639–656). London: Macmillan.

Brown, S., McNally, J., & Stronach, I. (1993). *Getting it together: Questions and answers about partnership and mentoring.* Stirling: Department of Education, University of Stirling.

Brown, T. (1987). *Language interaction patterns in lessons featuring mathematical investigations.* PhD thesis, University of Southampton.

Brown, T. (2001). *Mathematics education and language: Interpreting hermeneutics and post-structuralism* (2nd Rev. ed.). Dordrecht: Kluwer.

Brown, T. (2003a). Making mathematics inclusive: Interpreting the meaning of classroom activity. *Waikato Journal of Education, 9,* 113–128.

Brown, T. (2003b). One size does not fit all in school maths. *New Zealand Herald,* October 1st.

Brown, T. (2008a). Lacan, subjectivity and the task of mathematics education research. *Educational Studies in Mathematics, 68,* 227–245.

Brown, T. (2008b). Signifying "learner", "teacher" and "mathematics": A response to a special issue. *Educational Studies in Mathematics, 69*(3), 249–263.

Brown, T. (Ed.). (2008c). *The psychology of mathematics education: A psychoanalytic displacement.* Rotterdam: Sense Publishers.

Brown, T. (2008d). Desire and drive in researcher subjectivity: The broken mirror of Lacan. *Qualitative Inquiry, 14*(3), 402–423.

Brown, T. (2008e). Comforting narratives of compliance: Psychoanalytic perspectives on new teacher responses to mathematics policy. In K. Nolan & E. DeFreitas (Eds.), *Opening the research text: Critical insights and in(ter)ventions into mathematics education.* New York: Springer.

Brown, T. (2010). Truth and the renewal of knowledge: The case of mathematics education. *Educational Studies in Mathematics, 75,* 329–343.

Brown, T. (forthcoming). *Mathematics education and subjectivity.* New York: Springer.

Brown, T., Atkinson, D., & England, J. (2006). *Regulative discourses in education: A Lacanian perspective.* Bern: Peter Lang Publishers.

Brown, T., Eade, F., & Wilson, D. (1999). Semantic innovation: Arithmetic and algebraic metaphors in narratives of learning. *Educational Studies in Mathematics, 40*(1), 53–70.

Brown, T., & England, J. (2004). Revisiting emancipatory teacher research: A psychoanalytic perspective. *British Journal of Sociology of Education, 25*(1), 67–80.

Brown, T., Hanley, U., Darby, S., & Calder, N. (2007). Teachers' conceptions of learning philosophies: Some problems with consensus. *Journal of Mathematics Teacher Education, 10,* 183–200.

Brown, T., Hardy, T., & Wilson, D. (1993). Mathematics on Lacan's couch. *For the Learning of Mathematics, 13*(1), 11–14.

Brown, T. & Heywood, D. (in press). Geometry, subjectivity and the seduction of language. The regulation of spatial perception. *Educational Studies in Mathematics.*

Brown, T., & Jones, L. (2001). *Action research and postmodernism: Congruence and critique.* Buckingham: Open University Press.

Brown, T., Jones, L., & Bibby, T. (2004). Identifying with mathematics in initial teacher Training. In M. Walshaw (Ed), *Mathematics education with/in the postmodern.* Westport, CT: Information Age Publishing.

Brown, T., & McNamara, O. (2001). British research into initial and continuing professional development of teachers. In M. Askew & M. Brown (Eds.), *Teaching and learning: Primary numeracy, practice and effectiveness* (pp. 50–56). Southwell: British Educational Research Association.

Brown, T., & McNamara, O. (2005). *New teacher identity and regulative government: Discursive formation of primary mathematics teacher education.* New York: Springer.

Brown, T., McNamara, O., Basit, T., & Roberts, L. (2001). Project report: *The transition from student to primary teacher of mathematics.* Economic and Social Research Council, UK.

Brown, T., McNamara, O., Jones, L., & Hanley, U. (1999). Project report: Primary student teachers' understanding of mathematics and its teaching. Economic and Social Research Council, UK.

Brown, T., McNamara, O., Hanley, U., & Jones, L. (1999). Primary student teachers' understanding of mathematics and its teaching. *British Education Research Journal, 25*(3), 299–322.

Brown, T., & Roberts, L. (2000). Memories are made of this: Temporality and practitioner research. *British Educational Research Journal, 26*(5), 649–659.

Bulmer, M., & Rodd, M. (2005). Technology for nurture in large undergraduate statistics classes. *International Journal of Mathematical Education in Science and Technology, 36*(7), 779–787.

Butler, J. (1997). *The psychic life of power. Theories in subjection.* Stanford, CA: Stanford University Press.

Butler, J. (2005). *Giving an account of oneself.* New York: Fordham.

Byrne, C. (1983). Teacher knowledge and teacher effectiveness. Paper presented at the 14th Annual Convention of the *North-Eastern Educational Research Association.* Ellenville, NY: North-Eastern Educational Research Association.

CUREE. (2005). *Mentoring and coaching for learning: Summary report of the mentoring and coaching CPD capacity building project* (CUREE 2004–2005). http://www.cureepaccts.com/files/publication/1219313247/mentoring_and_coaching_capacity_building_final_report.doc (accessed January 20, 2010)

Cabral, T. (2004). Affect and cognition in pedagogical transference: A Lacanian perspective. In M. Walshaw (Ed.), *Mathematics education with/in the postmodern* (pp. 141–160). Westport, CT: Information Age Publishing.

Cady, J., & Rearden, K. (2007). Pre-service teachers' beliefs about knowledge, mathematics, and science. *School Science and Mathematics, 107*(6), 232–245.

Calderhead, J., & Robson, M. (1991). Images of teaching: Student teachers' early conceptions of classroom practice. *Teaching and Teacher Education, 7*(1), 1–8.

Campbell, J., & Husbands, C. (2000). On the reliability of OFSTED inspection of initial teacher training: A case study. *British Journal of Educational Research, 26*(1), 39–48.

Carr, W., & Kemmis, S. (1986). *Becoming critical: Knowing through action research.* London: Falmer.

Carré, C., & Ernest, P. (1993). Performance in subject-matter knowledge in mathematics. In N. Bennett & C. Carré (Eds.), *Learning to teach* (pp. 36–50). London: Routledge.

Carter, D., Carré, C., & Bennett, N. (1993). Student teachers' changing perceptions of their subject matter competence during an initial teacher training programme. *Educational Researcher, 35*(1), 89–95.

Carter, K. (1990). Teachers' knowledge and learning to teach. In W. Houston (Ed.), *Handbook of research on teacher education* (pp. 291–310). London: Macmillan.

Chamberlain, L. (2004). *Converting policies into practice in a primary school: examining school improvement and ethical-political dilemmas of a senior manager.* Doctor of Education thesis, Manchester Metropolitan University.

Cheng, H. (1990). *Student teachers' attitudes towards the humanistic approach to teaching and learning in schools.* Unpublished MA Thesis: University of York.

Christensen, O. R., Stentoft, D., & Valero, P. (2008). Power distribution in the network of mathematics education practices. In E. DeFreitas & K. Nolan (Eds.), *Opening the research text: Critical insights and in(ter)ventions into mathematics education* (pp. 131–146). New York: Springer.

Cobb, P. (1999). Individual and collective mathematical development: The case of statistical data analysis. *Mathematical Thinking and Learning, 1*(1), 5–44.

Connelly, F., & Clandinin, D. (1990). Stories of experience and narrative inquiry. *Educational Researcher, 19*, 2–14.

Convery, A. (1999). Listening to teacher' stories: Are we sitting too comfortably? *International Journal of Qualitative Studies in Education, 12*(2), 131–146.

Cooney, T. (1988). The issue of reform. *Mathematics Teacher, 80*, 352–363.

Corbin, B., McNamara, O., & Williams, J. (2003). Numeracy co-ordinators: Brokering change within and between communities. *British Journal of Educational Studies, 51*(4), 344–368.

Correa, C., Perry, M., Sims, L., Miller, K., & Fang, G. (2008). Connected and culturally embedded beliefs: Chinese and US teachers talk about how their students best learn mathematics. *Teaching and Teacher Education, 24*(1), 140–153.

Cotton, T. (2010). Diamonds in a skull. Unpacking pedagogy with beginning teachers. In M. Walshaw (Ed.), *Unpacking pedagogy: New perspectives for mathematics classrooms* (pp. 43–64). Charlotte, NC: Information Age Publishing.

Crozier, G., Menter, I., & Pollard, A. (1990). Changing partnership. In M. Booth, J. Furlong, & M. Wilkin (Eds.), *Partnership in initial teacher education* (pp. 44–56). London: Cassell.

Cruickshank, D. (1987). *Reflective teaching: The preparation of students teaching.* Reston, VA: Association of Teacher Education.

Dart, L., & Drake, P. (1993). School-based teacher training: A conservative practice? *Journal of Education for Teaching, 19*(2), 175–190.

Davies, B. (2006). Subjectification: The relevance of Butler's analysis for education. *British Journal of Sociology of Education, 27*(4), 425–438.

Davis, J. (2009). Understanding the influence of two mathematics textbooks on prospective secondary teachers' knowledge. *Journal of Mathematics Teacher Education, 12*(5), 347–364.

Davis, P., & Williams, J. (2009). Hybridity of maths and peer talk: Crazy maths. In L. Black, H. Mendick, & Y. Solomon (Eds.), *Mathematical relationships: Identities and participation* (pp. 136–146). London: Routledge.

DeFreitas, E. (2004). Plotting intersections along the political axis: The interior voice of dissenting mathematics teachers. *Educational Studies in Mathematics, 55*(1–3), 259–274.

DeFreitas, E. (2008). Enacting identity through narrative: Interrupting the procedural discourse in mathematics classrooms. In T. Brown (Ed.), *The psychology of mathematics education: A psychoanalytic displacement* (pp. 139–155). Rotterdam: Sense Publishers.

DeFreitas, E., & Nolan, K. (2008). *Opening the research text: Critical insights and in(ter)ventions into mathematics education.* New York: Springer.

Department for Education. (1993). *The initial training of primary school teachers. Circular 14/93.* London: Department for Education.

Department for Education and Employment. (1998a). *Teachers: Meeting the challenge of change.* London: Her Majesty's Stationary Office.

Department for Education and Employment. (1998b). *Teaching: High status, high standards. Circular 4/98.* London: Her Majesty's Stationary Office.

Department for Education and Employment. (1998c). *The Implementation of the National Numeracy Strategy: The final report.* London: Her Majesty's Stationary Office.

Department for Education and Employment. (1999a). *Framework for numeracy.* London: Department for Employment, Standards and Effectiveness Unit.

Department for Education and Employment. (1999b). *The National Numeracy Project: An annotated bibliography for teachers and schools.* London: Department for Education and Employment.

Department for Education and Skills. (2004). *Excellence and enjoyment: Learning and teaching in the primary years.* London: DfES.

Department for Education and Skills. (2006). *Primary framework for literacy and mathematics.* London: DCSF.

Derrida, J. (1994). Deconstruction of actuality: An interview with Jacques Derrida. *Radical Philosophy, 68*, 28–41, Reprinted in Derrida, 2002.

Derrida, J. (2002). *Negotiations: Interventions and interviews, 1971–2001.* Stanford: Stanford University Press.

Devine, N. (2003). Pedagogy and subjectivity: Creating our own students. *Waikato Journal of Education, 9*, 29–38.

Dewey, J. (1933). *How we think: A restatement of the relation of reflective thinking to the educative process.* Chicago: D.C. Heath.

Dowling, P. (1996). A sociological analysis of school mathematics texts. *Educational Studies in Mathematics, 31*, 389–415.

Drake, P. (2009). Mathematics for teaching: What makes us want to? In L. Black, H. Mendick & Y. Solomon (Eds.), *Mathematical relationships: Identities and participation* (pp. 161–172). London: Routledge.

Dunne, M., Lock, R., & Soares, A. (1996). Partnership in initial teacher training: After the shotgun wedding. *Educational Review, 48*(1), 41–53.

Earl, L., Watson, N., Levin, B., Leithwood, K., Fullan, M., & Torrance, N. (2003). *Watching and learning 3, final report of the external evaluation of England's National Literacy and Numeracy Strategies.* Toronto, ON: Ontario Institute for Studies in Education of the University of Toronto.

Easthope, A. (2002). *Privileging difference.* London: Palgrave Macmillan.

Edwards, A. (1995). Teacher education: Partnership in pedagogy? *Teaching and Teacher Education, 11*(6), 595–610.

Edwards, A., & Protheroe, L. (2003). Learning to see in classrooms: What are student teachers learning about teaching and learning while learning to teach in schools? *British Educational Research Journal, 29*(2), 227–242.

Edwards, A., & Protheroe, L. (2004). Teaching by proxy: Understanding how mentors are positioned in partnerships. *Oxford Review of Education, 30*(2), 183–197.

Eisenhart, M., Behm, L., & Romagnano, L. (1991). Learning to teach: Developing expertise or rite of passage? *Journal of Education for Teaching, 17*(1), 51–69.

Elbaz, F. (1990). Knowledge and discourse: The evolution of research on teacher thinking. In C. Day, M. Pope, & P. Denicolo (Eds.), *Insight into teachers' thinking and practice.* London: Falmer Press.

Elliott, J. (1987). Educational theory, practical philosophy and action research. *British Journal of Educational Studies, 35*(2), 149–169.

England, J. (2004). *Researching race: a psychoanalytic perspective.* Unpublished PhD thesis. Manchester Metropolitan University.

England, J., & Brown, T. (2001). Inclusion, exclusion and marginalisation. *Educational Action Research, 9*(3), 355–371.

Ernest, P. (1989a). The knowledge, beliefs and attitudes of the mathematics teacher: A model. *Journal of Education for Teaching, 15*(1), 13–33.

Ernest, P. (1989b). The impact of teachers' beliefs on instruction. In P. Ernest (Ed.), *Mathematics teaching: The state of the art* (pp. 249–254). London: Falmer Press.

Ernest, P. (1991). *The philosophy of mathematics education.* London: Falmer Press.

Ernest, P. (1998). *Social constructivism as a philosophy of mathematics.* Albany, NY: State University of New York Press.

Even, R., & Schwarz, B. (2003). Implications of competing interpretations of practice for research and theory in mathematics education. *Educational Studies in Mathematics, 54*(2–3), 283–313.

Felman, S. (1987). *Jacques Lacan and the adventure of insight: Psychoanalysis in contemporary culture.* Cambridge, MA: University of Harvard Press.

Fitzpatrick, M. (2009). Cognitive behavioural therapy plan is just wishful thinking. *Communitycare.co.uk.*

Forgasz, H. J., & Leder, G. C. (2008). Beliefs about mathematics and mathematics teaching. In P. Sullivan & T. Wood (Eds.), *Knowledge and beliefs in mathematics teaching and teaching development. The international handbook of mathematics teacher education* (Vol. 1, pp. 173–192). Rotterdam: Sense Publishers.

Foss, D., & Kleinsasser, R. (1996). Pre-service elementary teachers' views of pedagogical and mathematical content knowledge. *Teaching and Teacher Education, 12*, 429–442.

Foucault, M. (1997). *Ethics.* London: Penguin.

Foucault, M. (1998). *Aesthetics.* London: Penguin.

Frankenstein, M. (1997). *Ethnomathematics: Challenging eurocentrism in mathematics education.* Albany, NY: SUNY Press.

Freire, P. (1972). *Pedagogy of the oppressed.* Harmondsworth: Penguin.

Freud, S. (1991). The ego and the id. In A. Freud (Ed.), *The essentials of psychoanalysis,* 135–142. London: Penguin.

Freudenthal, H. (1978). *Weeding and Sewing.* Dordrecht: Reidel.

Fukuyama, F. (1992). *The end of history and the last man.* London: Penguin.

Furinghetti, F., & Pehkonen, E. (2002). Rethinking characterizations of beliefs. In G. Leder, E. Pehkonen, & G. Torner (Eds.), *Beliefs: A hidden variable in mathematics education?* (pp. 39–58). Boston: Kluwer Academic Publishers.

Furlong, J. (2001). Reforming teacher education, reforming teachers: Accountability, professionalism and competence. In R. Phillips & J. Furlong (Eds.), *Education, reform and the state: 25 years of policy, politics and practice*. London: Routledge.

Furlong, J. (2005). New Labour and teacher education: The end of an era. *Oxford Education Review, 33*(1), 119–134.

Furlong, J., Barton, L., Whiting, C., & Whitty, G. (2000). *Teacher education in transition: Reforming professionalism?* Buckingham: Open University Press.

Furlong, J., Campbell, A., Howson, J., Lewis, S., & McNamara, O. (2006). Partnership in English teacher education: Changing times, changing definitions – evidence from the Teacher Training Agency National Partnership Project. *Scottish Education Review, 37*, 32–45.

Gabriel, M., & Žižek, S. (2009). *Mythology, madness and laughter. Subjectivity in German idealism*. London: Continuum.

Gallagher, S. (1992). *Hermeneutics and education*. Albany, NY: State University of New York Press.

Galton, M. (1995). *Crisis in the primary classroom*. London: David Fulton.

Garetsky, E. (2004). *Secrets of the soul: A social and cultural history of psycho-analysis*. Toronto, ON: Knopf.

Gattegno, C. (1963). *For the teaching of mathematics*. Reading, MA: Educational Explorers.

George, P. (2009). Identity in mathematics: Perspectives on identity, relationships, and participation. In L. Black, H. Mendick, & Y. Solomon (Eds.), *Mathematical relationships: Identities and participation* (pp. 201–212). London: Routledge.

Gergen, K. (1989). Warranting voice and the elaboration of self. In J. Shotter & K. Gergen (Eds.), *Texts of identity* (pp. 70–81). London: Sage.

Giddens, A. (1999). *Runaway world: How globalisation is reshaping our lives*. London: Profile Books.

Gilroy, P., & Wilcox, B. (1997). OFSTED, criteria and the nature of social understanding: A Wittgenstienian critique of the practice of educational judgement. *British Journal of Educational Studies, 45*, 22–38.

Gipe, P., Richards, J., Levitov, J., & Speaker, R. (1991). Psychological and personal dimensions of prospective teachers' reflective abilities. *Educational and Psychological Measurement, 51*, 913–922.

Goldhaber, D., & Brewer, D. (2000). Does teacher certification matter? High school teacher certification status and student achievement. *Educational Evaluation and Policy Analysis, 22*(2), 129–145.

Goodson, I. F., & Sikes, P. (2001). *Life history research in educational settings*. Buckingham: Open University Press.

Goulding, M., Rowland, T., & Barber, P. (2002). Does it matter? Primary teacher trainees' subject knowledge in mathematics. *British Educational Research Journal, 28*(5), 689–704.

Graeber, A., & Tirosh, D. (2008). Pedagogical content knowledge: Useful concepts or elusive notion. In P. Sullivan & T. Wood (Eds.), *Knowledge and beliefs in mathematics teaching and teaching development. The international handbook of mathematics teacher education* (Vol. 1). Rotterdam: Sense Publishers.

Graham, J., & Nabb, J. (1999). *Stakeholder satisfaction: survey of OFSTED inspection of ITT 1994–1999*, UCET Research Paper no. 1. London: Universities Council for the Education of Teachers.

Green, S., & Ollerton, M. (1999). Mathematical anxiety amongst primary QTS students. *Proceedings of the British Society for Research into Learning Mathematics*, (June) Lancaster.

Griffiths, M., & Tann, S. (1992). Using reflective practice to link personal and public theories. *Journal of Education for Teaching, 18*(1), 69–84.

Grootenboer, P. (2003). *Preservice primary teachers' affective development in mathematics*. Doctor of Education thesis. University of Waikato.

Grossman, P., Wilson, S., & Shulman, L. (1989). Teachers of substance: Subject matter knowledge for teaching. In M. Reynolds (Ed.), *Knowledge base for the beginning teacher* (pp. 23–36). Oxford: Pergamon.

Grosz, E. (1990). *Jacques Lacan: A feminist introduction*. London: Routledge.

Gutstein, E. (2008). Building political relationships with students. An aspect of social justice pedagogy. In In. E. DeFreitas & K. Nolan (Eds.), *Opening the research text: Critical insights and in(ter)ventions into mathematics education* (pp. 189–204). New York: Springer.

Habermas, J. (1972). *Knowledge and human interests*. London: Heinemann.

Habermas, J. (1973). *Theory and practice*. Boston: Beacon Press.

Habermas, J. (1976). Systematically distorted communication. In P. Connerton (Ed.), *Critical sociology* (pp. 348–361). Harmondsworth: Penguin.

Habermas, J. (1987). *The philosophical discourse of modernity*. Cambridge: Polity.

Habermas, J. (1991). *Communication and the evolution of society*. London: Polity.

Haggarty, L., & Pepin, B. (2002). An investigation of mathematics textbooks and their use in English, French and German classrooms: Who gets an opportunity to learn what? *British Educational Research Journal, 28*(4), 567–590.

Hagger, H., Burn, K., & McIntyre, D. (1993). *The school mentor handbook: Essential skills and strategies for working with student teachers*. London: Kogan.

Hanley, U. (2007). Fantasies of teaching: Handling the paradoxes inherent in models of practice. *British Education Research Journal, 33*(2), 253–272.

Hanley, U. (2010). Teachers and curriculum change: Working to get it right. In M. Walshaw (Ed.), *Unpacking pedagogy: New perspectives for mathematics classrooms* (pp. 3–20). Charlotte, NC: Information Age Publishing.

Hanley, U., & Brown, T. (1996). Building a professional discourse of mathematics teaching within initial training courses. *Research in Education, 55*, 39–48.

Hanley, U., & Brown, T. (1999, February). The initiation into the discourses of mathematics education. *Mathematics Education Review, 55*, 1–15.

Hardy, T. (2004). 'There's no hiding place': Foucault's notion of normalization at work in a mathematics lesson. In M. Walshaw (Ed), *Mathematics education with/in the postmodern* (pp. 103–120). Westport, CT: Information Age Publishing.

Hardy, T. (2009). What does a discourse-oriented examination have to offer teacher development? The problem with primary mathematics teachers. In L. Black, H. Mendick, & Y. Solomon (Eds.), *Mathematical relationships: Identities and participation* (pp. 185–197). London: Routledge.

Harel, G. (1994). On teacher education programmes in mathematics. *International Journal of Mathematical Education in Science and Technology, 25*, 113–119.

Harre, R. (1989). Language games and texts of identity. In J. Shotter & K. Gergen (Eds.), *Texts of identity* (pp. 20–35). London: Sage.

Harris, S., Keys, W., & Fernandes, C. (1997). *Third international mathematics and science study: Second national report. Part 1*. Slough: National Foundation for Educational Research.

Hatton, N., & Smith, D. (1995). Reflection in teacher education: Towards definition and implementation. *Teaching and Teacher Education, 11*(1), 33–49.

Henriques, J., Hollway, W., Urwin, C., Venn, C., & Walkerdine, V. (1984). *Changing the subject*. London: Methuen.

Herscovics, N., & Linchevski, L. (1994). A cognitive gap between arithmetic and algebra. *Educational Studies in Mathematics, 25*, 59–78.

Hextall, I., Mahony, P., & Menter, I. (2001). Just testing? An analysis of the implementation of 'skills tests' for entry into the teaching profession in England. *Journal of Education for Teaching, 27*(3), 221–239.

Heywood, D., & Parker, J. (1997). Confronting the analogy: Primary teachers exploring the usefulness of analogy in the teaching and learning of electricity. *International Journal of Science Education, 19*(8), 869–885.

Heywood, D., & Parker, J. (2010). *The pedagogy of physical science*. New York: Springer.

Hobson, A., Malderez, A., Kerr, K., Tracey, L., Pell, G., Tomlinson, P., & Roper, T. (Eds.). (2005). *Becoming a teacher: Student teachers' motives and preconceptions, and early school-based experiences during initial teacher training*. Nottingham: DfES, [Available: http://www.dfes.gov.uk/research/data/uploadfiles/RR673.pdf. Accessed January 1 2008].

Hobson, A. J., Malderez, A., & Tracey, L. (2009). *Navigating initial teacher training: Becoming a teacher*. London: Routledge.

Hobson, A., Malderez, A., Tracey, L., Giannakaki, M., Kerr, K., & Pell, R., et al. (2006). *Becoming a teacher: Student teachers' experiences of initial teacher training in England*. Nottingham: Department for Education and Skills. Accessed January 1, 2008, from http://www.dfes.gov.uk/research/data/uploadfiles/RR744.pdf

Hobson, A., Malderez, A., Tracey, L., Giannakaki, M., Pell, R., & Tomlinson, P. (2008). Student teachers' experiences of initial teacher preparation in England: Core themes and variation. *Research Papers in Education, 23*(4), 407–433.

Hobson, A., Malderez, A., Tracey, L., Homer, M., Mitchell, N., & Biddulph, M., et al. (2007). *New teachers' experiences of their first year of teaching: Findings from Phase III of the Becoming a Teacher project*. Nottingham: Department for Children, Schools and Families. Accessed January 1, 2008, from http://www.dfes.gov.uk/research/data/uploadfiles/DCSF-RR008%20v2.pdf

Hollingsworth, S. (1988). Making field-based programs work: A three level approach to reading education. *Journal of Teacher Education, 39*(4), 224–250.

Holyoake, J. (1993). Initial teacher training - the French view. *Journal of Education for Teaching, 19*(2), 215–226.

House of Commons. (1999). *The work of Ofsted: other inspection frameworks. Select Committee on Education and Employment, report from the Education sub-committee: June 1999.* Accessed 20.09.2007, from http://www.publications.parliament.uk/pa/cm199899/cmselect/cmeduemp/62/6213.htm

Hurd, S., Jones, M., McNamara, O., & Craig, B. (2007). Initial teacher education as a driver for professional learning and school improvement in the primary phase. *Curriculum Journal, 18*(3), 307–326.

Husserl, E. (1989). The origin of geometry. In J. Derrida (Ed.), *Edmund Husserl's origin of geometry: An introduction*. Lincoln, NE: University of Nebraska Press.

Jablonka, E. & Gellert, U. (2010). Ideological roots and uncontrolled flowering of alternative curriculum conceptions. Keynote presentation. *Proceedings of the sixth international Mathematics Education and Society conference* (pp. 23–41). Berlin: Freie Universität.

Jagodzinski, J. (1996). The unsaid of educational narratology: Power and seduction of pedagogical authority. *Journal of Curriculum Theorizing, 12*(3), 26–35.

Jagodzinski, J. (2001). *Pedagogical desire*. Westport, CT: Bergin and Garvey.

Jaworski, B., & Watson, A. (Eds.) (1994). *Mentoring in mathematics teaching*. London: Falmer Press.

Jaworski, B., & Wood, T. (2008). *The mathematics teacher educator as a developing professional. The international handbook of mathematics teacher education* (Vol. 4). Rotterdam: Sense Publishers.

Jones, L., Brown, T., Hanley, U., & McNamara, O. (2000). An enquiry into transitions: Moving from being a learner of mathematics to becoming a teacher of mathematics. *Research in Education, 63,* 1–10.

Jones, L., Reid, D., & Bevins, S. (1997). Teachers' perceptions of mentoring in a collaborative model of initial teacher training. *Journal of Teacher Education, 23*(3), 253–261.

Jones, M. (2002). Qualified to become good teachers: A case study of ten new teachers during their year of induction. *Journal of In-Service Education, 28*(3), 509–526.

Jones, M., & Straker, K. (2006). What informs mentors' practice when working with trainees and new teachers? An investigation in mentors' professional knowledge base. *Journal of Education for Teaching, 32*(2), 165–184.

Kay, S. (2003). *Žižek: A critical introduction*. Cambridge: Polity.

Kiltz, G., Danzig, A., & Szecsy, E. (2004). Learner-centered leadership: A mentoring model for the professional development of school administrators. *Mentoring and Tutoring, 12*(2), 135–153.

Krainer, K., & Wood, T. (2008). *Participants in mathematics teacher education. The international handbook of mathematics teacher education* (Vol. 3). Rotterdam: Sense Publishers.

Krzywacki, H. (2009) *Becoming a teacher. Emerging teacher identity in mathematics teacher education*. Doctoral dissertation. University of Helsinki.

LaBoskey, V. (1993). A conceptual framework for reflection in preservice teacher education. In J. Calderhead & P. Gates (Eds.), *Conceptualizing reflection in teacher development* (pp. 23–38). London: Falmer Press.

Lacan, J. (1977). *Ecrits: A selection. London: Routledge.*

Lacan, J. (2006). *Ecrits*. New York: Norton.

Lacey, C. (1977). *The socialisation of teachers*. London: Methuen.

Laclau, W., & Mouffe, C. (2001). *Hegemony and socialist strategy*. London: Verso.

Lather, P. (2000). Reading the image of Rigoberta Menchu: Undecidability and language lessons. *International Journal of Qualitative Studies in Education, 13*(2), 153–162.

Lather, P. (2003). Applied Derrida (Mis)reading the work of mourning in educational research. *Educational Philosophy and Theory, 35*(3), 257–270.

Lave, J., & Wenger, E. (1991). *Situated learning: Legitimate peripheral participation*. Cambridge: Cambridge University Press.

Lawson, M. (2010). TV debate: Leaders' reputations left intact, *guardian.co.uk*, Thursday 15 April.

Leader, D., & Groves, J. (1995). *Lacan for beginners*. Bath: Icon.

Leat, D. (1995). The costs of reflection in initial teacher education. *Cambridge Journal of Education, 25*(2), 161–174.

Leatham, K. R. (2006). Viewing mathematics teachers' beliefs as sensible systems. *Journal of Mathematics Teacher Education, 9*(1), 91–102.

Leder, G., Pehkonen, E., & Törner, G. (Eds.) (2002). *Beliefs: A hidden variable in mathematics education?* Dordrecht: Kluwer Academic Publishers.

Leder, G., & Forgasz, H. (2002). Measuring mathematical beliefs and their impact on the learning of mathematics: A new approach. In G. Leder, E. Pehkonen, & G. Törner (Eds.), *Beliefs: A hidden variable in mathematics education* (pp. 95–114). Dordrecht: Kluwer Academic Publishers.

Lerman, S. (1990). Alternative perspectives of the nature of mathematics and their influence on the teaching of mathematics. *British Educational Research Journal, 16*(1), 53–61.

Lerman, S. (2002). Situating research on mathematics teachers' beliefs and on change. In G. Leder, E. Pehkonen, & G. Törner (Eds.), *Beliefs: A hidden variable in mathematics education?* (pp. 233–246). Dordrecht: Kluwer Academic Publishers.

Lester, F. K. (2002). Implications of research on students' beliefs for classroom practice. In G. C. Leder, E. Pehkonen, & G. Törner (Eds.), *Beliefs: A hidden variable in mathematics education?* (pp. 345–353). Boston: Kluwer Academic Publishers.

Li, Y., Ma, Y., & Pang, J. (2008). Mathematical preparation of prospective elementary teachers: Practices in selected education systems in East Asia. In P. Sullivan & T. Wood (Eds.), *Knowledge and beliefs in mathematics teaching and teaching development. The international handbook of mathematics teacher education* (Vol. 1, pp. 37–62). Rotterdam: Sense Publishers.

Li, Y., & Smith, D. (2007). Prospective middle school teachers' knowledge in mathematics and pedagogy for teaching. The case of fraction division. In J. H. Woo, H. C. Lew, K. S. Park, & D. Y. Seo (Eds.), *Proceedings of the 31st conference of the international group for the psychology of mathematics education* (Vol. 3, pp. 185–192). Seoul: The Republic of Korea.

Liston, D., & Zeichner, K. (1990). Reflective teaching and action research in pre-service teacher education. *Journal of Education for Teaching, 16*, 235–254.

Lopez-Real, F., & Kwan, T. (2005). Mentors' perceptions of their own professional develop during mentoring. *Journal of Education for Teaching, 31*(1), 15–24.

Lortie, D. (1975). *School teacher*. Chicago: University of Chicago Press.

Lunn, P., & Bishop, A. (2003). "'To Touch a Life Forever": A discourse on trainee teachers' perceptions of what it means to be an effective teacher in the primary school'. *Educational Studies, 29*(2/3), 195–206.

Ma, L. (1999). *Knowing and teaching elementary mathematics: Teachers understanding of fundamental mathematics in China and the United States.* Mahwah, NJ: Lawrence Erlbaum Associates.

MacAloon, J. (1984). Olympic games and the theory of cultural performance. In J. MacAloon (Ed.), *Rite, drama, festival, spectacle. Rehearsals towards a theory of cultural performance.* Philadelphia: Institute for the Study of Human Issues.

MacLure, M. (1993). Arguing for yourself: Identity as an organising principle in teachers' jobs and lives. *British Educational Research Journal, 19,* 311–322.

Mahony, P., & Hextall, I. (2000). *Reconstructing teaching.* London: Routledge Falmer.

Mansell, W., & Ward, H. (2003, May 9). A £400m failure. *Times Education Supplement,* 11.

Maynard, T. (2001). The student teacher and the school community of practice: A consideration of "learning as participation". *Cambridge Journal of Education, 31*(1), 39–52.

McEwan, H., & Bull, B. (1991). 'The pedagogic nature of subject matter knowledge'. *American Educational Research Journal, 28,* pp. 316–334.

McIntyre, D. (1993). Theory, theorizing and reflection in initial teacher education. In J. Calderhead & P. Gates (Eds.), *Conceptualising reflection in teacher development* (pp. 39–52). London: Falmer.

McLaren, P. (1995). *Critical pedagogy and predatory culture.* London: Routledge.

McLaughlin, T. (1994). Mentoring and the demands of reflection. In M. Wilkin & D. Sankey (Eds.), *Collaboration and transition in initial teacher training* (pp. 151–160). London: Kogan Page.

McLeod, D. (1992). Research on affect in mathematics education: A reconceptualisation. In D. Grouws (Ed.), *Handbook of research on mathematics teaching and learning.* New York: Kogan Page.

McNair, A. (1944). *Teachers and Youth Leaders* (The McNair Report). London: HMSO.

McNally, J. (2006). From informal learning to identity formation: A conceptual journey in early teacher development. *Scottish Educational Review Special Edition, 37,* 79–89.

McNally, J., Cope, P., Inglis, B., & Stronach, I. (1994). Current realities in the student teaching experience: A preliminary enquiry. *Teaching and Teacher Education, 10*(2), 219–230.

McNamara, D. (1990). Research on teachers' thinking: Its contribution to educating student-teachers to think critically. *Journal of Education for Teaching, 16*(2), 147–160.

McNamara, D. (1991). Subject knowledge and its application: Problems and possibilities for teacher educators. *Journal of Education for Teaching, 17*(2), 113–128.

McNamara, O. (2002). *Becoming an evidence-based practitioner.* London: Routledge Falmer.

McNamara, O. (2008). Initial teacher education: A(nother) decade of radical reform. In H. Gunter & C. Chapman (Eds.), *Radical reforms: Perspectives on an era of educational change* (pp. 91–103). London: Routledge Falmer.

McNamara, O., Brundrett, M., & Webb, R. (2008). *Primary teachers: Initial teacher education, continuing professional development and school leadership development. Primary Review Research Survey 6/3.* Cambridge: University of Cambridge Faculty of Education.

McNamara, O., & Corbin, B. (2001). Warranting practices: Teachers embedding the National Numeracy Strategy. *British Journal of Educational Studies, 49*(3), 260–284.

McNamara, O., Roberts, L., Basit, T. N., & Brown, T. (2002). Rites of passage in initial teacher training: Ritual, performance, ordeal and numeracy skills tests. *British Educational Research Journal, 28*(6), 861–876.

Menter, I., & Whitehead, J. (1995). *Learning the lessons: Reform in initial teacher education.* Bristol: University of West of England, and the National Union of Teachers.

Meredith, A. (1993). Knowledge for teaching mathematics: Some student teachers' views. *Journal of Education for Teaching, 19*(3), 325–338.

Meredith, A. (1995). Terry's learning: Some limitations of Shulman's pedagogical content knowledge. *Cambridge Journal of Education, 25*(2), 175–187.

Miller, K., & Baker, D. (2001). Mathematics and science as social practices: Investigating primary student teacher responses to a critical epistemology. *Ways of Knowing Journal, 1*(1), 39–46.

Millett, A., Brown, M., & Askew, M. (Eds.). (2004). *Primary mathematics and the developing professional.* Dordrecht: Springer.

Millett, A., & Johnson, D. (1996). Solving teachers' problems? The role of the commercial mathematics scheme. In D. Johnson & A. Millet (Eds.), *Implementing the mathematics National Curriculum: Policy, politics and practice* (New BERA dialogues series, 1) (pp. 54–70). London: Paul Chapman Publishing Ltd.

Monk, D. (1994). Subject area preparation of secondary mathematics and science teachers and student achievement. *Economics of Education Review, 13,* 125–145.

Morgan, C. (1997). Generic expectations and teacher assessment. Paper presented to the group on the *Research into Social Perspectives of Mathematics Education.* London: Institute of Education.

Morris, E. (1999). *In teacher training agency, national skills tests: A guide for trainee teachers.* London: Teacher Training Agency.

Moyles, J., & Stuart, D. (2003). Which school-based elements of partnership in initial teacher training in the UK support trainee teachers' professional development?' In *Research evidence in education library.* London: EPPI-Centre, Social Science Research Unit, Institute of Education, University of London.

Moyles, J., Suschitzky, W., & Chapman, L. (1998). *Teaching fledglings to fly. . . ? Mentoring and support systems in primary schools.* London: Association of Teachers and Lecturers.

Muijs, D., & Reynolds, D. (2001). *Effective teaching: Evidence and practice.* London: Paul Chapman.

Mullins, I., Martin, M., Gonzalez, E., & Chrostowski, S. (2004). *Findings from IEA's trends in international mathematics and science study at the fourth and eight grades.* Chestnut Hill, MA: TIMSS & PIRLS International Study Centre, Boston College.

Myers, T. (2003). *Slavoj Žižek.* London: Routledge.

Nolan, K. (2007). *How should I know?* Rotterdam: Sense.

Nolan, K. (2010). Playing the fields of mathematics education. A teacher educator's journey into pedagogical and paradoxical possibilities. In M. Walshaw (Ed.), *Unpacking pedagogy: New perspectives for mathematics classrooms* (pp. 153–173). Charlotte, NC: Information Age Publishing.

Noss, R. (1997). *New cultures, new numeracies.* London: Institute of Education.

Noss, R. (1998). New numeracies for a technological culture. *For the Learning of Mathematics, 18*(2), 2–12.

Office for Standards in Education (OfSTED). (1994). *Science and mathematics in schools: A review.* London: Office for Standards in Education.

Ofsted. (2002). *Framework for the inspection of initial teacher education 2002–2005, HMI 548.* London: Ofsted.

Ofsted. (2007a). *Annual report of Her Majesty's Chief Inspector of Schools 2006–2007.* London: The Stationery Office.

Ofsted. (2007b). *An employment–based route into teaching 2003–06, HMI 2664.* London: Ofsted.

Ongstad, S. (2006). Mathematics and mathematics education as triadic communication? A semiotic framework exemplified. *Educational Studies in Mathematics, 61*(1–2), 247–277.

Organisation For Economic Co-Operation And Development (OECD). (1999). *Measuring student knowledge and skills: A new framework for assessment.* Paris: Organisation For Economic Co-Operation And Development.

O'Connell Rust, F. (1999). Professional conversations: New teachers explore teaching through conversation, story and narrative. *Teaching and Teacher Education, 15,* 367–380.

Pepin, B. (2009). The role of the textbook in the 'Figured Worlds' of English, French and German classrooms: A comparative perspective. In L. Black, H. Mendick, & Y. Solomon (Eds.), *Mathematical relationships: Identities and participation* (pp. 107–118). London: Routledge.

Pepin, B., & Haggarty, L. (2007). Making connections and seeking understanding: Mathematical tasks in English, French and German textbooks. Paper presentation at AERA 07, Chicago, April 2007.

Perry, B. (1985). The system's response to the challenge of CATE. In C. Mills (Ed.), *The Impact of CATE. Report of teacher education study group*. Guildford, Society for Research into Higher Education, Teacher Education Study Group.

Phelps, C. (2010). Factors that pre-service elementary teachers perceive as affecting their motivational profiles in mathematics. *Educational Studies in Mathematics, 75*(3), 293–309. DOI: 10.1007/s10649-010-9257-2.

Pinker, S. (2002). *The blank slate: The modern denial of human nature*. London: Penguin.

Pitt, A. (1998). Qualifying resistance: Some comments on methodological dilemmas. *International Journal of Qualitative Studies in Education, 11*(4), 535–554.

Pitt, A., & Britzman, D. (2003). Speculations on qualities of difficult knowledge in teaching and learning; an experiment in psychoanalytic research. *International Journal of Qualitative Studies in Education, 16*(6), 755–776.

Potari, D., & Georgiadou-Kabouridis, B. (2009). A primary teachers' mathematics teaching: The development of beliefs and practice in different "supportive" contexts. *Journal of Mathematics Teacher Education, 12*(1), 7–25.

Povey, H. (1997). Beginning teachers' ways of knowing: The link with working for emancipatory change. *Curriculum Studies, 5*(3), 329–342.

Power, M. (1994). *The audit explosion*. London: DEMOS.

Presmeg, N. (2002). Beliefs about the nature of mathematics in the bridging of everyday and school mathematics practices. In G. Leder, E. Pehkonen, & G. Törner (Eds.), *Beliefs: A hidden variable in mathematics education?* (pp. 293–312). Dordrecht: Kluwer Academic Publishers.

Prestage, S., & Perks, P. (1999). Towards a pedagogy of teacher education: A model and a methodology. MER11 Editorial. *Mathematics Education Review, 11*, 1–5.

Price, A., & Willett, J. (2006). Primary teachers' perceptions of the impact of initial teacher training on primary schools. *Journal of In-Service Education, 32*(1), 33–45.

Putnam, R. T., & Borko, H. (2000). What do new views of knowledge and thinking have to say about research on teacher learning? *Educational Researcher, 29*(1), 4–15.

Raffe, D., Brannen, K., Croxford, L., & Martin, C. (1999). Comparing England, Scotland, Wales and Northern Ireland: The case for 'home internationals' in comparative research. *Comparative Education, 95*(1), 9–25.

Reynolds, D. (1998). 'Schooling for literacy: A review of research on teacher effectiveness and school effectiveness and its implications for contemporary educational policies'. *Educational Review, 50*(2), 147–162.

Reynolds, D., & Farrell, S. (1996). *Worlds apart: A review of international surveys of educational achievement involving England*. London: Ofsted.

Ricoeur, P. (1981). *Hermeneutics and the human sciences*. Cambridge: Cambridge University Press.

Ricoeur, P. (1984). *Time and narrative* (vol. 1). Chicago: Chicago University Press.

Ricoeur, P. (1985). *Time and narrative* (vol. 2). Chicago: Chicago University Press.

Ricoeur, P. (1987). *Time and narrative* (vol. 3). Chicago: Chicago University Press.

Roberts, L. (2004). *Shifting identities: an investigation into trainee and novice teachers' evolving professional identity*. PhD thesis. Manchester Metropolitan University.

Robertson, J. (1997). Fantasy's confines: Popular culture and the education of the female primary school teacher. *Canadian Journal of Education, 22*(2), 123–143.

Rose, J. (2006). *Independent review of the teaching of early reading*. London: Department for Education and Skills.

Rose, J. (2009). *Independent review of the primary curriculum*. London: Department for Children, Schools and Families.

Ross, D. (1989). First steps in developing a reflective approach. *Journal of Teacher Education, 40*(1), 22–30.

Roth McDuffie, A. (2004). Mathematics teaching as a deliberate practice: An investigation of elementary pre-service teachers' reflective thinking during student teaching. *Journal of Mathematics Teacher Education*, 7(1), 33–61.

Rowland, T. (2008). Researching teachers' mathematical disciplinary knowledge. In P. Sullivan & T. Wood (Eds.), *Knowledge and beliefs in mathematics teaching and teaching development. The international handbook of mathematics teacher education* (Vol. 1, pp. 273–298). Rotterdam: Sense Publishers.

Rowland, T., Huckstep, P., & Thwaites, A. (2005). Elementary teachers' mathematics subject knowledge: The knowledge quartet and the case of Naomi. *Journal of Mathematics Teacher Education*, 8(3), 255–281.

Rowland, T., Martyn, S., Barber, P., & Heal, C. (2000). Primary teacher trainees' mathematics subject knowledge and classroom performance. *Research in Mathematics Education*, 2, 3–18.

Rowland, T., Martyn, S., Barber, P., & Heal, C. (2001). Investigating the mathematics subject matter knowledge of pre-service elementary school teachers. In *Proceedings of the 23rd Conference of the International Group for the Psychology of Mathematics Education* (Vol. 4, pp. 121–128). Utrecht, The Netherlands: Freudenthal Institute, Utrecht University.

Rowland, T., & Turner, F. (2007). Developing and using the 'Knowledge Quartet': A framework for the observation of mathematics teaching. *The Mathematics Educator*, 10(1), 107–124.

Rowland, T., Turner, F., Thwaites, A., & Huckstep, P. (2009). *Developing primary mathematics teaching: Reflecting on practice with the Knowledge Quartet*. London: Sage.

Schoenfeld, A. (1992). Learning to think mathematically: Problem solving. metacognition, and sense making in mathematics. In D. A. Grouws (Ed.), *Handbook of research on mathematics learning and teaching* (pp. 334–370). New York: Macmillan.

Schwab, J. (1978). Education and the structure of the disciplines. In I. Westbury & N. J. Wilkof (Eds.), *Science, curriculum and liberal education* (pp. 229–272). Chicago: University of Chicago Press.

Schön, D. (1983). *The reflective practitioner*. London: Temple Smith.

Schön, D. (1987). *Educating the reflective practitioner*. Oxford: Jossey-Bass.

Schütz, A. (1962). *The problem of social reality*. The Hague: Martinus Nijhof.

Sfard, A. & Linchevski, L. (1994). A tale of two students, the interpreter and the doer. *Proceedings of the eighteenth conference of the group on the Psychology of Mathematics Education* (Vol. 4, pp. 257–264), Lisbon: University of Lisbon.

Sfard, A., & Prusak, A. (2005). Identity that makes a difference: substantial learning as closing the gap between actual and designated identities. Keynote presentation. *Proceeding of the twenty-ninth conference of the international group on the Psychology of Mathematics Education*. Melbourne: University of Melbourne.

Shulman, L. (1986). Those who understand: Knowledge growth in teaching. *Educational Researcher*, 15(2), 4–14.

Shulman, L. (1987). Knowledge and teaching: Foundations of the new reform. *Harvard Educational Review*, 57(1), 1–22.

Simco, N., & Wilson, T. (2002). *Primary initial teacher training and education: Revised standards, bright future?* Exeter: Learning Matters.

Simon, S., & Brown, M. (1996). Teacher beliefs and practices in primary mathematics. In L. Puig & A. Guitierrez (Eds.), *Proceedings of twentieth conference of the international group for the Psychology of Mathematics Education*. Valencia: University of Valencia.

Singer, M. (1959). *Traditional India: Structure and change*. Philadelphia: American Folk Law Society.

Sinkinson, A., & Jones, K. (2001). The validity and reliability of Ofsted judgements of the quality of secondary mathematics initial teacher education courses. *Cambridge Journal of Education*, 31(2), 221–237.

Skemp, R. (1976). Relational understanding and instrumental understanding. *Mathematics Teaching*, 77, 20–26.

Skovsmose, O. (1994). *Towards a philosophy of critical mathematics education*. Dordrecht: Kluwer Academic Publishers.

Skovsmose, O. (2005). *Travelling through education: Uncertainty, mathematics, responsibility.* Rotterdam: Sense Publishers.

Skovsmose, O. (2008). Mathematics education in a knowledge market. Developing functional and critical competencies. In E. DeFreitas & K. Nolan (Eds.), *Opening the research text: Critical insights and in(ter)ventions into mathematics education* (pp. 159–174). New York: Springer.

Smith, D. (1991). Educating the reflective practitioner in curriculum. *Curriculum, 12,* 115–124.

Smith, K., & Hodson, E. (2010). Theorising practice in initial teacher education. *Journal of Education for Teaching, 36*(3), 259–275.

Sokefeld, M. (1999). Debating self and culture in anthropology. *Current Anthropology, 40*(4), 417–447.

Solomon, Y. (2009). *Mathematical literacy: Developing identities of inclusion.* New York: Routledge.

Sparks-Langer, G., & Colton, A. (1991, March). Synthesis of research on teachers' reflective thinking. *Educational Leadership,* 37–44.

Speer, N. (2005). Issues of methods and theory in the study of mathematics teachers professed and attributed beliefs. *Educational Studies in Mathematics, 58*(3), 361–391.

Stinson, D., & Powell, G. (2010). Deconstructing discourses in a mathematics education course: Teachers reflecting differently. In M. Walshaw (Ed.), *Unpacking pedagogy: New perspectives for mathematics classrooms* (pp. 201–222). Charlotte, NC: Information Age Publishing.

Stipek, D., Givvin, K., Salmon, J., & MacGyvers, V. (2001). Teachers' beliefs and practices related to mathematics instruction. *Teaching and Teacher Education, 17*(2), 213–226.

Stones, E. (1992). *Quality teaching: A sample of cases.* London: Routledge.

Strathern, M. (2000). *Audit cultures: Anthropological studies in accountability, ethics and the academy.* London: Routledge.

Stronach, I. (1999). Shouting theatre in a crowded fire: Educational effectiveness as 'cultural performance'. *Evaluation, 5*(2), 173–193.

Stronach, I., Corbin, B., McNamara, O., Stark, S., & Warne, T. (2002). Towards an uncertain politics of professionalism: Teacher and nurse identities in flux. *Journal of Educational Policy, 17*(1), 109–138.

Su, C. (1992). Sources of influence in pre-service teacher socialization. *Journal of Education for Teaching, 18*(3), 239–257.

Sullivan, P., & Wood, T. (Eds.). (2008). *Knowledge and beliefs in mathematics teaching and teaching development. The international handbook of mathematics teacher education* (Vol. 1). Rotterdam: Sense Publishers.

Swars, S., Smith, S., Smith, M., & Hart, L. (2009). A longitudinal study of effects of a developmental teacher preparation program on elementary prospective teachers' mathematics beliefs. *Journal of Mathematics Teacher Education, 12*(1), 47–66.

Sztajn, P. (2003). Adapting reform ideas in different mathematics classrooms: Beliefs beyond mathematics. *Journal of Mathematics Teacher Education, 6*(1), 53–75.

Szydlik, J., Szydlik, S., & Benson, S. (2003). Exploring changes in pre-service elementary teachers' mathematical beliefs. *Journal of Mathematics Teacher Education, 6*(3), 253–279.

Tahta, D. (1993). Editorial. *For the Learning of Mathematics, 13*(1), 2–3.

Tahta, D. (2008). Sensible objects. In N. Sinclair, D. Pimm, & W. Higginson (Eds.), *Mathematics and the aesthetic: New approaches to an ancient affinity.* New York: Springer.

Tann, S. (1993). Eliciting student teachers' personal theories. In J. Calderhead & P. Gates (Eds.), *Conceptualising reflection in teacher development.* London: Falmer.

Tauer, S. (1998). The mentor–protégé relationship and its impact on the experienced teacher. *Teaching and Teacher Education, 14*(2), 205–218.

Taylor, P. (1996). Mythmaking and mythbreaking in the mathematics classroom. *Educational Studies in Mathematics, 31,* 151–173.

Taylor, W. (2000). The role of the providers. In I. Reid (Ed.), *Improving schools: The contribution of teacher education and training: an account of the joint UCET/HMI Symposium,* Edinburgh, December. (UCET, Occasional Paper).

Teacher Pathways project. (2003–2007) Accessed April 20, 2007, from http://www.teacherresearchpolicy.org

Teacher Training Agency. (1999). *National Skills tests: A guide for trainee teachers*. London: Teacher Training Agency.

Teacher Training Agency. (2002). *Qualifying to teach: Professional standards for qualified teacher status and requirements for initial teacher training*. London: Teacher Training Agency.

Teacher Training Agency. (2000a). *QTS numeracy skills test trainee support materials*. London: Teacher Training Agency.

Teacher Training Agency. (2000b). *QTS skills test in numeracy, June and July 2000: National results summary for initial training providers*. London: Teacher Training Agency.

Thompson, A. (1984). The relationship of teachers' conceptions of mathematics teaching to instructional practice. *Educational Studies in Mathematics, 15*, 105–127.

Thompson, A. (1992). Teachers' beliefs and conceptions: A synthesis of the research. In A. D. Grouws (Ed.), *Handbook of research on mathematics teaching and learning* (pp. 127–146). New York: Macmillan.

Tickle, L. (1994). *The induction of new teachers: Reflective professional practice*. London: Cassell.

Tirosh, D., & Wood, T. (Eds.). (2008). *Tools and processes in mathematics teacher education. The international handbook of mathematics teacher education* (Vol. 2). Rotterdam: Sense Publishers.

Todd, S. (Ed.). (1997). *Learning desire: Perspectives on pedagogy, culture, and the unsaid*. London: Routledge.

Training and Development Agency. (2007) *The revised standards for qualified teacher status*. Accessed 20.04.2007, from http://www.tda.gov.uk/upload/resources/doc/draft_qts_standards_17nov2006.doc

Tripp, D. (1993). *Critical incidents in teaching: The development of professional judgement*. London: Routledge.

Troman, G. (1996). The rise of the new professionals? Restructuring of the primary teachers' work and professionalism. *British Journal of the Sociology of Education, 17*(4), 473–487.

Troman, G. (1999). Researching primary teachers' work: Examining theory, policy and practice through interactionist ethnography. In M. Hammersley (Ed.), *Restructuring school experience: Ethnographic studies of teaching and learning* (pp. 33–50). London: Falmer.

Turkle, S. (1978). *Psychoanalytic politics*. London: Free Association Press.

Twiselton, S. (2004). The role of teacher identities in learning to teach. *Educational Review, 56*(2), 157–164.

Tzur, R. (2001). Becoming a mathematics teacher-educator: Conceptualizing the terrain through self-reflective analysis. *Journal of Mathematics Teacher Education, 4*(4), 259–283.

United States Department of Education. (2008). *Foundations for success: The final report of the National Mathematics Advisory Panel*. Washington, DC: United States Department of Education.

Universities' Council for the Education of Teachers. (2007). *ITE Inspection Burdens*. London: UCET.

Valli, L. (1993). Reflective teacher education programs: An analysis of case studies. In J. Calderhead & P. Gates (Eds.), *Conceptualizing reflection in teacher development* (pp. 11–22). London: Falmer Press.

Van Manen, M. (1977). Linking ways of knowing with ways of being practical. *Curriculum Inquiry, 6*, 205–228.

Walkerdine, V. (1988). *The mastery of reason: Cognitive development and the production of rationality*. London: Routledge.

Walls, F. (2009). *Mathematical subjects: Children talk about their mathematical lives*. New York: Springer.

Walls, F. (2010). The good mathematics teacher. Standardized mathematics tests, teacher identity, and pedagogy. In M. Walshaw (Ed.), *Unpacking pedagogy: New perspectives for mathematics classrooms* (pp. 65–86). Charlotte, NC: Information Age Publishing.

Walshaw, M. (2004). The pedagogical relation in postmodern times: Learning with Lacan. In M. Walshaw (Ed.), *Mathematics education with/in the postmodern*. Westport, CT: Praeger.

Walshaw, M. (2007). *Working with Foucault in education*. Rotterdam: Sense Publishers.

Walshaw, M. (2008). Developing theory to explain learning to teach. In T. Brown (Ed.), *The psychology of mathematics education: A psychoanalytic displacement* (pp. 119–138). Rotterdam: Sense Publishers.

Walshaw, M. (Ed.). (2010a). *Unpacking pedagogy: New perspectives for mathematics classrooms* (pp. 201–222). Charlotte, NC: Information Age Publishing.

Walshaw, M. (2010b). Learning to teach: Powerful practices at work during the praticum. In M. Walshaw (Ed.), *Unpacking pedagogy: New perspectives for mathematics classrooms* (pp. 109–128). Charlotte, NC: Information Age Publishing.

Walshaw, M. (2010c). Mathematical pedagogical change: Rethinking identity and reflective practice. *Journal of Mathematics Teacher Education, 13*(6), 487–497.

Watkins, C. (1992). An experiment in mentor training. In M. Wilkin (Ed.), *Mentoring in schools* (pp. 95–115). London: Kogan.

Weber, S. (1993). The narrative anecdote in teacher education. *Journal of Education for Teaching, 19*(1), 71–82.

White, J. (1989). Student teaching as rite of passage. *Anthropology and Educational Quarterly, 20,* 177–195.

Wilkin, M. (1993). Initial training as a case of postmodern development: Some implications for mentoring. In D. McIntyre, H. Hagger, & M. Wilkin (Eds.), *Mentoring: Perspectives on school-based teacher education*. London: Kogan Page.

Williams, A., & Soares, A. (2002). Sharing roles and responsibilities in initial teacher training: perceptions of some key players. *Cambridge Journal of Education, 32*(1), 91–107.

Williams, J. (2008). *Keeping open the door to mathematically demanding programmes in further and higher education. Teaching and Learning Research Briefing*. Swindon: Economic and Social Research Council.

Williams, J. (in press due out Dec 2010). *Mind, culture and activity*. Towards a political economy of education: use and exchange value of mathematically enhanced labor power.

Wilson, M., & Cooney, T. (2002). Mathematics teacher change and development. In G. Leder, E. Pehkonen, & G. Törner (Eds.), *Beliefs: A hidden variable in mathematics education* (pp. 127–148). Dordrecht: Kluwer Academic Publishers.

Wilson, S., Floden, R., & Ferrini-Mundy, J. (2001). *Teacher preparation research: Current knowledge, gaps, and recommendations*. Washington, WA: University of Washington, Center for the Study of Teaching and Policy.

Wilson, S., Shulman, L., & Richert, A. (1987). 150 ways of knowing: Representations of knowledge in teaching. In J. Calderhead (Ed.), *Exploring teachers' thinking* (pp. 104–124). London: Cassell.

Wragg, E., Bennett, S., & Carré, C. (1989). Primary teachers and the national curriculum. *Research Papers in Education, 4*(3), 17–45.

Zeichner, K. (1987). Preparing reflective teachers: An overview of instructional strategies which have been employed in preservice teacher education. *International Journal of Educational Research, 11*(5), 565–575.

Zeichner, K., & Liston, D. (1987). Teaching student teachers to reflect. *Harvard Educational Review, 57*(1), 23–48.

Zeichner, K., Tabachnick, B., & Densmore, K. (1987). 'Individual, institutional and cultural influences on the development of teachers' craft knowledge'. In J. Calderhead (Ed.), *Exploring teachers' thinking* (pp. 21–59). London: Cassell.

Zuber-Skerritt, O. (Ed.). (1996). *New directions in action research*. London: Falmer.

Žižek, S. (1989). *The sublime object of ideology*. London: Verso.

Žižek, S. (2000). *Did somebody say totalitarianism?* London: Verso.

Žižek, S. (2001). *The fright of real tears: Krzysztof Kieslowski between theory and post-theory*. London: British Film Institute.

Žižek, S. (2006). *The parallax view*. Cambridge, MA: The MIT Press.

# Index

9 789400 705531